Bruce Ansley is one of New Zealand's pre-eminent storytellers. For more than two decades he was a writer for the *New Zealand Listener*, before becoming a full-time author in 2007. He has held fellowships at Oxford and Cambridge universities, and has won a number of journalism awards. He is the author of ten books, including *Coast: A New Zealand Journey*, which won Best Illustrated Non-fiction Book at the New Zealand Post Book Awards in 2014. His other books include *A Fabled Land: The Story of Canterbury's Famous Mesopotamia Station* and *Wild Roads: A New Zealand Journey*.

He loves tramping and has roamed the South Island's back country. For many years he lived in a tiny traditional bach in Golden Bay, and he once built a house in the far reaches of Pelorus Sound. He has worked as a commercial fisherman in Fiordland and as a deer farmer on Banks Peninsula, but has also called each of the four main cities home. On a good day he can usually be found out on the water in his Norwegian motor-sailer, but his favourite occupation is simply poking around New Zealand, which he regards as the wildest, most beautiful, most romantic country in the world.

Ansley has three sons and lives with his wife, Sally, on Waiheke Island.

BRUCE ANSLEY

HarperCollins*Publishers*

HarperCollins*Publishers*

Australia • Brazil • Canada • France • Germany • Holland • Hungary
India • Italy • Japan • Mexico • New Zealand • Poland • Spain • Sweden
Switzerland • United Kingdom • United States of America

First published in 2018
This edition published in 2021
by HarperCollins*Publishers* (New Zealand) Limited
Unit D1, 63 Apollo Drive, Rosedale, Auckland 0632, New Zealand
harpercollins.co.nz

ISBN 978 1 7755 4184 4 (paperback)
ISBN 978 1 7754 9151 4 (ebook)
ISBN 978 1 4607 9891 1 (audiobook)

Cover design and illustration by Julia Murray
Typeset in Sabon LT by Kirby Jones
Author photograph by Jane Ussher
Printed and bound in Australia by McPherson's Printing Group
The papers used by HarperCollins in the manufacture of this book are a natural, recyclable product made from wood grown in sustainable plantation forests. The fibre source and manufacturing processes meet recognised international environmental standards, and carry certification.

CONTENTS

Journeying

New Zealand was built on adventure. It was extraordinarily difficult getting here for a start. Waka and sailing vessels created a catalogue of disaster.

Once here, why, fierce escapades lay all around. Early adventurers were confronted by an unruly country. They had mountains and rivers to cross, glaciers, forests, volcanoes to conquer. The nation's early history is one of battling raw nature, of privation and fierce determination and, of course, wild journeys. It made a lasting impression on us. Sturdy self-reliance remains one of the markers in New Zealand's perception of itself. High-country farmers and wilderness women have a legend to support. One of our most unlikely heroes, the prison escapee George Wilder, captured the nation's imagination for his ability to elude pursuing forces, vanish into the bush and survive on his own.

What is a wild journey now? Well, the classics remain rugged enough. Try, for example, following the path of the doomed surveyor John Whitcombe across the Southern Alps. I did, and as

I dangled in something like a tea tray above a West Coast river I considered calling this book *Teetering on the Edge*.

The country hasn't lost its edge. If you sail around North Cape, or South Cape, you encounter exactly the same seas, the same perils as Captain James Cook did, your advantage being that you at least know where you are. You can walk through the valley under the Two Thumb Range and know just how it felt to Samuel Butler, the first European to set eyes on it.

But wild journeys in modern New Zealand can both traverse unexpected territory and take you by surprise. I set out one day to drive from my home on Waiheke Island to Wanaka in a hurry. It developed into a wild journey. So did the usually placid State Highway One, riven by earthquakes in the top half of the South Island. Even Queen Street in Auckland can blow its cover. Or getting to a wild journey can be wilder than the journey itself, as in a blighted hunt for the South Island kokako.

Wild journeys depend on perspective. I'm not full of derring-do. I don't dress in camo, strap on a knife and take on the wild. I'm an average, easily scared man who has to brace himself. The wildest journey I've ever done was as a Boy Scout launched upon an unknown landscape. For what seemed days, weeks, we were lost in the wilderness, terrified by things that went bang in the night. Years later I retraced my steps. It was just a short walk in the hills.

1

Chasing George

New Zealand in 1962 was a nation of just two and a half million people, who prided themselves on knowing everyone else by their first names.

Keith Holyoake was Prime Minister, Dove-Myer Robinson Mayor of Auckland. Peter Snell ran a world-record mile. Wilson Whineray captained the All Blacks. George Wilder escaped from prison.

George broke out of prison three times. He fooled the police. He lived in the bush. He swam rivers, crashed through roadblocks. He was polite and apologetic to people he stole from.

What else? Well, nothing really. He's like a frame that has lost its photograph. Only a murky background remains.

Yet George was once the most celebrated man in the country. People followed his tracks. They applauded his escapades. They diminished his crimes: oh, a few counts of burglary and car conversion. Nothing, really. Just a young man feeling his oats.

They even sang songs about him, or at least, sang along with Howard Morrison's 'George The Wild(er) NZ Boy'.

Even today he is elusive. He got away from the police dozens of times. Now he escapes the public. He lives near a tiny settlement at the bottom of Hawkes Bay. It is as much a bolthole as you could find in this country. Some people know where he lives, but not many. Oh, and he plays golf.

Half a century on from the days when every newspaper marvelled over the way he stayed out of sight, George Wilder is still lying low. He remains fleet. In fact, he seems to have got rather better at it over the years. His tracks remain on the land nonetheless.

George first escaped on 17 May 1962. He climbed a ten-metre wall to break out of New Plymouth prison. It was quite a feat; the hopelessness of the place must have lent him wings. New Plymouth prison was built around 1870 in an era of Victorian prisons. New Zealand favoured, then, dreadful stone dungeons, although at least this one didn't become a backpackers' hostel like Christchurch's Addington jail, or a tourist attraction like Napier's.

These prisons fascinate the public because of their meanness, their sense of bread and water. They are the deepest, darkest dungeons of fairy tales. People look at their barren cells and shiver deliciously. They ask to see the places where people were hanged.

Only two people were executed in the New Plymouth prison, both in the late nineteenth century, both Maori, one for killing a surveyor parcelling up his land for sale, the other for murdering his wife.

The jail stands on the corner of Downe and Robe streets, prime CBD real estate in New Plymouth, a sad place with its blank stone walls broken by tiny windows. As with all the other relics of grim justice, no one wants to stay very long.

Neither did George Wilder. Hard-labour convicts were still breaking rocks there in the late 1950s, not long before George escaped. He was in for burglary, car conversion (a Jaguar, one of his favourites) and shop-breaking.

The cells were tiny, only 2.1 metres by 3 metres, the smallest in the land, too small to swing a cat or hold a man. So over the wall went George, and you only have to stand outside this stone pile to sympathise: he was a creature of bush and space.

He was said to have changed out of his prison clothes on the jail's roof, putting on a check shirt and air-force blue trousers, although there's no record of where he got them. A small car was reported to have broken through a police road checkpoint on the New Plymouth to Waitara highway shortly thereafter and, chased by a traffic officer, it disappeared. Police said it was a green 1935 Chevrolet Junior with primrose grille and wheels; George always liked his cars. Police said George was a tough man but not dangerous.

The legend began at that moment.

He might have been seen here, he was reported there, but essentially he disappeared.

At the time, Scott Carpenter was orbiting the earth and winning a reputation for disobeying orders. Adolf Eichmann, who stood trial for Holocaust atrocities inside a glass cage in Jerusalem, was on his way to the gallows.

George Wilder was creating his own reputation. A stolen Thames Trader he was believed to be driving crashed through a roadblock near Tokaanu. A policeman fired two shots at him.

They missed. 'Crashing through roadblocks' was to become the most-used phrase of his escapes.

Police gave chase at speeds of up to 75 miles an hour (120 kilometres per hour) — not too bad for an old Trader. They found the van abandoned. Wilder had 'escaped into the bush', the second most-used phrase of his escapes.

Police believed he'd doubled back to Tokaanu. They set up a roadblock at Moerangi, not far from Tokaanu. A light-blue Austin A50 slowed, almost stopped, then crashed through the roadblock and roared away. Next day the car was found bogged in mud some ten kilometres to the north. Police began searching the western shores of Lake Taupo.

Well, Moerangi is still named on the map, but on the ground it is no more than a sign pointing to a nearby station. I reach the top of the Waituhi Saddle, driving through bush, before realising I've gone too far, although the view is worth it. Then back, past Moerangi and through Karatau Junction, whose perfect old school is now the community hall, with the new school beside it.

But Tokaanu has seen better days. The petrol pumps have gone but the little church is well-cared-for, unlike in some small towns. If there are people here, they're staying indoors.

Tokaanu was once a popular thermal resort but it is eclipsed by nearby Turangi now. The grand hotel still dominates the town, giving the empty streets an air of gravitas. When George Wilder was on the run, the Tongariro power scheme and the Tokaanu power station were in full swing and the area was thriving.

I begin to realise that half a century ago is light years away for New Zealanders. The country has changed so much in that time. This is a journey through a New Zealand that once was but no longer is, just as the George Wilder character could no longer exist.

George was a child of his time. I first heard of him at school. The teacher asked what we thought of him. One boy said he was a crook who should be back behind bars. Oh, the indignation. The world, or at least our world as contained in Room 13, rose up against the heretic.

George was a bit like the Lone Ranger, without his horse. He wasn't a crook, not really, he'd hardly done anything wrong, and what about all of those nice notes? On the other hand, look at his courage, his cunning, his great thirst for freedom. For life!

In those days an ability to live in and off the bush was one of the great New Zealand dreams. To go off on your own, to survive without help from anyone, to run rings round the cops, to be your own person absolutely. The cold? The loneliness? The almost complete lack of food? Nah. In that age of nuclear paranoia all of us believed that when the big one struck, why, we'd just strike out for the bush. Exactly as George Wilder had done. He was our hero.

By 18 July, when George had been on the run for two months, police speculated publicly that hunger could force him to give up. He had only roots and ferns for food, they said. They believed him to be somewhere along the western shores of Lake Taupo, in rough, scrub-covered country — 'Tough going all the way,' said the search controller. They'd placed cordons of men and dogs. Launches had joined the hunt, and an aircraft.

Essentially, they were right. George was ensconced in Waihaha, a bay on Taupo's western shore which still can only be reached by water or walking track.

Much later Antonios Papaspiropoulos, a writer and poet, moved into an old, derelict cottage in Waihaha with his wife,

Victoria, and their three children. He wanted a refuge, a sanctuary where he could recoup, recover, find a new direction in his life. The cottage had not been lived in for at least ten years. Its owner told him that George Wilder had hidden there.

As the family cleared and cleaned and painted, they found four pencil sketches by George Wilder inside a wardrobe. That find led them several ways. Antonios found his sanctuary there, and his new direction. And, he wrote, 'simplicity, serenity, and large doses of reprieve'. He felt a resonance with George Wilder, whom he believed had found both refuge and his creative muse in the cottage. The poet grew 'a thief's eye for detail'. He dubbed his home the 'George Wilder Cottage.' He began writing.

When the local newspaper ran a story about Antonios's interest in the famed escapee, people dropped in notes of their experiences. George's reputation had flourished in the half-century since his escape. He'd been invested with strange powers.

One man wrote of him escaping police by faking his footprints: he put his boots on back to front, so his pursuers thought he was heading in the opposite direction. Those who want to test this theory should try it.

Those stories are part of the enduring Wilder legend. He is said to have stolen cars and performed amazing stunts in them, to have crashed through roadblocks and fled into wild country, to have lived off the land, to have hidden from searchers under their noses and even to have joined them in searches for himself, to have swum wild rivers and leapt over tall mountains, probably in a single bound.

Some of those stories are verifiable; at least, they were reported in the nation's newspapers, which in those days took a sober view of their responsibilities, named their sources and reported them accurately, if sometimes dully. (Though George Wilder was never dull: how could he be, on the run, police at his heels, for months at a time?)

An essential part of the narrative, and of his enduring popularity with the New Zealand public, was the notes he was said to have left in the houses and baches he broke into for food. They were said to be apologetic, humble, even sweet. Very sorry about the damage, sorry for taking your food, needs must etc.

But none of the newspaper accounts of the many episodes in his escapes reported these notes, none of those I read at least. I begin to wonder why he left them. They seem dangerous, for two reasons. First, they would alert the police to his whereabouts, and second, they would be, effectively, confessions to further crimes for which, sooner or later, he'd be called to account.

Did George leave those notes? Perhaps, perhaps not. Legends feed upon themselves and grow in the telling. The best I can say is that I haven't seen one, or found anyone who did, or read a contemporary newspaper account which mentions them.

Yet George's public insisted upon them. One of the tales related to Antonios came from a bride upset because George had stolen the bridegroom's suit off the line on their wedding day. (Who would *wash* a suit? On the day of the wedding?) Another came from a woman whose parents had been burgled by Wilder, who quaffed her mother's collection of miniature bottles of whisky, gin and so on, and left an apologetic note saying he'd been so hungry — and thirsty.

On the other hand, *something* had alerted the police and led them to his whereabouts, and what could be a better clue than the notes? Antonios felt there was an element of folklore in the stories, but certainly, he believed, the notes existed: there were simply too many people talking about receiving them.

George could settle the account one way or the other, but he's not saying.

Another point in the story seems clear enough: the Waihaha house was his base, for quite a while. Antonios's account of finding drawings inside the wardrobe drew a rare, if indirect, response from the legend himself, holed up somewhere near Cape Turnagain: according to his sister, who contacted the poet, they weren't George's. Evidently he never drew inside wardrobes. Why this, of all the stories that circulate about George Wilder, should elicit a contact, even a denial, is anyone's guess. Perhaps he simply objected to the notion that he might be in the closet, in any sense.

Another point: she didn't dispute the fact that he had lived in the cottage for some time, marking off the days on the wall. Clearly he'd made the house in Waihaha his base.

Much later, I read a review by John Horrocks of Gerard Hindmarsh's book *Outsiders: Stories from the Fringe of New Zealand Society*. The book included a piece about George Wilder, an outsider if ever there was one. Horrocks included a story of his own in the review: one of the houses in Waihaha was owned by the Richwhite family, whose scion David went on to become a very public merchant banker. They kept a plywood dinghy there. George took it and rowed across the lake to Kinloch, where he was said to have broken into baches for supplies.

I go to Kinloch and think about that voyage across the lake.

Kinloch has that affluent, self-satisfied air of lakeside subdivisions, flush rather than flash, every lawn mowed, all hedges trimmed, the lake's Wanaka to Taupo's Queenstown, with not too much space for visitors.

Sir Keith Holyoake, then Minister of Agriculture and later Prime Minister, first made it famous when he bought a sheep station there in 1953. Perhaps as a result, Kinloch was subdivided in 1959, and one of its best pieces of architecture remains the relaxed mid-century house which Holyoake is said to have described on his deathbed as his pride and joy.

In 1962, when George came raiding, the settlement was still embryonic, a scattering of baches, but it had one relevant feature. It lay 17.5 kilometres in a direct line from Waihaha, a long voyage by dinghy.

Horrocks told me that his family had bought the dinghy from the Richwhites. It was a small, heavy, blunt-nosed vessel, not easy to row.

Taupo is as much inland sea as lake. It is huge, the biggest lake in New Zealand. Fierce winds can sweep across it, creating a chop very much like a stormy sea. In 1962 there'd have been few lights around it, apart from Taupo on the other side.

George would have shoved off into darkness. Much worse, he faced a round trip of thirty-five kilometres. He'd have wanted to go there and back in the dark; the trouble with isolated places is that someone intruding upon them is much more visible. They're difficult to hide in.

He'd have launched the dinghy from the beach at Waihaha, taken a fix on the odd light across the lake, and shoved off. Nothing in the legend says anything about seamanship — it's all about his skills in the bush.

Well, rowing a dinghy is easy enough. But rowing a blunt-nosed one, a heavy old thing, a very long way on a lake which might have been calm enough but quite possibly was not, is an astonishing feat.

I take my own dinghy for a row in Putiki Bay at Waiheke Island as a test. It is a light, fibreglass dinghy, perhaps a little short to make a decent rowing boat, but then the Horrocks's dinghy wasn't long either. As a rough estimate, I reckoned I could row at a walking pace, perhaps three knots. But not against a wind. And for how long? After just a couple of kilometres, out to the bay entrance and back, I am quite ready to go home for a rest.

Without stopping, the journey would have taken Wilder at least ten hours there and back. In the dark. With only a rest at half time, perhaps lying back in some bach's easy chair, opening a can from a kitchen cupboard. The thought of the row back certainly would have spoiled my appetite.

Perhaps, as John Horrocks suggested, he crept around the edge of the lake and hid in one of the many bays on the way. Either way the man wasn't just a fugitive. He was a miracle.

There are two ways of getting to Waihaha now. One of them wasn't there in George's day, for now tourists on foot or on bikes traipse past the bay on the Great Lake Trail.

The way George probably arrived there was along the Waihaha Road. It must have been a pretty safe bet then — remote, little used, rough. He could have sneaked along it in the dark unseen. Even these days the road starts well. I drive past farms and through an increasing number of gates, growing lumpier and bumpier all the way. Sheep and cattle take a close interest.

Eventually, after a final, indignant twitch of a bull's tail, I can go no further.

I abandon the car, go through one last gate, and find a few young Italians camped in a clearing.

Waihaha? They look puzzled. One of them thinks it is five hours' walk away. (A Department of Conservation worker had told me the same thing, but it turned out she was talking about the Waihaha hut, which was in the opposite direction.) I don't bother asking if they know anything about George Wilder. They are here for the scenery, and there is plenty of that. The green land slopes gently before it dives through bush down to the lake.

Taupo, the resort city, glitters across the lake. It seems a very long way away. Half a century has created another world. The town has grown and grown. New subdivisions are everywhere. Is there anything more jarring than the accommodation industry en masse? The rule is, the more beautiful the place, the more dire the architecture, and Taupo does its best here.

George's side of the lake, though, would still be recognisable to him.

I take an unmarked track which seems to lead in the right direction, downwards, and find the Waihaha track not far away. The sign assures me Waihaha is only 15 minutes away, but it takes longer. The old track to the baches below is now used also by anglers, who are asked to first register with a local Maori trust board. It angles down the hill and dives into a stream bed. All around, bush birds tsk and chatter.

I shuffle over rocks and around boulders. The bed is dry, but must be a precipitous, dangerous route in the wet. More bush in George's day, more runoff, more water in the stream. As for doing it in the dark, you'd have to be a mug — or a prison escapee. Yet this is probably the path George used.

The track lands on a flat and threads through bush, emerging beside a simple, attractive house, the Richwhite place. A sign has that ring of patronage: it is private property. I am welcome to pass through but not to camp, light fires or leave litter, which seems fair enough.

Along the foreshore several other cottages poke their fronts through the bush. The George Wilder cottage is a simple affair down at the end. A few dinghies lie about. The lake is full of trout. Plenty of baches in other bays all nicely stocked. Would he have been living off roots and ferns, as the police suggested? Oh dear, no. Only a week after his escape police were confident that starvation would force him out of hiding and perhaps it did, baches and homes around Lake Taupo becoming his larder. But he was at large for another two months and no one ever grabbed him as he was pinching a feed.

Police complained of the rough country they were searching in. Fifty men were hunting for him, but on his side George had bushcraft, cunning and a degree of desperation too.

His hideout must have seemed safe enough. Waihaha is closed in by cliffy headlands on two sides. Anyone coming in from the lake by boat would be easily seen. It is a long noisy walk through the bush and along the foreshore. Plenty of time for a man on his guard to slip away.

George would have been very happy here. I wanted to escape to this place myself.

But the net was closing. Police had got wind of him. They were concentrating their search along Taupo's western shore, where Waihaha lay. Police cordons of men and dogs were joined by launches, even an aircraft. Residents were asked to search their houses and make sure their cars were locked.

The search became a national sport. All of the wild money was on George.

He broke cover next at Mangakino, in a stolen Land Rover, another favourite of George's. Brian Main, the policeman who later arrested him, reckoned he kept a fleet of cars in the bush, and he would amuse himself doing wheelies.

This time newspapers reported he 'flashed past' a police checkpoint near Mangakino. Can you flash in a Land Rover?

The vehicle was found abandoned near the top of Titiraupenga, 1042 metres high. Police admitted that the task of finding him up there was formidable. The mountain was surrounded by a logging area and heavy bush. It was criss-crossed with bush tracks and hunters trails, gouged by creeks and gorges.

Millworkers, forestrymen, farmers and soldiers joined the hunt. This was becoming a national pastime, and oh, the drama of it.

George was said, again, to be exhausted and desperate for food. But, police said, the chances of him being caught while on the mountain were not high. This was Wilder country and George was at home in it.

Yet they *did* almost catch him. He was spotted near Whakamaru, a little way down the road from Mangakino, and quite close to the road leading up the mountain. 'Net closes', proclaimed the newspapers.

One moonlit, frosty, misty night he broke into a farmhouse. He smashed a back window of the house. The farmer thought the noise was his cat. 'But then I heard footsteps,' he told reporters. 'I grabbed my rifle from beside the bed, tiptoed out to the back room and kicked the door open. George must have heard me coming because he wasn't there.

'I moved outside meaning to fire a couple of shots in the air to alert the police and the Army men. But I'd forgotten to put the bolt in the rifle and load it.'

The farmer was sanguine enough. He went back inside and telephoned the police instead. He thought Wilder was probably starving but he wasn't going to get any more involved in the search: 'If he tries again tonight he can have it. I'm not going to stay here.'

Four Alsatian police dogs and a posse of more than thirty police, prison officers, soldiers and bushmen gave chase. George threw them off by doubling back on his tracks (possibly giving rise to the backwards boots story), leaping into the Huiarau Stream and swimming across it. The stream was perhaps ten metres wide, the very stuff of legend!

Next day George was back on the front page: 'Wilder tears through cordon on bicycle.' He'd pinched a bike and crashed a cordon, racing down a steep hill on the Whakamaru straight and onto the Mangakino Stream bridge. Cars formed a roadblock. He nipped through a gap between them, pedalling all the faster, flying like a bird, because a policeman fired a shot allegedly in the air to alert searchers, and George may have thought the rifle was pointed at him.

But a *bicycle*? For a man as keen on cars as George Wilder?

Perhaps the locals had obeyed police advice and locked their cars, every one of them, although a practised car converter should have had no trouble with that. More likely he was improvising. Cars can be heard from afar on quiet country roads. Bicycles are silent.

He threw police dogs off the scent by wading through a freezing, knee-deep stream and at 4.30 that morning broke into a farmhouse, again in nearby Valley Road.

The farmer heard him. 'At first I thought it was one of our three young sons in the bathroom,' he told reporters. 'I called out something about getting back to bed, then heard Wilder bolt through the window.'

He tried to start the farmer's car but the canny cocky had removed the rotor, an old-fashioned device essential to cars of that era.

Again George escaped. This time he confounded the police dogs by walking through a mob of sheep to kill his scent.

My, it was cold. Frosts of minus eight to minus fourteen degrees had whitened the land for a week. How long could George stand it?

Not very much longer.

A day or so later, a Saturday afternoon, he was caught. Constables Hamilton and Gyde, with police dog Bruce, found him hiding in a hole ten metres from a logging road.

A famous newspaper photograph shows him in a police car, flanked by policemen, in irons, handcuffs being a lame term for the heavy steel bracelets on his wrists. He doesn't look worn-out, or cold, or at the end of his tether. He doesn't even look resentful, just resigned. The headline says, 'Got him!'

One newspaper described him as hungry and tired, but lean, fit and far from exhaustion. He was clean-shaven and dressed in black jeans with a black jersey and boots with no soles (perhaps he'd ruined them by wearing them back to front). They took him to the Mangakino Police Station and fed him his first meal in two days. Then, back to the pokey he went.

More than half a century later he would still find his way around Whakamaru and Mangakino without any difficulty at all, even on a bicycle. The two small towns are in their own time capsules. Both began their later life as hydro villages, both of them bustling and busy when George was scooting around.

You get to Whakamaru across the top of the power station's dam, Lake Whakamaru quiet behind it. Black swans and blue herons poke about carefully. Grassy slopes run up to the inevitable pine forest. George could not have chosen a more dramatic backdrop, although having other things on his mind, probably he didn't give it much thought.

Unbelievably strong forces shaped this country. Whakamaru is the oldest of eight volcanic centres, some twenty-eight eruptions over thousands of years spraying the area with burning debris. Volcanic rock forms monuments, sculptures, cathedrals, cliffs, bluffs, all around it.

The last upheaval, a mere sixty or so years ago, shaped an entire village: the Whakamaru power scheme. State houses are laid out in curving streets of such beauty it is hard to believe now, in an age of geometrical subdivisions, how government planners could have been so derided. A little further on lies the village centre, with its store, café, takeaway, garage — everything a modern society needs.

The turnoff to Titiraupenga lies along the modern road the hydro workers built between Whakamaru and Mangakino. The mountain rises at the edge of the Pureora Forest Park, where fifteen years after it gave refuge to George Wilder protesters took to the treetops to save the ancient rainforest — podocarps which sheltered the rare northern kokako among other species. Unusually, they won. Trampers, mountain bikers and guided tours follow George's tracks now.

From the north the mountain looks like a child's sandcastle, sloping sides, flat top with a perfect cone sitting on it. Its reputation is more severe. Its points and planes glower over the land. Shadows lie across valleys and ravines, giving it a ravaged look.

The road leading towards it, Sandel Road, is a pleasant, storybook sort of road, not quite wide enough for a centre line, but tarsealed for much of its length and running through farmland and the remains of plantations until it ends quite suddenly and becomes the gravel Bush Road, the name hinting at what the country must once have been like up here.

The landscape changes at about the same time and starts to show its volcanic bones. Little bluffs, odd bumps and turrets begin poking out of the paddocks. The road ends in private property now.

Huiarau Stream flows through it. Frankly, it doesn't look much. It's early spring now. Perhaps the stream is quieter, but its banks show no sign of it running rampant.

George was said to have leapt into a raging torrent and swum to safety, but now, even at his age, he could wade across without getting his shorts wet. Sharp cliffs, gorge-like, show where the stream was in its heyday.

Farmers around here evidently take the view that any tree not a pine is taking up good grass space.

Valley Road, home to the farmhouses George broke into, is nowhere to be found.

I go down to Mangakino, a town of charming cottages where power-scheme workers once lived, now painted pink and yellow and pale blue and green, with verandas and trellises and flowers, the kind of place where people stop what they're doing and peer at your passing.

The town centre accommodates a big tavern, which locals boast has the first and largest island bar in the country. They might have mentioned something more important: it was one of two towns designed by the famed émigré, modernist architect and town planner Ernst Plischke, making the town truly unique. The other town was Kaingaroa.

Mangakino has a café and store, and a real estate office where I pop in to ask about people with long memories. A nice woman there points me towards Robert Dwane, said to know a lot about the place.

Robert tells me his father lived in the town before him. Robert, though, was away during the George Wilder affair, returning a little while after and staying there ever since. But he remembers a lot, confirming the newspaper stories, and he says I couldn't find Valley Road because it is now McDonald Road and he knows of no one from Wilder's era still living there.

We stray from the subject. He tells me about his hair. He is seventy-two and it is still pure auburn without a trace of grey. Somehow, without any chemical help, he has reversed the ageing process. His hair was pure white until he got married. Then it took on its present hue, a pure, unflecked, dusky Titian. Unbelievable — but then, so is George.

I surreptitiously question his wife, Gwen. It is true, she says. If she ever discovers his secret, she'll patent it.

Somehow, this seems to fit. The town looks topsy-turvy, as if anything can happen here, and probably has. It exists in a bubble of its own. George could sneak in tomorrow and feel at home. Some, quite a few possibly, would recognise him immediately. Hello George. How've you been?

***

George's next escape lasted almost six months: 172 days. He was serving six and a half years for burglary, shop-breaking, theft and, of course, escaping.

In the early hours of 30 January 1963, prison officer R.H. Grubb was knocked unconscious as he was checking cells in the east-wing basement of Mount Eden prison, then bound and gagged. Grim Victorian piles evidently did not suit George at all well and this one was worse than New Plymouth. Thirty-six people had been executed there, latterly on a scaffold known as 'the meccano', its steel pieces bolted together in a thin space resembling a rocky gorge. The last was Walter Bolton, also the last person to be executed in New Zealand: the hanging in 1957 is said to have been botched so he was effectively strangled to death. That was only six years before George and his three companions, all of them seasoned prison escapees, made their break. No modern notions permeated the grey walls of 'The Rock': it was designed to intimidate. Its gaunt walls still rise above the motorway like a spectre. The prison might have cowed its inmates, but it also gave them a strong incentive to depart.

George and the others went over the wall on a rope made of sheets, of course: next to letting down their hair, which would have made it a short journey, sheets were the traditional way to immortality. The record is currently held by one Ahmad Shelton who, while awaiting trial in a Los Angeles jail, rappelled fourteen storeys down a rope made of sixty bedsheets, calling the *Los Angeles Times* to boast about the feat even before his escape was announced.

Two shots were fired at the Mount Eden desperadoes, one when a small green car failed to stop. Police warned that one of the escapees, Frank Matich, could be dangerous when cornered.

A prison officer told newspapers that Wilder must have worked all night, using a hacksaw to cut away steel facing around the architrave of his cell door then patiently chipping through the wood around the lock with either a chisel or a steel knife. Clearly the New Zealand prison system gave him every reason to rehabilitate himself in society, if a little ahead of his time.

The prison's forensic description of the escape continued. George nailed a twenty-five-centimetre length of leather belt into the wood above the lock and used it as a lever for his knife or chisel. As soon as he got the cell door open he used an 'improvised key' to free the other three.

They ambushed Prison Officer Grubb, knocked him out, bound him with lengths of towelling and a leather belt, took his keys and opened the heavy wooden door to the detention block. They locked that door behind them and used a hacksaw to cut a padlock on the door leading to the exercise yard. Obviously they weren't short of tools. They dragged poor Officer Grubb into a lavatory in the exercise yard beside the prison wall.

'Standing on each others' shoulders', they threw the rope of sheets through the light steel mesh covering the top of the yard, forced a hole through it, climbed six metres up the sheets, through the hole and down a lesser drop on the other side.

When Prison Officer Grubb (who was later treated and discharged) failed to make his next routine phone call to the officer in charge, the break was discovered. The hunt began.

George was described as 1.8 metres tall, of sallow complexion, with fair hair, grey eyes and scars on both knees.

The scars were of no use, of course, for George seems never to have worn shorts, and the description was pretty useless too. All photographs of George show him with dark hair.

The New Zealand Herald published several pictures of him, all different, all looking little like the photographs taken after his arrest. The newspaper suggested he might be hard to identify. His face in the later photographs seems to be made up of triangles: his nose, his ears, his countenance itself the face of a pixie rather than a gnome, always a hint of humour; heavy eyebrows; big, sharp eyes wide-spaced; anxious lines etched into his forehead beneath a mop of dark hair. Not a face you'd be scared of, more someone you used to know.

The four disappeared into the blue. The green car proved a false lead, as did a launch missing from its Hobson Bay mooring. The sure and certain sightings of George began, lots of them, many putting George in several different places at the same time.

A citizen was waiting in his car on Ponsonby Road when two men came along, spotted the car and its driver, put hands to their faces, muttered, 'We'd better get out of here,' turned around and headed off in the opposite direction. The man had time to observe that one of them was Wilder, 'beyond a doubt'. The other was said to be Rueben Awa, another of the escapees.

Obviously Ponsonby Road was different then. In today's eclectic crowd the pair would never be noticed.

Half an hour later 'an Islander' complained that two men had attacked him and stolen his car on Ponsonby Road. Police were looking for a 1954 green Ford Zephyr.

The escapees shared the front page with the Queen, who wrapped herself in furs and boarded an airliner with the Duke of Edinburgh, bound for Fiji at the start of her Royal Tour of Australia and New Zealand, an event which later was to eclipse even George.

On 2 February, the same day that gales across the Pacific forced the Queen and Duke back to Canada, Rueben Awa walked into a Newmarket butcher's shop 'famished and unkempt' and said he wanted to give himself up.

He chose well. The butcher, a Mr N. Stratton, bought him a couple of bread rolls from the baker next door. The candlestick maker was not needed that day.

A couple of days later Frank Matich was recaptured in scrub at Whata Whata in the Waikato, 'hungry, barefoot and exhausted', but still defiant and 'prepared to fight' — until police dog Jon dissuaded him.

Now the royal visit was depleting the searchers' ranks as police concentrated on escort duties. The Queen knocked everything else off the front page. 'Fresh and cool as a summer breeze,' she was said to be, unlike George on the run. A 'triumphant tour' trumped the mad escape.

Until: drama in the Hunua Ranges. Near the little town of Kaiaua the fourth escapee, Patrick Wiwarena, was surprised on the road by two pig-hunters, who offered him a lift (of course). Another man with him dived off the road and down a steep bank. Police believed the diver was George. Several baches between Kawakawa and Kaiaua had been burgled in the previous few days, and food taken. Police were fair about that: they weren't sure the two escapees were responsible, they said.

Then, as a gale prevented the Royal Yacht *Britannia* from entering Wellington Harbour, police dog Duke gashed a leg climbing through a barbed-wire fence on the Wilder hunt. This was a quandary. Police dogs weren't as newsworthy as the Queen, but they weren't far behind. A disabled girl crawling on hands and knees to see the Duke carried the day for the royals.

As the royal couple left New Zealand, a crowd of 5000 roaring goodbye, Wiwarena was recaptured at a bach between

Lake Rotoehu and Lake Rotoma. It was not much more than a kilometre from search headquarters. He appeared in court with a black eye and his right arm in a sling. Police said he had injured himself eluding pursuers.

Pine forests now darken the land here, but bush still forms a tunnel as you drive from Lake Rotoiti to Rotoehu. Rotoma has more baches, many of them appearing more than fifty years old. Perhaps George looked them over. A beautiful, still place, very quiet, and I would have thought he'd have been exposed here.

I take a curly side road to the shadowed valleys on the northern side of Rotoehu. Secluded, with many classic Kiwi baches — pale green, the further back from the lake the older, waterfront property being a more recent maxim of real estate. The place would have suited George, I think.

Police next focused their search on Murupara, where police believed he and Wiwarena had arranged to meet. I go there.

Road workers are rebuilding the bypass, and I wonder why the town needs one. Surely there couldn't be great numbers of cars heading for the Ureweras, probably the wildest road in the country? Besides, Murupara never seemed prosperous enough to lose its through traffic. A roadman gestures furiously at the ground as I drive through. Slow down? Stop? Then why the bypass? Perhaps I'm being blamed for Murupara's woes.

This was Wilder country in the 1960s: remote, sparsely populated, a wild expanse of New Zealand sweeping into the all-but-impenetrable Ureweras.

Yet the police soon lost interest in the town. A car was stolen from Kawerau and later found at Whakatane. Nothing to connect the theft with Wilder, but it was their only fresh clue. They cast about. They searched on the Coromandel after a report that a horse-float driver may have picked him up and dropped him near Paeroa. Another sighting placed him back at Lake Rotoma.

A bach-owner found her door jammed, and upon pushing it open, saw a man standing inside. In her fright she fell, hurting her arm. Police were 'almost certain' it was George.

By the end of February, George had disappeared altogether.

Frank Matich had another crack at freedom, trying to hacksaw his way out of his cell again. He made too much noise and was nabbed. George was better at it. Hacksaws seemed to be freely available in New Zealand jails then.

Around 10 April, when George had been at large for more than three months, police reported a positive sighting — in the Waitakeres. A car reported missing in Gisborne had passed a police patrol car on Scenic Drive near Swanson. Police gave chase. The car pulled up. A man hopped out. Wilder. Police were *certain*. They said he looked slim and was shaven. He dived into nearby bush (George always 'dived').

Police dog Duke gave chase, lost him. They found an apple core, so fresh 'it hadn't turned brown'. Had George stopped for a bite?

Then a man who had been seen looking into the garage of a Titirangi resident was tracked by police dogs until they lost his scent in a creek.

Over eight days, thirty police checked more than 400 houses in Karekare, Piha and all the way up to Anawhata. Whoops! A man looking Wilder-like bought milk and doughnuts from a Jervois Road dairy back in Herne Bay. A constable gave chase but the man ran into Shelly Beach Road and disappeared.

After a taxi driver saw a man dive (of course) into bush, police dog Duke was on the case again. He tracked down a fourteen-year-old boy.

Four months after the escape Mr Justice Gresson gave Matich and Wiwarena 'an exemplary sentence which will demonstrate the futility of these escapes, and perhaps help strip them of the false sentimentality and even glamour with which they are sometimes imbued by foolish and irresponsible persons'.

Ah, too late. Sentimentality and glamour were limpet-like on George. People were humming along to the Howard Morrison Quartet's 'George, the Wild(er) N.Z. Boy'. It was sung to the tune of 'The Wild Colonial Boy', the traditional ballad which had the same outcome in both Australian and Irish versions: romantic Robin Hood bushranger hunted down and shot dead.

However, George was still very much alive, somewhere, for he'd vanished again.

At the end of May, newspapers reported that he had been at large for four months. The *New Zealand Herald* ran a photograph of him. It looked vaguely like George. 'He could be anywhere,' the newspaper said, wisely. He was reported to possess a good knowledge of bush craft — 'but that did not mean he was sitting around in the bush'.

By then, he probably was.

In his absence, we had other things to read about. Gordon Cooper, the US astronaut, was rocketing around Earth in his space capsule, setting a new endurance record. The bodies of Dr Gilbert Boyle and Mrs Margaret Chandler were found on the banks of a Sydney waterway, cause of death unknown. The Profumo affair was in full light. A rise in Golden Kiwi prize money was front-page news.

That June, Wiwarena escaped from Mount Eden a third time.

In July a National Airways Corporation DC3 crashed in the Kaimai Ranges killing all twenty-three aboard. Aucklanders were outraged by the proposed purchase of a Barbara Hepworth sculpture, *Torso II*, for 950 guineas, which, in terms of its current value, was next to nothing. City councillor Tom Pearce compared the sculpture with 'the buttock of a dead cow'. It was eventually bought by businessman George Wooller and donated to the art gallery.

On 16 July Wiwarena was recaptured not far from Tokaanu. He was said to be 'well-dressed, well-fed and clean-shaven'.

A day later, George Wilder was caught near his old haunt, Taupo. He was recaptured at 11 p.m. on a cold, showery night, almost exactly a year after his first escape ended at Mangakino.

He had last been seen on 9 April, when he abandoned the stolen car near Swanson; at least, police thought it was George. For more than three months, he'd vanished. The most common newspaper story had been along the lines of 'nothing to report'.

He'd disappeared into the blue and that was his most remarkable feat. New Zealand was a much smaller country in the 1960s. We were a nosier place. Everyone knew not only their neighbour's business, but the comings, goings, attitudes, ages, incomes, sports, politics, marital states and IQs of their entire suburb.

You didn't get someone like George, bad photographs or not, wandering about without anyone noticing, especially when any poll (had there been one) would have shown that three quarters of the nation wanted to clap him on the back and the others to dob him in, without any 'don't knows'.

In the end he was nailed by — a bird. Well, the combination of a bird and a concerned citizen. A ranger, Don Main, employed by what, in those pre-Department of Conservation days, was the Department of Internal Affairs, knew that someone had been killing kereru, native pigeons, in an area called Runanga. It lay beside the Napier highway, about fifty kilometres from Taupo. Up to then it was noted only for the Runanga stockade, built like a Maori pa, one of a chain of small fortresses thrown up by Pakeha troopers in 1869–70 against Te Kooti's dwindling forces, and abandoned in 1876. After that the area was given over to farming and logging.

Main inspected a rough old wooden hut, sagging, missing some of its weatherboards, evidently part of a defunct logging operation, but found no one there. (Wilder later said he saw the man approach and took to the bush until the coast was clear.) But he must have suspected something. Soon afterwards, at nine in the evening, he and three policemen, one of them his brother Brian, left Taupo. It was a cold, wet night. They turned off the Napier–Taupo highway a few kilometres south of Rangitaiki onto a rough pumice road leading to bush on the foothills of the Ahimanawa Range and sneaked along the track.

'We could see a light inside,' Main told reporters. 'Fortunately I know the track well and we were able to reach the hut without tripping over anything.'

As Brian Main described it later, they kicked down the door and charged into the hut. They found George inside, dozing beside a fire, a couple of candles burning on a shelf over the fireplace, his radio playing soft music.

In this romantic setting George must have been feeling warm and comfortable, his usual instincts snoozing with him, his sixth sense put away for the night. In Ranger Main's account, 'He tried to get up at first, but then he realised he was properly caught and he just lay there. He was sullen after his arrest, and did not have much to say.'

George's wildest journey had come to an end. The handcuffs went on 172 days after he escaped, the longest New Zealand escape on record, beating Trevor Nash's 158 days from two years before.

The officer in charge, Sergeant Marson of Taupo, said that George was in very good physical condition but uncommunicative. He offered no resistance. He denied being George Wilder at first but Marson knew him from his recapture at Mangakino.

He had three loaded rifles and a dozen rounds of ammunition with him. He had apparently been living in the hut for some time, trapping possums, living off the land, using the rifles to get his dinners, maybe the kereru which led to his downfall.

Compare his arrest with the twenty-first century version. Wilder was known to be armed. In a modern version, the Armed Offenders' Squad would go in with body armour and assault weapons and dogs and a helicopter or two. Here, a trio of cops and a wildlife ranger tiptoed up a bush track in the dark and rushed in, no shots fired, fair's fair, everything's jake, a testimonial from the arresting officers, Sergeant Marston declaring there was nothing sinister about Wilder's weapons and Constable Main averring that he wasn't a violent person.

That was more than half a century ago but worlds away, and now I am traipsing through the events — and the deeper into it I go, the more I am immersed in its essential decency.

Did I have the sense of following in his footsteps? Nah. He trod too lightly, too easily.

So I go to Rangitaiki. The road passes Opepe, another of the stockades built during the Te Kooti campaign, where on 7 June 1869 some of Te Kooti's force surprised a detachment of fourteen Bay of Plenty militia camped in the abandoned village. Nine militia men were killed, but no Maori. I walk up through damp bush to their graves, heavy, cold, wet, even in summer.

The sky lowers over the landscape and it begins to rain. The road tracks through arid pine forests that would not have kept George in kereru for very long. In fact, it doesn't look the kind of place where anyone would worry about pigeons now. Is there any country more depressing than a place where pines have been? A formless landscape, without landmarks, and I am lost in it. No sign of anything that once was, and especially no trace of George.

I follow this track and that, to the place where I calculate, or guess, George had been caught, but the land has been turned over. The old mill has long gone and George's hut was already falling down when he was found in it. I float around in this modern wilderness and come to an oasis: the Rangitaiki Tavern, 'home of the famous bugger burger'.

A bloke there remembers George being caught 'on one of the blocks up the road'. Lots of bush mills were working then, all gone now. He has a sharper memory of coming home over a bridge after a session and, bugger, there was a roadblock on the other side and he was bound to be snapped. But the police just looked inside the car and waved him through. They were looking for George. George had saved his bacon.

It is 7.30 a.m. I sit in a long room with the TV on the wall going, eating poached eggs on big square pieces of white-bread toast with thick bacon. The cook tells me he'd thought George was OK. He remembers the Howard Morrison song and looks as if he might break out a line or two.

I put my dishes on the counter. 'Thanks, boss,' he says.

George escaped from jail once more, for a only a few hours, but this seems the place to end the quest, except for some postscripts. For a start, how did George survive so well for so long within easy reach of Taupo? Someone must have known he was there, someone must have given him a hand.

Someone did.

I encounter a woman I once worked with in Christchurch, June Peka. She spent her childhood in Taupo. Here is what she told me:

I was eleven, I reckon. We lived in Taupo. I had a horse and all the freedom in the world.

We were quite feral. We didn't get into trouble but we weren't overseen much.

I was riding my horse in the bush when I found this beautiful, shiny black Buick. I was mad about cars so I was sure of it. Flash cars like that were few and far between. Later I saw George had a liking for Buicks and Jaguars and I know this one was a Buick. I think it might have been owned by Henry Johnson, who had a milk bar/restaurant in Taupo. Mum and Dad had the pie shop, the Cindy Lou restaurant and later the Le Mans hamburger bar.

I rode my horse up to it, and there was a bloke sleeping in the front seat. I thought he'd been injured and he needed help. I rode home and got Dad.

We went back in his old Fordson van. We parked it and had to walk into the bush a few hundred yards. Dad told me to stay back.

He opened the door, and the bloke woke up, and they talked for half an hour or so.

I didn't know who he was. But I think that was how George and Dad met. Dad was a bit of a wide boy; he was on the fringes, but he was never involved in anything seriously criminal.

Later, after George had been caught and was in jail, he made contact with Dad again. Dad was a cook up at The Terraces hotel out of Taupo. He told me about meeting up with George again after he escaped. He took a waitress called Luvvie with him.

George was hiding in a hut, a cabin way up in the bush. It was pretty bare, just somewhere to sleep in. On the walls he'd drawn light switches, a calendar, he'd even drawn a light hanging from the ceiling. It was very realistic.

Dad was taking out food from the Terraces for some time. He must have given George my mother's rifle.

My mother's name was Ngaire, my father's Sonny. We were a shooting family.

The cops gave it back to us. They said they found it when they caught George.

It has words carved into the stock. They're quite faint: 'George Wilder.' I never really examined it, but now, I can see, faintly, underneath, ' C/- Sonny.' Dad almost definitely would have given it to him. He went out there to the hut quite a lot.

I still have the rifle. I've never used it since. I put the bolt away many years ago. It's lost now, so it can't be fired.

My brother and I always wondered why Dad didn't get into trouble. They wouldn't have been surprised to know Dad was involved.

I remember Brian Main too. I was in awe of him. He threatened to kick my arse once or twice.

I probably went up to the hut where he was caught, but I can't remember it. Taupo was the wild west in those days. We lived in the bush, even in the town streets — we lived in Tamatea Avenue — and half the houses were holiday houses. Most were batten and board baches or two Ministry of Works huts joined. Most you couldn't see from the road. You'd follow a track and there'd be a holiday house at the end of it. George would have had no trouble getting into them. Some weren't even locked. At others the key would be under the mat.

My friend Raymond and I did things like that and we were only kids. No one would be there for six months, or a year, and they were very easy to get into in those days. We didn't vandalise them, but we'd quite often get into those places, cook up some rice, make some cocoa.

I think everyone thought George was harmless. He was certainly not someone you'd be afraid of.

I remember the talk around town, people saying George was out there searching with the buggers last night, it was raining like hell, everyone had parkas on and George was with them with a big grin on his face hunting for himself.

That's another story for the George Wilder file, and here's one more. George is said to have had his hair cut by a well-known Taupo barber. He had no money, so the two made a deal: George would pay for his haircut with the skins of animals he'd shot.

Brian Main later went much further. By his own account he got George a job at Poronui Station, now a glamorous sporting lodge in the Taharua Valley, south-west of Taupo: 'He was a bloody good worker, did earthworks, built bridges, did anything and enjoyed it. He was just a young fella sowing his oats.'

Main died in March 2017, a little after his brother Don. His widow, Anne, told me he'd always liked George: 'If you'd asked him about George, you wouldn't have been able to get away. He would have gone on and on. You get the nasty, vicious ones now, but George? He was just a ratbag.'

**

His story lies astride another one, of what makes a New Zealand hero, of the characteristics we most admire in ourselves: enterprise, self-sufficiency.

In the great New Zealand literary tradition he loved small towns, small places. Where he lives now is near one of the smallest, Herbertville, a tiny place on the border of Hawkes Bay and Wairarapa. It was once a much busier place, when steamers put into nearby Cape Turnagain and the big coastal sheep stations were in their prime, loading wool onto schooners beaching on the sand and refloating with the tide. Pub, shops, police station. The grand old pub down the road at Wimbledon was built in 1869.

Now Herbertville is a place people have left, for it's more a holiday-home settlement, with a camping ground that was bought by its campers.

In his own fashion George reversed the trend and boosted the permanent population by one. *The Evening Post* reported that when he was finally freed from Paparua Prison in Christchurch on 20 June 1969, 'Wilder disappeared after his release … as silently and efficiently as he glided into the bush after his escapes.'

He's still lying low. He's not looking for publicity, although publicity is looking for him. Journalists, writers and TV producers have tried to entice him out. I wrote him a letter care of the local golf club, where, in a photograph of a golf team, published some forty years after his final release from jail, he is instantly recognisable. It was returned unopened.

George's wild journey continues. He has made his greatest escape of all.

2

Voyaging north

Capes are the loneliest places in the world. They are a country's extremities, jutting into the ocean at its corners, places where the winds clash and the cold gathers, feared by sailors, shunned. They both end and begin the land in wells of fear and despair.

The land-bound stand on them with feelings of vertigo, as if the world has changed and they may never find their way back, while below them the seas clash and the rocks grind.

At sea level capes become mythical. Bernard Moitessier, the French sailor who saved his soul by refusing to finish the first non-stop round-the-world yacht race in 1968–69 and instead sailed half-a-globe more, saw them like this:

A great cape is both a very simple and an extremely complicated whole of rocks, currents, breaking seas and huge waves, fair winds and gales, joys and fears, fatigue, dreams [...] A great cape, for us, can't be expressed in longitude and latitude alone. A great cape has a soul, with very soft, very

violent shadows and colours. A soul as smooth as a child's,
as hard as a criminal's.

Moitessier wrecked three boats, two on reefs and one on a beach, but none on capes, perhaps because he held them in such reverence.

The world's great capes are not just the circumnavigating sailor's landmarks, but signposts of history. They form elegies, mnemonics: Horn, Good Hope, Leeuwin.

New Zealand has added to the ballad in its own, no-nonsense way. Certainly we have Palliser, Maria van Diemen, Farewell, Foulwind, Turnagain, Reinga and Egmont. But our main capes, the ones at the very top and bottom of the mainland, are simply North and South. Both are named with a complete lack of romance and entirely in keeping with the nation's love of practicality. North Cape lies at the top of North Island, South Cape at the bottom of Rakiura or Stewart Island (known as South Island, before it was renamed for an adventurous sealer).

If North Cape is the head of the New Zealand universe, does that make South Cape the bottom end, with all its connotations? Or is it the other way round? Essentially, it depends on which one you're tackling at the time, for both can be beguiling, and ferocious, and you round either one with fingers crossed or cursing.

Other capes in New Zealand's half of the world reflect the mystery and magic of their breed, and the conflicted souls of their explorers. The Cape of Good Hope in South Africa is a rocky, nasty place, home of the *Flying Dutchman,* crewed by more-than-usually unhinged sailors spending eternity trying to round it.

Cape Horn in Chile, the most famous of them all, was 'discovered' by the Dutch navigator Willem Schouten, who rounded in a dreadful storm in January 1616 and named it after Hoorn in his homeland, a beautiful city with a civility entirely at odds with its namesake.

Early explorers were typically arrogant: various groups of people already inhabited the Tierra del Fuego region, and doubtless had their own names for its most distinctive feature. So it was with North Cape. Maori called the cape at the end of their universe Otou, but Captain James Cook preferred sticking to the point: North Cape it was.

Cook spied a pa on the cape, and even saw a few of its people, but a strong current was belting into the *Endeavour* and conspired with wind to carry the ship well to the north. On this brief acquaintance, North Cape it remained.

When Cook rounded the cape at the bottom of Stewart Island, until then named Whiore, it duly became South Cape. Stewart Island itself was named after the first officer of the sealer *Pegasus,* who'd been busily charting the southern coast, his name supplanting Te Punga o Te Waka o Maui, 'the anchor stone of Maui's waka', and the even more poetic Rakiura, 'isle of the glowing skies'. So the northernmost and southernmost points of New Zealand were set in true two-by-four fashion without any of that nonsense of homesickness or demented sailors — nor any nod towards their inhabitants.

Both North and South capes, essentially, are knobs of rock all but inaccessible by land and certainly best avoided by sea. The permanent population of both is zero, usually.

I am not an intrepid sailor, nor even a very good one. But I have rounded both capes by sea, South Cape twice (see Chapter 9). The second time was accidental.

***

My brother Craig owns a fine boat, the *Crocus*, which he built over two decades or so. It was shipped unfinished from his then home in the United States to his new one in Auckland, where he completed it, and has sailed happily ever since. The *Crocus* was based on a design by the Norwegian naval architect Colin Archer, famous for his seagoing yachts.

So I was perfectly happy to entrust my life to it when Craig rang one day and asked if I would crew his boat on the second half of a North Island circumnavigation. We were to sail from Picton up the west coast of the North Island and yes, around North Cape. We would then sail down the east coast to Auckland.

I'm not a very good sailor mainly because I can't be bothered with the essential detail: I love boats but I muck around in them and let someone else handle chores such as making sure we're heading in the right direction, commonly known as navigation. I follow Toad's philosophy in *The Wind in the Willows* that 'there is nothing — absolutely nothing — half so much worth doing as simply messing about in boats'. My main talent, as a sailor, is that I don't get seasick, although another common sailing dictum is that someone who hasn't been seasick simply hasn't sailed far enough.

I travelled from Christchurch to Picton by bus, the only passenger from Kaikoura onwards, chatting with the driver. Picton lay dark that evening, the boat lying massively in the quiet water: the solidity of her, the romance of her mast and rigging. She looked as if she'd just come around the world, shaken off the salt water like a dog, and was ready to jump back in again. A determined-looking bowsprit jutted in front and her solid rudder hung off the canoe stern that Archer boats were famed for.

Without any messing around, off we went up the knobbly Queen Charlotte Sound, past Blumine Island, and Pickersgill, and Long Island, and Motuara Island, where Cook raised the flag and took possession of the South Island for King George III, and Cannibal Cove where a boatload of sailors from the *Adventure*, sister ship to Cook's *Resolution*, were cooked and eaten, and into a full gale blasted by the bellows of Cook Strait.

Small-boat voyages are the stuff of dreams, of sailing blue seas with one hand on the tiller and the other clutching a tall drink, one eye on the horizon and the other seeing palm trees beyond. I've yet to have one like that. The truth is that, particularly belting into a fresh wind and a short sea, you think of dice in a cup so sympathetically you fancy you may never play Snakes and Ladders again.

You can experience your own offshore voyage by blindfolding yourself, getting someone to spin you around a dozen times then topple you into a cave, one of those with rocks dangling from the roof, sticking from the sides and lying ready to trip you at every step. A simple journey to the ship's lavatory, full of pipes, tubes, valves and levers like a medieval torture chamber in which you cling to the nearest protuberance and balance as best you can, is the kind of wild journey that seldom makes the sailing pages.

The most seaman-like way of dealing with the situation is to set the self-steering, which works through a wind vane and enables the boat to steer itself; check the radar detector, which detects other vessels' radar and sets off an alarm; hop into your sleeping bag and put up something called a lee-cloth, which stops you from falling out of bed; and pop out every so often to check that all is well. And since by now it was dark, that is what we did.

In this way we snored deep into the South Taranaki Bight until, on one of my trips into the cockpit to gaze blindly around, terrify myself with the masses of water which towered one moment then passed harmlessly underneath, and convince myself all was well, I noticed that we were sailing into the middle of a large city. I said so, loudly.

My brother, a much better sailor, who knew exactly where we were and what lay ahead, told me these were oil rigs.

Oil rigs? They were sea-borne skyscrapers, monsters full of lights and ill intent. Bugger the lee-cloth. If we were going to hit one of those, or its pipelines or the boats which I was sure were clustering around them like flies, I was going over the side like an undersize snapper when the fishing inspector comes by.

I checked my inflatable lifejacket, which from that moment on was pyjamas and deck attire combined.

The sun rose, and as it often does after dark and stormy nights, the wind died, the sea flattened and the oil rigs became well, just oil rigs. Taranaki took its graceful shape and Cape Egmont, whose every headland once boasted a pa, turned into its cracked and crenellated self.

Six knots or so is quite a decent speed for a tubby, heavy boat in what was now a good breeze and a smooth sea. The rule of thumb for sailing ships was to calculate voyage times at 160 kilometres a day. The *Crocus* could do much better, but still, going around the coast on a yacht is rather like jogging beside a mountain range. Nothing changes very much for a long time, but the next time you take notice, everything is different.

New Plymouth went by and there was sea, and more sea, all of it empty, and night fell again.

We had a fair breeze, and everything was nice and quiet, and the boat moved easily through the water, making scarcely a sound. We divided the night into watches, which meant that one of us was responsible for the boat at certain times of the night, and it was during Craig's watch that I got out of bed to go to the toilet and check the chart-plotter while I was about it. This was an excellent instrument which showed exactly where the boat was, and where it was going, and a red line showed where it had been. The line showed that at some point in the night the wind had changed and the vane had turned the boat through a neat right angle and we were now heading for Australia. I woke Craig and told him so. He seemed unimpressed. What was he going to do about it? I asked. He was thinking about that, he replied.

I went on to the toilet and passed his bunk on the way back. He snored in a carefree sort of way. Oh well, I decided, it was his boat, and I went back to bed.

The sun rose on a small boat out at sea with no land in sight. We turned around, and slowly, magically, New Zealand reappeared. I was relieved. There was always the possibility that those dark forces which inhabit dreams had spirited it away.

We passed a fishing boat, quite close, but if we expected some salty camaraderie, some companionship on the ocean — for after all we were the only two boats in the world as far as we could see — we were disappointed. The crew worked on deck without so much as looking up. Were they poaching?

Cape Maria van Diemen began to take shape, one of the world's most beautiful capes, white sand reaching through bones of rock to a knuckle at its end and Motuopao Island settling just offshore, the remains of its old lighthouse symmetrical as a castle keep.

Beautiful like a yellow-bellied sea snake.

The sea rose up off this cape and swallowed the collier *Kaitawa* and her twenty-nine crew on 23 May 1966. The *Kaitawa* was not a big ship, but a ship nonetheless. That dark night she just disappeared, leaving a single, faint radio call for help hanging in the ether. No one knows what happened. The best guess is that a giant wave swept the ship and gulped her down, shoving the crippled hulk onto the awful Pandora Bank, which completed the job.

Water frolicked over Pandora Bank today. We stayed away.

Cape Reinga was now in sight. It is not New Zealand's most northerly point, but it *is* the nation's northernmost tourist attraction.

Two great seas meet right there, the Tasman Sea on the west side, the Pacific Ocean on the east. It is not a friendly meeting. The two clash and bash.

The result is often called a 'confused sea'. I don't think it is at all confused. The two staunch up to each other and, since neither will give way, turmoil ensues. White waters twist and whirl and dump like wrestlers.

I stood up there on the cape once, sheltering beside the famous lighthouse with a busload of tourists in a gale, and all of us were awed. It was strange, and distant, as if we were in another place. We were peering into the devil's hole, and we felt so light upon the ground that we looked for something to hold on to. No one so much as reached for a phone. The fury of it scared everyone. None of us stayed long.

I resolved never, ever, to go anywhere near that place by sea.

Yet here I was, sailing around it — and the frothing water leapt, danced around in the sun, and the tourists up by the lighthouse packed the fences and took photographs and were probably saying, 'Look at that little boat down there. What a great view they must have, lucky things,' and we passed by just as quickly as we possibly could.

Now the perfect sweep of Spirits Bay lay on our starboard side. The Maori name for Spirits Bay is Kapowairua. It was once home to Tohe, a Ngati Kahu chief. He left his people to make a last visit to his daughter, who lived on the Kaipara, enjoining his people to grasp his spirit should he die. He *did* die before reaching his daughter, and the bay took the name he bequeathed, 'spirit'. It's said to be the place where spirits of the dead leave for the afterlife, and if that is so, then they'll depart with fond memories.

From the land, on a good day, the bay is a perfect curved beach, Northland's bluey-green sea pumping delicious waves onto its pale sand. From the sea it is more mysterious. A Department of Conservation camp site, said to be one of the best in New Zealand, lies at its eastern end under Hooper Point. Beyond lies Tom Bowling Bay, and a light shone in its corner. A house? Here? Tom Bowling Bay is not only uninhabited, it is very hard to get into. I resolved to check later.

Almost there. But the top of New Zealand has a quirk. Despite the mythology, North Cape to the Bluff and so on, North Cape is not the northernmost part of New Zealand.

The Surville Cliffs occupy that spot. With the colonial habit of calling landmarks after European passers-by rather than using the names bestowed by the locals for centuries, these commemorate a French captain, Jean-Francois-Marie de Surville, who saw them just a few days before Captain Cook did.

By now dusk was gathering and by any name at all the Surville Cliffs were gloomy. They rose sheer from the sea, white foam lighting their base. They are formed by rock called ultrabasic, which means, essentially, something pretty barren. It takes a special kind of plant to grow there, which from the sea seemed to be stunted creatures clinging desperately to life — and that is what they are, both rare and endangered.

The cliffs looked a place no one wanted to go to, and that was true also.

North Cape lay just around the corner.

It was quite dark now. Some people are sanguine about approaching a coast in a small boat at night. I am not one of them. I find a dark coast frightening and a black cape truly terrifying, being both extremely hard by nature and difficult to climb by shipwrecked sailors, even scared ones with large waves up their backsides.

North Cape, or Otou, seemed alarmingly close, and waves crashed and banged as they do. And what was that beyond? An island? No one had mentioned that. But here it was, Murimotu, where the cape's lighthouse (a residual stump replacing the cast iron classic of old) flicked on and off.

Many sailors welcome lights. They're a symbol of hope, a metaphor for life, love, a path to salvation. They scare me. I know that beneath them lies something dark and savage.

My grip on the tiller was firm, in the way a dead man's clutch has to be pried loose. Below, in the cabin, Craig peered into his chart-plotter, and reeled off the course, a few degrees this way, a couple of degrees that. I halved the number of degrees towards the cape and doubled the number away from it. I was quite certain we were heading for the rocks.

Surf rumbled. Black rock loomed. The light winked. *Come closer, big boy.*

And we were round. We would anchor for the night, said Craig. My god, here?

No, off a sandy beach that lay beyond. He'd anchored there before. It was good. Safe.

We eased around the cape in darkness so deep, so profound: it was as terrifying as the small hours when you wake blind, not knowing where you are.

Now the sound of the cape behind us was being drowned (oh, that awful word) by the noise of waves breaking on a beach. That was not good, I knew. Waves could suck in a yacht and spit it onto the beach in several bits. 'Close, just a little closer,' said my brother on the chart-plotter. But he could feel my nervousness.

'This'll do,' he said, and we dropped the anchor off Waikuku Beach. The Waikuku Flats are a tombolo which join North Cape, once an island itself, to the mainland. He slept soundly, I woke often. On land waves shush in a soothing way. At sea they hiss.

***

Later, I met Charlie Petera. A kaumatua of the Ngati Kuri, he was the last surviving Ngati Kuri soldier to have fought in World War II, and one of the last veterans of the 28th Maori Battalion to have seen action overseas when he died in June 2016, at the age of ninety-two.

Charlie and his wife Katerina were New Zealand's northernmost residents, owning a house at the north end of Parengarenga Harbour, a little south of Waikuku Beach and the cape. He was born there, crossing the harbour to go to school at

Te Hapua. Only a couple of houses remained, and his was the only occupied one, New Zealand's northernmost house.

I asked about the light in Tom Bowling Bay. 'There was once a community in Tom Bowling Bay,' he said, 'but it vanished a long time ago.'

I asked other people. No house there, everyone said, and no light either. Who then owned that ghostly spark of light in the night?

The map showed a road leading past Tom Bowling Bay and stopping above the Surville Cliffs. North Cape itself is a reserve, a forbidden zone. You must cross Maori land to reach Tom Bowling Bay, or Waikuku Flat. I asked the iwi, the Muriwhenua (North Cape) Incorporation, for permission to drive in and see for myself. No deal. The mystery remained unsolved.

But that morning, when I awoke off Waikuku Beach, the world was a magical place where anything could happen. The sun shone on dunes a creamy white, housing the bones and artefacts of former residents. Wild horses galloped along Waikuku Beach. We were the only living creatures in our universe. North Cape was just a shape.

3

Raiding south

Tuturau lies deep in the Southland green. It is more a name on
a map than a settlement. You take a side road from Mataura
to Wyndham. The road follows the Mataura River and about
halfway along you pass Tuturau, if you're alert.

On a bare hill above the road, with a fine view over Southland's
lush land, a stone monument juts out from a scattering of te kouka,
cabbage trees. The monument is a war memorial, like hundreds
of others in towns and lonely places. It is a little different from
the rest, however.

The pillar was erected to mark the centennial of the 'battle'
of Tuturau. The northern chief Te Puoho died here, at the end
of the longest overland raid in New Zealand history. The raiders
marched 1500 kilometres through dense bush and raging rivers,
over mountain passes and impossible headlands. This wasn't just
a wild journey. It was an incredible one.

At the end of it Te Puoho was killed. He died uselessly, in
a doomed and futile quest. His death was so inconsequential

that in the twenty-first century he might have been described as 'collateral damage'.

Ah, but his raid. That was different. It is his true memorial, an epic adventure ranging the length of the South Island. He hacked, scrambled and climbed his way through country seldom tracked then and still, the best part of two centuries later, unknown to many. There's a reason for that. I set out to see just how formidable a journey it was, and was beaten to a standstill almost immediately.

Te Puoho's plan was simple. He intended to destroy an entire people, the South Island Ngai Tahu.

Even then Ngai Tahu had been masters of Te Wai Pounamu, the South Island, for some eight centuries. They owned the gold standard of the time, pounamu, jade or greenstone. By the early nineteenth century they'd become successful traders with whalers too.

Te Puoho planned to lead a taua, a war-party, from Golden Bay down the West Coast, through bush and over mountains, to attack Ngai Tahu settlements along the southern coast and their island strongholds in Foveaux Strait, then force-march the survivors back up the South Island's east coast, mopping up other settlements as he went. He intended to enslave them all in a great pen he would build at Paturau, on the coast a little south of Farewell Spit.

Te Puoho was a Ngati Tama chief. The Taranaki iwi were allies of Ngati Toa and enemies of Ngai Tahu. Te Puoho first ran his plan past his ally and de facto superior, Te Rauparaha.

The Ngati Toa chief wasn't sure it was a good idea. He'd beaten up the Ngai Tahu along the east coast of the South Island, taken their great pa at Kaiapoi then struck down the mighty Onawe fortress in Akaroa Harbour. But the southerners were regrouping, fighting back, and Te Rauparaha was too good at his work to underrate them.

Perhaps he felt the Mordor-like eye of the Ngai Tahu chief Tuhawaiki on Ruapuke. Tuhawaiki was known among Pakeha as 'Bloody Jack', his reputation enhanced by the massacre of a sealing gang, the sealers killed and eaten.

Ruapuke is a grim island in Foveaux Strait. Passengers on the Stewart Island ferry pass its dark bulk and might wonder if anyone ever lived there, for Ruapuke hunkers down in this fierce strait, fair square in the path of every storm. Yet Ngai Tahu still inhabit the island, depending on the season.

At that time, 1836, Ruapuke was the de facto capital of the Ngai Tahu empire. Te Rauparaha's raids had forced the Ngai Tahu power base southwards into Murihiku. Tuhawaiki's power had grown with the shift, and some say it was he who'd grabbed Te Rauparaha at Lake Grassmere in Marlborough and forced him off the South Island. The Ngati Toa chief slipped out of his cloak and swam for his life.

Now Tuhawaiki glared balefully north from his Ruapuke stronghold. Te Rauparaha could see the flaws in Te Puoho's plan clearly enough. He knew that the Ngati Tama chief was committing the classic mistake of underestimating his enemy. Ngai Tahu would not be easy targets, he warned.

Te Puoho disagreed. He took a Napoleonic view of his enemy: softies, he declared. Historians have dickered over the details, but he gathered around him a force of somewhere between fifty and one hundred warriors, and some women. From the perspective of the twenty-first century the notion of taking on an entire iwi with so small an army seems optimistic, even without taking into consideration the route they took.

Historians have also differed over their path, but the scope of the journey is clear enough. In a sentence, they marched down the West Coast, over the Haast Pass through Otago and into Southland. That is talking the talk. Walking the walk was entirely different.

This was New Zealand in the raw. If they were lucky there'd be a faint track through primeval forest, with its barbed entanglements of understorey. No bridges crossed what are still the roughest rivers in the land. They had no blankets, no food stores, no shoes, no shelter tents, parkas, no solace of any kind unless you count the mad ambition of their leader.

Well, Te Puoho may have been a deluded tyrant, but no one can doubt his ability to forge his way and leap all hurdles in his path.

I fell at the first of them.

The route was easy enough at its beginning. The starting point, Puturau, where Te Puoho planned to set up his holding pens for captured slaves, lies high on the West Coast, a little south of Whanganui Inlet. Today you get there quite quickly, turning off the highway to Farewell Spit at Pakawau and driving over a low saddle. Already you are on the track Te Puoho probably used to reach the coast, for the road follows an old Maori trail.

You reach a fork. One branch heads north, stopping short of Cape Farewell. The other turns south, clinging to the edge of Whanganui Inlet. The scene starts rearranging itself. You feel dislocated. This might be the twenty-first century, but it could as easily be one hundred years ago.

The road is narrow, unsealed. The surroundings seem unfamiliar. Forest runs down to the inlet. It's thick, and green, of the kind that if left to itself wants to be much thicker. The rata is bright red.

Mangarakau appears, suddenly. Time goes into reverse. Going on two centuries ago this would have been a busy little town. Maori were already living here when the first Europeans arrived in the 1830s. The colonists mined coal, shipping it out through the nearby Whanganui Inlet, whose narrow entrances provided the only shelter on this part of the coast.

Three decades later the inlet accommodated coal mining, flax and timber milling. Gold was discovered. Mangarakau became a boom town: ships in the harbour, a tramway, shops, school, post office, farms. But eventually everything ran out, although sawmilling dragged on until 1968. Only the town hall remains, with a visitor centre and museum. The hulk of the scow *Kohi*, once one of a fleet of uniquely New Zealand craft designed for river bars and shallow harbours, still lies beside the old jetty.

Te Atiawa groups allied to Ngati Tama had invaded this land, ensuring that Te Puoho would not have to fight his way south past hostile iwi. The terrain, however, remained implacable.

The road runs from Mangarakau to Paturau, still following the old Maori trail. The centre of civilisation, once. A big Maori village stood here, supplying the hundreds of diggers who came after gold.

The Maori trail ran onto the beach but the lonely road clings to slightly higher ground, growing ever more meagre.

Now you're in no doubt at all. This is another country. The Tasman roars on one side. Waves bash the coast. You can feel salt on your lips. The scrub tilts crazily, barbered by the fierce west wind. Limestone faces rise high.

At the Anatori River, you stop. The road crosses the river, perhaps. You need a serious four-wheel drive. Even then it stalls four kilometres south, at the Turimawiwi River and its baches.

Otherwise from here, you walk. As you look south along this lonely landscape, your heart drops another notch. You're on your own here, in every sense. The first obstacle is the Anatori bluffs, and you have the drop on Te Puoho here, for the road bypasses them.

You also have the tide tables, because the mouths of the Anaweka River and Big River are dangerous, safe to cross only at low tide, and that's if the Tasman Sea is not wild — which is rather like hoping an elephant is not big. Beyond them are rock tablelands reaching into the sea.

At the foot of Kahurangi Point lies a Department of Conservation hut first made from the old lighthouse keepers' houses. You look around and think, Well, at least Te Puoho didn't have to live here. Lighthouse keepers and their families did. Their lives were always dramatic. They relied on boats and packhorses to bring supplies, and schedules on this wild coast were erratic. Once, a spat with a landowner prevented supplies getting to the lighthouse at all, stranding a keeper's wife in Collingwood until it was resolved.

The 1929 Murchison earthquake smashed the keepers' house altogether. James Mackay, the government agent infamous for his role in land purchases from Ngai Tahu (he did them far more damage than Te Puoho ever did) investigated this route as a possible bridle track linking Nelson to the West Coast goldfields. He reported, in 1860, that the coast from here to the Heaphy River was 'a most frightful rocky and precipitous' one which should be avoided by taking the track inland by the valleys of the Heaphy and Aorere rivers to Collingwood. That, of course, is the route now trodden by thousands on the Heaphy Track.

Charles Heaphy and Thomas Brunner, the surveyors and explorers, came here, and bargained their right of way down the coast with Te Niho, one of Te Rauparaha's chiefs, following Te Puoho's tracks a decade or so later. They reported rocky beaches passable only at low water, and precipitous points 'which had to be ascended by ropes of flax and supplejack'.

Very little has changed. Golden Bay author Gerard Hindmarsh called it 'the impassable coast' in his book *Kahurangi Calling*, 'an area so harsh and inaccessible it remains virtually untouched to this day'. He and three companions bashed their way along it, nevertheless, risking terrain that sometimes terrified them, and joined the select few who'd survived the journey.

Everything I'd read about this coast, written by trampers more experienced and better equipped than I, came to me as I considered it. Hut book entries record: 'Whatever you do, do not try to walk down this coast.' 'Karamea or bust, and I bust.'

Perpendicular cliffs. Dense bush, all but impenetrable. Dangerous fords. Gales. Waves of Hokusai proportions. Vertiginous sense of unreality. Seals furious at intrusion. Rocks whose size is measured in storeys. Impracticable. Appalling. Terrifying. Exhausting. No sign of human life present or past. Most of all, beyond help. Many turned back. People who made the journey came out scratched, bruised and scared.

I considered all of this. I was not Te Puoho, or Heaphy, or Brunner, or Mackay. I was a storyteller. Ahead lay thirty kilometres of the nastiest, bitiest (sandflies compete with seals for the honour), rockiest, riskiest, smelliest (seals), loneliest, wettest country in all New Zealand. Was I stupid enough? Well, yes, but not this time.

I decided on a detour. I went back up the coast to my car and drove a giant loop through Golden Bay and over the Takaka Hill to Motueka, then down the Motueka River valley and over the Hope Saddle to the Buller and Murchison, then through the Buller Gorge to Westport and up to Karamea to rejoin Te Puoho's path on the first part of the Heaphy Track, which was very beautiful and oh so civilised, even over the once-feared Kohaihai Bluff. It was the long way round but an easy one and it would have won Te Puoho's vote as he bashed and crashed his way down the Kahurangi coast.

My brother Neil knew that coast well. He'd worked in the environmental arm of what was then the Forest Service. He always looked to me as if he'd been made of rata vine himself. He could do the Heaphy Track in a day. One of his stories was about the wreck of the *Marudai Maru No 2*, a Japanese squid boat. She ran aground on the reef surrounding the Bluff. The crew was winched off and dropped at the Heaphy Hut among surprised trampers.

Two Forest Service workers and one tramper claimed salvage rights and held off all comers for a couple of days, until the wreck became Crown property and was sold off. But a fair amount of the ship's gear was circulating by then: my own memento of the wreck was a beautiful braided line which became my anchor warp for the next twenty years.

Te Puoho must have felt pretty good as he emerged from that part of the coast and surveyed the territory ahead. Well, as good as a man might feel when his mission in life is to wipe out an entire people.

The Heaphy Track stops at the Kohaihai River and a nice safe swing bridge takes you across to join the road. In the late nineteenth century, well after Te Puoho had been and gone, colonists contemplated a town here on the Kohaihai. The spot was surveyed, and a little map shows what was going to be what: a school here, cemetery there, roads throughout, even a zone for 'landless natives', possibly those robbed of their land by Mackay himself. It remained a paper town only, but who knows? Business interests have long lobbied for a road to run from here to Golden Bay, slicing through pristine bush and mountains.

The Ngatirarua chief Niho rampaged down this coast in the early 1830s, capturing the Ngai Tahu chief Tuhuru and taking him back to Paturau where he was ransomed, the deal including his daughter's marriage to Niho and the establishment of strongholds controlled by Niho at Mawhera (now Greymouth) and Hokitika. Te Puoho regarded him as an ally.

A straight road runs along the coast to Karamea. The way south seems wonderfully clear after the thick bush of the Kahurangi coast. A microclimate warms the air. The taua must have revelled in it.

Lone nikau now stand sentinel. Karamea lies amid its maze of estuaries and its leftover harbour, dried up by the 1929 earthquake. It was completely isolated for two years, because the road was cut too, and it has never shaken that feeling of loneliness. Southwards went the taua, on to Mawhera, along a route by and large followed by today's highway for the same reason: it was the easiest way.

A decade after Te Puoho passed this way Heaphy and Brunner crossed the trail of a war-party, almost certainly the Ngati Tama chief's. They could not get past the Te Miko cliffs north of Punakaiki. A famous sketch by Heaphy shows Brunner at the 200-metre sheer bluff climbing a rata-and-vine ladder, 'very shaky and rotten', perhaps Te Puoho's work, with their dog Rover and rifle being hauled by a flax rope.

At Mawhera, Te Puoho got a shock. His putative ally Niho would not let him into the pa there, nor the one at Hokitika. No trace of either pa remains now. The north side of the Hokitika entrance, the more likely site for a pa, is now taken up with mementoes of the old port which early Europeans built there.

I walked down a track to the southern side of the entrance. It is a whitebaiters' stronghold now, their palisades made of corrugated iron and plastic and wooden stakes, whatever materials are at hand. The first airline in New Zealand to fly scheduled air services was based at an aerodrome here. A memorial marks the spot, but Niho's great enterprise has gone for good.

Some of Niho's men joined the taua, and with two young Ngai Tahu women to show him the way through the Alps, Te Puoho pressed on down the West Coast. Oh, the determination of the man.

The coastline south of Hokitika is long and straight, until you reach the Wanganui River at least. Then it becomes cliffy, pierced by the vast rolling West Coast rivers that are still capable of sweeping away the best concrete and steel bridges engineers can devise.

Te Puoho and his party crossed them all. His exact route has been lost in time, but he must have stuck to the coast as his main source of food. Past the Okarito lagoon where the kotuku breed, past the glaciers pouring icy water into the sea, the mountains squeezing the coast, their black-and-white hulks threatening, past Bruce Bay where Maui is said to have first landed at the end of his epic voyage, over the rocks and cliffs and points and bluffs until he reached the Haast River.

Most agree that Te Puoho turned away from the coast here, pressing upriver to the Haast Pass, Tioripatea. That route climbs upwards, following the Haast River to the Pass. Even now the place is dangerous. Te Puoho would have followed the track used by the southern people for generations before the first Europeans came along, the Haast River a broad highway leading into mountains green and grim.

Julius von Haast, explorer and geologist, claimed to have been the first European over the Pass, although a prospector named Charles Cameron reckoned *he* was the true pioneer. Cameron was vindicated a few years later when his powder flask was discovered on Mount Cameron directly to the west of the Pass. Both would have been following the Maori route, for there simply was no other way. Road-makers of every era follow the same paths, the easiest.

That track evolved into a packhorse route and remained the main route through these mountains until 1929, when hundreds of men displaced by the Great Depression were put to work pushing a road north from Hawea. Work stopped at the Gates of Haast when World War II broke out, and did not start again until 1956. The road eventually opened in 1965. Thirty years later it was even sealed.

For all that, the Pass remains dark and dangerous and peopled by spectres. Ghosts haunt the place: the unsolved murder of Jennifer Mary Beard, the terrible deaths of two Canadians swept off the road into the roaring Haast River. The world's best roading technology can scarcely restrain the tremendous forces trying to hurl great slabs of rock into this void.

Tioripatea was a suitably awful route for a taua intent upon killing. Even now its dank atmosphere smells of death. The road nestles beside the river, in some places all but in it. The mountainsides close in, dripping. Is it better to go over the Pass in the daylight when you can see it, or in the dark, when you cannot? That's a moot point, but Te Puoho's party didn't have the choice. They sneaked past the cliffs, where waterfalls spout from sheer walls and every rock wants to become a rolling stone, then over the Pass, probably cold and wet, certainly hungry.

An old bridle path cut in the late nineteenth century, once part of the drovers' route, runs off from the Pass towards the lakes. A swing bridge takes it over the Fish River; it rejoins the road at Davis Flat below. It follows the old Maori track used by Te Puoho, and later by Cameron and Haast too. It's strange, walking through a silent forest whose trees once stood by as the taua padded past. Boughs drip above me. That tree there must have been just a sapling, that big one already half a century old. The mossy ground is silent and soft. The raiding party must have loved that path. They knew they were past the worst, the country gentler to the east.

They descended onto the flats of the Makarora Valley and headed down the Makarora River on its southern side. They were in very different country now. Probably the sun was shining, the dark green bush giving way to golden tussock. The wind blowing whitecaps across Lake Wanaka. Mountain peaks topped with winter snow rising above the clouds, but they were on the good side of them now. Across a low saddle to Lake Hawea. The rockscape of Central Otago spread before them, a strange place then, invested with taniwha, fiends and demons. Now it is haunted more by real-estate agents and speculators, just as carnivorous.

Maori lived there for part of the year, usually over summer, just as people do now. They built several settlements around the two lakes, including one on the peninsula jutting into the water beside Wanaka town. They ate eels, duck, fern root, weka, and they went after local pounamu, greenstone.

Te Puoho's raiders fell upon these peaceful people, first striking a tiny settlement at Makarora near the present-day pub. Nine people were said to live there, including two infant girls. The hungry taua killed and ate the two children.

Te Puoho had to keep going lest word of the raid get out and alert locals. He captured a young man called Pukuharuru from the next tiny settlement, at the saddle between the two lakes where the road now crosses. Te Puoho sent him ahead, with two of his warriors, to capture his father Te Raki. But Pukuharuru managed to escape and alert Te Raki, who wasted no time finding and dispatching the two guards.

Te Puoho realised the game was up. Unless he cleaned up the locals he was going to face a well-organised Ngai Tahu taua with something other than forgiveness on their minds. They would be in good shape, and his own warriors were not. They'd marched through hell and high water and besides, they were still hungry. Even now, he reasoned, accurately, Te Raki, his family and others from nearby settlements would be racing down the Clutha Valley to present-day Tarras then up the Lindis, intent on raising the alarm.

The Maori summer trail followed the present road, past what is now the ruin of the old Lindis Hotel, around the enormous bluff to the Lindis Pass, over to the Waitaki Valley then down to the coast and southwards. It is still lonely country whose mysterious golden folds are portrayed in a thousand watercolours, and it's easy to imagine here the Ngai Tahu fleeing noiselessly, hiding their tracks as they ran from Te Puoho.

The Ngati Tama chief had to move quickly southwards if he was to win this race. He took the five inhabitants of the Wanaka settlement prisoner, bringing the total to twelve, and forced them to guide him south over another Maori trail. He chose to head up the Cardrona Valley.

It is an easy journey at first, the route leading up a wide scrubby valley, but it soon turns severe, as is the way with mountain passes. Today it is the Crown Range Road, carrying traffic between Wanaka and Queenstown. You'll have noticed a pattern here. All the way from Golden Bay this man has followed routes which became the absolute innards of scenic New Zealand. Two centuries later he might have been employed by the Tourist and Publicity Department.

Now here he is climbing the Crown Range. Did a man bent on warrior-upon-warrior action stop to admire the view, among the finest by any world standard, the golden brown spread below him and the sharp white peaks? Or did he simply say, as many a snowbound motorist has, 'Let's get off this bloody mountain and back to the warm'? No snow poles to guide him. He is thought to have ducked over a saddle and into another valley and descended by way of the Roaring Meg, beside the Gibbston Valley.

He and his band have walked two thirds of the length of the South Island through and over what was then, and still is, New Zealand's most difficult territory. A tramper going away for a week is advised to take some sixty items of gear as well as food. Te Puoho had none of them: no boots or gaiters, no waterproof clothing, no polar fleece nor polypropylene, no sleeping bag or GPS, not even scroggin.

But I'm carrying some of that gear, as I stand on the Crown Range road with a small party of trampers working out which way he would have gone. He was aiming for the Roaring Meg on the other side, and he wanted the simplest, most direct route. Which, I think, as I stand looking at the Pisa Range, is also the easiest.

Behind me is the warmth and comfort of the Cardrona Hotel. Smoke is rising from a few cottage chimneys. It is late in the season but a little further down people are coming off the Cardrona skifield with the well-padded look of skiers after a good day. Cows stare in the manner of animals for which humans usually mean some sort of unpleasantness, but otherwise it is a contented scene.

We aim for a low-ish saddle. We walk up a long, quite gentle valley, idyllic in the spring sun. The spaniard springs golden from the ground: an orange, spiky plant, it is capable of spearing through anything save a suit of armour, although the armour theory is still untested. The long thorns of grey matagouri warn us away: matagouri can live for much more than a century. Did Te Puoho give these same plants a wide berth too? Almost certainly this is the route he would have used. Early stockmen used Maori trails and this was once a stock route too.

We reach the top of the range easily enough. The track descends into the rocky canyons of Central Otago, the hills dotted with rock spikes, like the armour of dinosaurs, weathered by eons. I wonder what Te Puoho would have made of this landscape with its pillars and fortresses and gargoyles. If he'd been an imaginative man he might have thought it premonitory. It is a lonely place, but a lovely one, a long, spectacular but quite easy descent down the valley of the Roaring Meg.

Which stops us completely, almost exactly halfway along the track. In the spring thaw the stream is just too high and fast to cross. It is living up to its name.

I stand beside the ruin of an old hut, the rubble of a fireplace with a broken iron dixie and an iron stove and a sheet of corrugated iron half-buried, all jammed between two precipices alongside a tributary stream. People were hardy then; me less so.

Nothing for it but to turn back, plod up and over the Pisa Range again. I cannot imagine Te Puoho giving up so easily, but on the other hand I've already lived much longer than he did. I catch a sneaky grin from his ghost.

Instead, I drive over the Crown Range and through the Kawarau Gorge to the Roaring Meg and climb the track from the opposite direction. It is a straightforward tramp of a few hours to the point where we stalled then back again, but satisfying.

Not long after Te Puoho passed through, a goldminers' hotel, the Kirtleburn, stood beside the Kawarau River at the foot of this track. It burned down in 1880, leaving its owner with a bag of flour, a case of spirits and little more. Some of its patrons might have used Te Puoho's route across the river, if they'd drunk enough at the bar.

He crossed the river by way of a natural rock arch, known to Maori as Whatatorere and to Pakeha as the rock bridge, or Chalmer's Leap. It cannot have been a popular way of crossing the river, for one of the stories about the Roaring Meg is that it was named after a woman carried through the torrent by diggers.

The Kawarau is a wild river. The rock arch was the only easy crossing and it had been used by Maori for centuries. Goldminers used it too, leaping over a gap in its middle. It is said that this amazing geological construction was blown up by gold prospectors, but remnants remain and intrepid souls still use the crossing.

Te Puoho probably climbed the spur of Mount Difficulty opposite the rock bridge, and descended to the Nevis River valley. The Nevis has cut its groove between the Hector Mountains on one side and the Garvie Mountains on the other. What little traffic there is through the valley passes through Bannockburn, once a gold-rush town and still booming, for wine is now bringing in more money than gold ever did.

One thing has hardly changed since Te Puoho put his cold feet upon the ground, and that is the nature of the valley. A good winter here can still throw up three weeks of twenty-degree frosts.

A Maori track is said to have run between Bannockburn and Garston, a little settlement in the Mataura River valley below Lake Wakatipu. Moa hunters left traces of a summer hunting camp with ovens. Maori used it as a path between Southland and Central Otago, and told early European settlers of the route.

It was a hard road then, and it still is. It is not much used and anyway is closed from mid-June until the end of September. Even at the outset signs announce, rather unnecessarily, that the grade is steep for the next nine kilometres, and that Mount Cook is 198 kilometres to the north. You can see it peeking over the far ranges.

The route runs over Duffers Saddle, at 1300 metres among the highest public roads in the land. It is probably the loneliest too. From there it drops into the wilderness of the Nevis Valley.

But Te Puoho is believed to have taken the shorter route from the Roaring Meg. The two meet at the Nevis Crossing at what seems to be the bridge to nowhere.

The entire Nevis Valley has always been a crossing. The gold miners came and went, leaving few traces: the remains of a gold dredge on Schoolhouse Flat, an old stone village on the Lower Nevis where a few people still live, lots and lots of clay and rock jumble from their endeavours. Farmers have endured, as they always do. All they ask of passers-by is that they close the bloody gates, for there are lots of those. It's anybody's guess who they'd prefer crossing their land, a band of warriors hell-bent on violence or day-trippers leaving their gates open, but I think the tourists would lose by a neck.

Modern traffic still has to ford, officially, twenty-seven rivers. Te Puoho and his band must have been even wetter and colder than usual. The first goldfields warden here described his territory, accurately, as a 'cold, sequestered and ice-bound region'. The taua had another problem: food was so scarce it was all but non-existent, and they were starving.

One account says they were so weak that when they sat down to rest they had trouble getting up again. One older man wandered off and died. His skeleton was found years later by a shepherd, his taiaha beside him.

At the southern end of the valley lies the Nokomai River, whose own valley would have carried the raiders down to the Mataura and into Southland over the broad green valleys to the Waimea Plains where fat cows now amble. No ambling for Te Puoto though: his was a race, for he would have been certain that the Ngai Tahu fleeing from Lake Hawea, over the Lindis and down the Waitaki would waste no time warning people of his advance and summoning Bloody Jack from his lair.

In his book *Te Puoho's Last Raid*, Atholl Anderson describes how Te Puoho spotted the smoke of an eeling party beside the Mataura, between the present-day Wendon and Otama. They captured the party and fell upon their eels with equal zeal.

Then they passed by what is now Gore, then Mataura, and came to Tuturau. The kainga sat on a low hill, a few huts, a few old people looking after the place until eeling parties returned. The raiders simply took it over and moved in. Te Puoho was confident that no one yet knew the raiders had reached the far south.

But word had reached Tuhawaiki, who was visiting the whaling station at Bluff at the time. He immediately thought that Te Rauparaha must again be at his gate. That mistake was fatal for Te Puoho. Tuhawaiki was not going to trifle with such a warrior. He rushed back to Ruapuke and marshalled his forces.

From the perspective of the twenty-first century it's the scale of this confrontation which startles. Te Puoho's force seems tiny for such an ambitious raid. But the mighty Tuhawaiki may have had even fewer men willing and able to fight: Anderson estimates sixty poorly armed warriors, perhaps fewer.

Still, a fleet of waka and a whaleboat set forth from Ruapuke. They landed on the mainland, marched north and surrounded Tuturau. At dawn, two armed men climbed on the roof of a hut. Te Puoho woke, shouting a warning. One of the attackers fired his musket, hitting the northern chief in the arm. The other fired too. Te Puoho fell back, dead.

Te Puoho's head was cut off and stuck on a pole. Few survived the subsequent massacre. They were enslaved and later killed. And that was that. The huge adventure was over, with a whimper.

In a way, Te Puoho's brother-in-law Ngawhakawa drew the shortest straw. He managed to escape then retraced the raiders' steps, up through Central Otago, over the Alps, up the coast, all the way back to Golden Bay, where he delivered the news. A retaliatory attack on the southerners petered out. By any standards the raid was a complete failure.

Henry Samuel Chapman, Supreme Court judge, newspaper owner and editor and historian, later met the man said to have fired the fatal shot that Killed Te Puoho, Topi-Patuki. Topi is still a revered name among southern Maori. Judge Chapman wrote the event's epitaph: 'Thus ended in disaster this ill-advised expedition, which must have caused a great deal of suffering, hardship, and starvation to its members for no result whatever. [But it] really was a very wonderful undertaking considering the terrible country the taua had to pass through, and has not been equalled by any other in Maori history.'

Yes, what an epic! Some of that wild journey can still only be done on foot, the Kahurangi coast, sections of the West Coast below, parts of the Central Otago trek. Roads follow some of it, and in places like the Haast Pass it is easy to imagine a force of desperate men scrambling over rocks and through the forest; cars or not, time there has stood still.

One hundred and one years after the event, in December 1937, Southlanders raised a memorial to the raid. They named the place the Maori Centenary Reserve. They built an obelisk on a hill where the tiny Tuturau settlement once stood, and beside it a thatched wharenui, or meeting house. Built of wooden slabs and roofed with tussock, it soon decayed and collapsed.

The memorial declared: 'The last fight between North and South island Maoris, in which the Southerners were victorious, took place in this locality in December 1836.' One-nil. Go the south! Some of the descendants of Topi, the man who shot Te Puoho, were at the unveiling. The unfortunate chief might have been gratified by the crowd. About 3000 people turned up, far more than ever attended his raid.

One last thing: Te Puoho's only monument here by the Mataura River does not so much as mention his name.

4

Pointing down

Puysegur Point lies at the most south-westerly point of New Zealand. You can get there by sea, or by a hard tramp along the bottom coast. Either way, you have to be keen. It is a wild place, the edge of the void. The mountains running all the way down the South Island's spine stop the wild westerly winds crossing the Tasman and bat them downwards. They collect here and spit through Foveaux Strait.

The average winds here are gale force. They are more than a gale for a third of the year, hurricanes for at least two weeks. The West Coast is the wettest area in New Zealand and, politely put, Puysegur Point is at its end.

Who would want to go there? Well, hardly anyone, although I've been at the Point quite often. Not once was it easy. The first time, I arrived in what I thought was a roaring gale but greater experience taught me was just a breeze by Puysegur standards.

I was the accidental partner in a fishing boat, the *Nina*. Accidental because I was a reporter on the *Otago Daily Times* and my immediate boss was a man called Ian. He had been a commercial fisherman and was now settling for a shore life after a serious injury. He noticed me reading a boating magazine and our shared interest drew us together.

We were working the night shift then, both a little bored, and one night he came up with a proposition, which essentially came to this: why didn't we build a boat and go cray-fishing? We could make money and have fun. Was I interested?

Yes, I was. I was unattached and looking for adventure.

We borrowed the money for the boat. It was the first time I'd been inside a bank manager's office and I sat in mute horror as Ian listed his assets. Mine took less time. Essentially, I owned an old car.

No matter. The bank manager smiled upon us and lent us the money, to me a fortune, enough to buy a house and another car. Oh yes, those were the days.

The boat took shape at a Kaikorai Valley engineering works. It was built of steel. I quit my job and became a labourer. I did the awful jobs, like cleaning off rust and painting the inside of fuel and water tanks. I was and still am claustrophobic.

I was beaten up by a fat bully of a welder and saved by a skinny Australian with a ball hammer. I used up all my money and bludged a bed and food from friends who never blinked once. I wondered whether this was such a good idea, not for the last time.

When you're young you're not unattached for all that long. I met Sally. She took the long view. I might be filthy and broke, and my immediate job prospects were bizarre, and I proposed to go away for quite a long time, but heck, you couldn't have everything. We didn't know each other very well, and to her it was an act of faith for which I've been forever grateful.

Surprisingly, to me, one day the boat was finished, painted orange (Ian said it was a great colour if you were going to be rescued), christened the *Nina* (Ian said short names were easier to spell) and launched. In a very short time we were heading for Fiordland. We were elated. We were going to make our fortunes on the high seas.

We were stuck in Bluff for a week or so by bad weather, which down there meant the kind of weather which in other places would bring on a Civil Defence emergency.

One night, when it seemed a little less stormy, we set off, dodging Dog Island in the dark and heading into Foveaux Strait. We were wrong. It was not less stormy. The further west we went, the worse it got. Great lines of white-capped waves marched upon us. I inspected them closely, from the inside. I rolled around like a marble in a tin can.

We sought refuge in Port Craig, cut into the western edge of Te Waewae Bay and once a small logging town of bushmen, outlaws and their families, all of them evidently hardy. The sea was smoother in there, but that made the whitecaps prowling outside more fierce. A couple of other boats huddled with us. They said the weather would only get worse and we should give it a go.

We steamed along the south coast and the waves got bigger and they crashed on black rocks and their spray was hurled into the air and the coastline was horrifying and I understood the true meaning of the word 'godforsaken'.

Suddenly the seas parted. Moses must have felt the same way. We sailed into tranquillity.

Above us a white lighthouse looked down kindly. We had rounded Puysegur Point and sailed into Rakituma, Preservation Inlet. I knew exactly why it had been so named. This had been a haven for centuries. We anchored alongside other fishing boats in a place called Otago Retreat on the chart but known to fishermen as Shallow Passage.

It goes without saying that we didn't make any money. Oh yes, we caught crayfish, packed their tails into twenty-two-kilogram bags and stacked them in the boat's freezer, and on stormy days we explored the long reaches of this amazing sound, and I fell in love with it forever, the sweet smell, the dark heavy air, the pale gold beaches above the black water, the piles of pale green kina shell lying like jewels.

We were always within sight of Puysegur Point. Across the narrow passage from the Point lay Coal Island. One of the lighthouse keepers, Philip Payn, discovered coal and gold here in the late nineteenth century and a town, tiny and remote even by the standards of the day, sprang up on the island. At the peak of the gold rush, around 1890, more than seventy miners, some with families, lived here, and remnants of that enterprise could still be found everywhere.

Once we were almost wrecked on the outside coast of Coal Island, and I gave thanks for the orange paint. Not for the last time.

The Puysegur Point lighthouse lay up a short steep track from the Passage. It had a weird reputation which seemed to fit perfectly. In 1943, a man lived on Coal Island among the ruins from that old community. He objected to the light on Puysegur Point across the water on the grounds that it kept him awake at night. Three lighthouse keepers and their families lived there then. He took them hostage at gunpoint and burned the wooden lighthouse to the ground.

Now the light sat on a concrete tower and the keepers had gone, but you could see where they'd been. I sat beside the tower in the wind looking over the Tasman and thinking about the remarkable people who liked this life.

Much later I met one of them, Warren Russell, who had lived there with his wife. He'd get out of bed every two or three hours to do a weather report. He didn't just like the life, he loved it. He finished his lighthouse keeper career on Dog Island outside Bluff Harbour where the gales sometimes whipped spray right over the tower. Keepers were a select company, gone now.

I was keen to go too. Living on a small boat can get tedious, and tetchy. Also, I was in love, to be married that very March, and I can report that Preservation Inlet in the wildest, loneliest, most inaccessible part of New Zealand is no place for the lovelorn.

February dragged by on leaden feet, and March sprang upon us on sprightly ones, and I was increasingly alarmed. We were ready to go, waiting in Shallow Passage with a bunch of other boats, and after months of solitude every one of us wanted desperately to be gone. But oh, the weather. It was awful. It was beating the average by a serious margin on the Beaufort scale.

Communications were terrible. There was no way I could tell my intended of my situation. We had known each other for only a few months and I could hear the words 'I told you so' gusting over the mountains from her nearest and dearest.

One day the wind eased. The assembled fleet popped from its prison. We rounded Puysegur Point as an armada and zipped along Foveaux Strait with a great swell behind us. The boats were surfing down the waves and how exhiliarating it was. Bow waves sprang into the air for joy, exhausts let loose with a cheer.

Nina had been racing along for an hour when we noticed something odd. As the boat reached the bottom of the wave which was carrying it along, it would tilt to one side and turn.

The helmsman would swing the wheel the opposite way and the boat would correct itself and steam on.

For a while, we took no notice. The price of crayfish, the long showers we were going to have, the warm beds of home. But the problem (for by now we realised we had one) got worse, until the man at the wheel was bracing himself as the boat sped down the face of each wave and did its best to turn at the bottom.

This is known as broaching: at its worst the boat could turn side on to the wave and be capsized by it. By now we had a pronounced list to one side. Something had to be done.

With my commanding experience of one season's fishing, I thought I knew the cause. The bags of frozen crayfish in the refrigerated hold must have shifted, weighing down one side of the boat. Ho, yes. Without telling Ian, I went out of the wheelhouse, lifted first the heavy steel hatch-cover, then the foam-filled plug that stopped the cold air escaping, and wedged them against the surrounding crayfish pots stacked on the deck.

Dropping into the hold, I looked around.

The bags of crayfish, frosty white, were exactly as we'd stacked them. Odd, I thought. Still, while I was down here, I'd move some bags to the high side of the hold which might correct the list. First one, then two, then half a dozen, cripes, it was cold down here, and kind of spooky, and ... *clang!*

A particularly nasty roll shook the hatch-cover loose. It swung free and, in that particular way in which these disasters gain momentum, collected the big square plug on its way, wedged it into the hatch opening, and fell on top of it to make sure of the job.

It happened with the speed of a gunshot. One moment I was down below doing good deeds, the next I was captive in the dark, with all the machinery of the boat performing as designed, and freezing me solid in as short a time as possible.

I considered my position. That is, I thought rationally for a fraction of a second before my claustrophobia set in, followed closely by panic.

I beat the plug with my fists. I lay on my back and kicked it. I cursed it so fervently any decent object would have shrivelled, but that damn plug took absolutely no notice. I knew how the crayfish felt. One moment they were in their natural environment, happily going about their business, the next they were frozen stiff with no prospects at all.

I don't know how long I was down there. It can't have been very long, for a fishing boat is not very big and Ian was bound to notice my absence.

He did. He came out on deck, looked around, and shouted, 'Bruce!'

'I'm down here,' I shouted back. My cry sneaked past the bung and the hatch-cover and squeaked into the open air.

'Where?'

'*DOWN HERE!*'

I heard the hatch cover being yanked open. An eye appeared beside the plug. 'Wha—?'

He pulled. I pushed. The plug did not move. It had been hammered by the hatch-cover and it liked its new possie. It wasn't going anywhere.

'Doesn't matter,' Ian shouted. 'The boat's going to sink anyway.' He grabbed a screwdriver, jammed it through the crack into the hold, and went back to saving the ship. I hoped. I was not at all reassured by his closing sentence. Sinking was one thing, bad enough for sailors to avoid if they possibly could. Sinking while trapped in a freezer … Well, even as avid a storyteller as I was probably wasn't going to get around to telling that one.

I grabbed the screwdriver and attacked the plug in a frenzy. It didn't move. A tiny bit of reason appeared, no more than a glint in the dark. Where was the plug stuck? Over there in the corner? What if I got the screwdriver in here, levered it just so?

Whap! The plug popped free and I popped out in the same split second.

Never had the crowded deck of a small fishing boat in the middle of one of the world's most feared straits felt so good. Oh, yes. Nothing could be that awful, could it? Capsizing? Poof.

Ian did not agree. Upside down was not good. He wanted to avoid it. He waited for the right moment and with considerable skill managed to turn the boat around. A nearby vessel which knew we were in trouble and was standing by turned around to escort us back.

Now that it was not surfing, but going into the waves, the *Nina* was steadier. Both boats turned for Puysegur Point. The white stump of the lighthouse appeared. None of us had expected to see it again for a while and certainly not so soon.

It was the very definition of mixed feelings. On one hand, we were safe. On the other, we were safe in a place far from the home we'd been looking forward to.

We rounded the Point and dropped anchor in the calm below. Our immediate problem was quickly fixed: a fault had pumped fuel from one tank to another on the opposite side of the boat, weighing down that side. But our escape had used up the one day of calm weather we could reasonably expect in a fortnight or so. The gale returned. We were stuck.

The crew of the other boat took it calmly, considering that they'd been looking forward to going home too, resuming family life, living the way normal people do. But all things happened at sea.

I was not calm at all. The prospect of missing my own wedding, without explanation, seemed so awful that sinking into the depths while locked in a freezer seemed a promising way out.

We spent another ten days stuck behind Puysegur Point. At last, the weather stilled. We raced around the Point in the dark, set a course for home, and never stopped before we tied up in Careys Bay, Port Chalmers.

I spruced up. I'd towed my jeans behind the boat for a hundred kilometres and reckoned them ship-shape.

Good fortune set in. I did not know where my wife-to-be, Sally, was living, but I marched hopefully up Princes Street, Dunedin. The very first person I met was her sister Donna. She told me Sally's new address and, what was more, did not look the least bit surprised that I'd appeared out of the blue two days before the wedding. Oh, all right, Sally *did* look surprised when she opened the door and before her stood a man with a ginger beard wrapped around a sunburned, flaking face, dressed in clothes that looked as if they'd been dragged behind a boat for a hundred kilometres. Even after I identified myself she seemed a little ... unsettled.

Well, to cut a long story down a little, we got married, I made no money from my fishing adventure, and the boat sank. A long marriage ensued, and continues, although marriage is always a wild journey itself. Given its delicate balance, however, perhaps that's a story for another day or, safer still, another life.

Strangely, I still longed for Puysegur Point. The mysterious twists of Preservation Inlet, its still green water, its bays, intricacies and complete strangeness had been preserved in my memory amid the slow crumbling of age, a period of my life so full of adventure I sometimes think I must have been down there for years.

When the chance came to go back, I seized it. My transport was the good ship *Argus,* piloted by Colin (Wobbles) Gavan.

We steamed up from an anchorage on Big South Cape Island, Taukihepa, passing the jelly-mould shape of Solander Island, once home to five men, two parties of sealers first marooned then abandoned by their captains.

They were rescued in 1813 by the ship *Perseverance,* whose captain concluded they could only have survived on that lonely rock for four years or so by 'divine interposition'. Ingenuity may have played a greater role:

> They were cloathed in seal skins, of which their bedding also was composed, and their food had been entirely made up from the flesh of the seal, a few fish occasionally caught, and a few sea birds that now and then frequent the island [...] They had attempted to raise cabbage and potatoes, of which plants one of them happened to have some of the seed when unhappily driven upon the island; but their first and every subsequent experiment failed, owing to the spray of the sea in gales of wind washing over the whole island, which rendered culture of any kind impracticable.

This was no place to linger, although our destination seemed hardly better: mountains grim in the fading light, waves crashing white on the Marshall Rocks beneath the Puysegur Point light. The *Argus* rolled in the big swell, pitching into it and taking it on its shoulder, passengers bracing themselves against furniture and doorways.

The captain believed that a golden lode ran between Coal Island and its immediate neighbour, Steep-to Island. It seemed likely to stay there for a while, Preservation Inlet now being part of the Te Wahipounamu–South West New Zealand World Heritage area, and listed as the Rakituma/Preservation Inlet Historic Area by Heritage New Zealand to boot. Digging for gold was frowned upon.

Captain Cook's voyage cleared the way to exploiting this new land. The usual crowd of chancers was on his heels, hoping to strike it rich.

A memorial, a small plaque, was set in Cuttle Cove where a whaling station flourished in the early nineteenth century. Sixty men worked there in what was then Southland's biggest town. Until the 1830s they killed right whales and seals. The seals were all but wiped out. The whales survived, barely, but the Cuttle Cove settlement did not.

Gold miners followed.

In October 1908 the *Clutha Leader* reported: 'The Tarawera Company claims to have proved by extensive and careful prospecting that their property contains vast bodies of very rich ore. Old miners consider there is sufficient to last the company fifty years.'

Miners drove shafts through solid rock, hallways and caverns. The lust for gold, for treasure in a new land, must have driven these men hard. They carved their way through rock with basic food and little comfort in the windiest, wettest, wildest, loneliest land any storyteller in their northern homelands could ever have created. Was it poverty that drove them, or imagined riches? Either way, it was a monkish life, without the enlightenment.

The rich seams promised by the Tarawera Company's 'careful prospecting' were as ephemeral as the old miners' stories. The gold simply wasn't there.

A much more modern settlement scarcely fared better. The whalers, sealers and miners had left behind them pockets of freehold land, extremely rare in this southern fastness. A syndicate built a lodge on one of them near Cuttle Cove, and called it Kisbee Lodge. Surely tourists would snap up the opportunity to stay in the nation's most remote wilderness, admire the primeval forest, live in a New Zealand that once was and never would be again, walk soundlessly on the soft carpet of moss and lichens, and eat lots and lots of fresh fish?

Alas, tourists did what tourists do and went to Bali. When we were there the lodge was owned, it was said, by an Auckland syndicate which used it more or less as a bach. A rather baronial one.

Colin Gavan told the story of an old gold miner here who hid his stash in a gumboot, buried the gumboot under a tree, and marked the tree with an iron spike. Then he sailed away to find a doctor, for he was ill — very ill, as it proved, because he died. Alas, the forest in that spot was felled. No one ever found the gold, but the spike turned up: it stripped the teeth from a saw in the timber mill.

More interesting were the cave networks where Maori once lived. They were subdivided by stone walls, marking off living and sleeping areas. Middens, heaps of shells, often stood outside their entrances, for they always had an escape route and somewhere to land a waka.

We spent a night moored next to the iron hull of the *Stella*, the steamship that brought supplies to these lonely communities, now another fascinating wreck. Then we rounded Puysegur Point with the lighthouse sentinel above and went home in a flat calm, with that sneaking sense of relief. Adventures are fun, as long as you emerge from them intact.

5

Rolling on One

State Highway One carries New Zealanders from the top of their country to the bottom. It is as adventurous as the Great Ocean Road in Australia, as exotic as America's Route 66, as scenic as Norway's Atlantic Road, which is sometimes called the most beautiful journey in the world, but only by people who don't know about SH One. It is our Appian Way, although a bit longer and a whole lot more bendy.

It joins all the dots, the cities and the small towns. It is vital to the nation's health and well-being, like an artery. When something blocks it, the country clutches its breast and falls to its knees.

Something *did* block it, thoroughly. On 14 November 2016, an intricate network of faults ruptured around Kaikoura. The huge earthquake lifted parts of the seabed clear from the water and brought down hillsides in a rain of rocks. Squeezed between mountains and sea, SH One was buckled and buried. The critical link between Christchurch and the north, even the lifeline between the South and North islands, was broken.

SH One was transformed from a sedate trip, if a spectacular one, into a wild journey. Or *several* wild journeys. The road split into two. Then two and a half. Then maybe three and a half or even four, according to which vision for the future was in vogue. It frayed in its middle, unravelled.

It became so complicated trip computers couldn't cope. The closest they could get to a decent guess was that you'd get there sometime, somehow.

I'd never thought of SH One as a wild journey, except as a kid on Sunday afternoons when the world shrivelled to a back seat and time stood still.

The main road north of Christchurch was the Main North Road. Everyone who lived in Christchurch knew it well. Their Sunday mornings were spent driving north to the Pegasus Bay beaches, Brooklands, Kairaki, Woodend, Waikuku, sometimes further, where the names rolled on your tongue, Amberley, Cheviot, Parnassus, and on exceptional, wonderful days, all the way to Goose Bay and, oh joy, Kaikoura.

Why not? Petrol was cheap and the roads wide and empty, except on Sunday afternoons when everyone drove home at once. Then from Saltwater Creek all the way to the city, they queued. Traffic stopped, then started again, but never at much more than a walking pace. Dogs panted. Radiators boiled. Cars died on the roadside. Kids grizzled. Fathers did that strange one-handed scything thing over the back of the front seat. Kids ducked.

Through Woodend the cars crept, then Kaiapoi, inching (for these were pre-metric days) over the Waimakariri, past all the fruit and veg stalls of Marshlands and finally, exhaustedly, home, where we'd fight over who had to unload the car.

The Main North Road became State Highway One. They — those faceless people who did these things — put a new bridge over the Waimak. They built a four-lane motorway (*four* lanes!) from Belfast on the city outskirts to Kaiapoi. There it ended, and still does, although there are plans to extend it around Kaiapoi to Pegasus, which is a new town-in-progress to the north getting a fillip from Christchurch popping outwards after its earthquakes.

State Highway One was a joyous business then, and I always felt like Toad in *The Wind in the Willows*: 'Here to-day, up and off to somewhere else to-morrow! The whole world before you, and a horizon that's always changing!'

After the Christchurch earthquakes State Highway One became the fairway, the shining path. Hitting the road was a huge relief after queuing for petrol. Escape!

When earthquakes slammed Kaikoura too, everyone had had quite enough of them. We were thoroughly experienced in fault lines, and magnitudes, and seismologists and their arcane language of fault geometry and seismic moment. We were far too familiar with the EQC and the insurance companies. Many of a lifetime's treasures lay broken on floors and we were scared to bits too.

But it wasn't the fear, or the damage, or the bureaucracy, which mattered most. It was the loss, of community, city, history, those places our parents had loved and their parents too. That's why the Kaikoura earthquake hurt so badly. It wasn't fair. We didn't live there, but we'd grown up with the town. It had always been part of our lives. We loved it, and what then seemed the endless journey to reach it.

The highway had forked at Waipara. You took the left fork if you wanted to sit in the hot pools at Hanmer, or drive over the

Lewis Pass to sit in more hot pools at Maruia Springs, or turn left at Springs Junction for the West Coast, or go straight ahead over the Shenandoah to Nelson.

If you were heading for Kaikoura you went straight-as-a-die past Waipara and through the long gentle valleys below the ranges which blotted out the sea. You went through Cheviot, that neat little North Canterbury town where only the shopkeepers changed.

Much of the South Island's early European history, the vast sheep stations literally given to the wealthy and adventurous, was summed up here by William Robinson. He owned a huge sheep run that ran over the hills and far away and even had its own harbour, Port Robinson, where ships loaded his wool. He was known as Ready-Money Robinson. One story said he carried the money to pay for his land in a wheelbarrow; another insisted that after his cheque had been declined by land officials, he cashed it at a bank, demanded small change and notes, put everything in a sack, returned to the land office and dumped it on the counter.

One way or the other, he built a vast mansion just outside the town, and bought another in Christchurch. A model of his country seat has pride of place in the Cheviot Museum. It was a huge affair of 1418 square metres, built around a central courtyard, surrounded by a park ranging over the rolling hills. When Robinson died in September 1889 his estate ran over more than 37,000 hectares of prime North Canterbury country.

The mansion went up in flames in 1936, and was so thoroughly burned only its chimneys remained. His first Christchurch house was fated, too. In 1871 his butler, a man called Cedeno, stabbed a housemaid to death and tried to kill another. At his trial he said he'd wanted to kill Robinson as well. Cedeno became the second (of seven) to be hanged at Lyttelton Gaol.

Now you could trace the mansion's foundations in the green grass of the Cheviot Hills Domain, where the cricket pavilion stood on what had been its front steps. Not far away the old manager's house, a rather grand place too, was kept in good shape. The remains of Port Robinson slowly disappeared into the sea.

The Cheviot Museum speaks of the moa-hunters who once ranged along the coast, troves of adzes, huge ovens, piles of moa bones. Near the coast lies a great slab of sandstone whose hollowed centre sheltered moa-hunters, its edge serrated with slits where ancient adzes were sharpened.

A little north of Cheviot a road branched off inland and made its way over a low range of hills to Waiau, an isolated country town soon to become its own headline.

Once, SH One traffic was carried over the Waiau River into Parnassus by a one-way wooden bridge. Much later I discovered the name, Parnassus, was the whim of another runholder, this time a man who fancied himself as a classical scholar and imagined a likeness between a nearby hill and Mount Parnassus in Greece. Instead of the god Apollo and the Muses, however, Parnassus was home to the classical country-town triumvirate: garage, store and tearoom. But in 1980 road-builders replaced the wooden bridge with a curvy concrete one which carried the highway past poor Parnassus in a flash. Now a few buildings huddled on the old road. Ahead lay the Conway River and the Hundalees.

The Hundalees were as much a part of the South Island highways legend as the Otira, or the Lindis, or the Takaka Hill, roads feared by drivers in the old days of single carburettors and three-speed column shifts. You could get stuck on the Otira, snow-bound on the Lindis, or boiled dry on the Takaka Hill. Back-seat passengers were merely in a lather as they climbed over the Hundalees, four long, slow summits, one, two, three, and an eternity later four, and as you reached that final summit and looked down, oh my.

The Kaikoura coast sparkled below. It always shone, no matter what the weather. The sea changed from aqua near the rocks to indigo in the Kaikoura Canyon where the great whales feasted.

As you drove down that hill, yellow kowhai lay like sunshine on the land and the world seemed so happy that nothing bad could ever happen again. The road rocked back and forth and around until with a sigh it levelled and you were at Oaro. Contented baches gazed at the sea, where a perfectly white rock rose from the blue. How many generations, centuries of birds had painted that rock? High on the bushy headlands falling sheer to the sea lay the earthworks of the mighty Omihi pa where Ngai Tahu once guarded their territory, an eyrie whose defenders could see far up and down the coast.

They took refuge there from the invading Ngati Toa chief Te Rauparaha but not even Omihi could save them. The Ngai Tahu were sheltering the chief Kekerengu, unwisely. Kekerengu had been having an affair with a wife of Te Rangihaeata, Te Rauparaha's nephew and right-hand man. Te Rangihaeata was not someone to cuckold. He and the Ngati Toa took the pa and killed almost everyone inside it before rampaging south. Kekerengu got away.

The road threaded along this coast, around the bays, clinging to the buttresses, through road tunnels where as children we'd clamour for our father to honk the horn, as I did for my own children and forever thereafter.

Every turn of the road held a memory. Over there was the high rock which you could climb and throw your fishing line through a hole like a window down into the sea below. Not far from the road was the hidden pool, as big as the learners' pool at my school, where you could swim among purple and translucent-green seaweed and (once) watch the feelers of crayfish waving like wands from their crevices in the rocks. I swam there until, well, the catastrophe overtook all.

On one straight stretch a railway tunnel ran beside the road, with a concrete outer wall, vents like a castle's arrow-slits.

Then came the Kahutara river mouth at the end of the cliffs, where surf crashed onto a black-sand beach piled high with driftwood and running along to the mouth of the Kowhai River. My father fished there, casting a long line into the surf and sitting hunched for hours, sometimes catching a moki and dancing on the wet stones. We camped in the blue borage near the river bridge, in a huge square tent with a green top and sides that lifted to make extra rooms. I struggled through the driftwood looking for the kauri logs I was going to make into a boat, like my hero Johnny Wray of *South Sea Vagabonds*.

Kauri forests did not grow in the South Island, but I didn't know that then, and if someone had told me I would not have believed them, the South Island being not just my universe but the synthesis of every good thing in the entire world.

Not long ago I climbed Mount Fyffe, the beautiful little mountain beside Kaikoura, and saw far below a lake I'd never known despite a lifetime of poking around this place. It lay secret in a wobbly basin near the Kahutara. As I stood there in the snow on the peak a helicopter suddenly thumped up and landed and disgorged tourists. They'd done my day's climb in a few minutes. My quiet sense of achievement and joyous aloneness vanished.

There it was. Tourists and whales. Their collusion had transformed Kaikoura. The tourists came to see the whales and the whales came to see what they could find in the canyons that lay so close offshore.

Yet not long ago Kaikoura was a little town where fishing boats clung to precarious moorings and the cinema showed old flicks on Saturday nights. I once stayed in the posh Adelphi Hotel with my father. I thought it very grand, with a big lounge and deep armchairs whose inhabitants could barely be seen, and the bathroom not far down the hall. On the way to the Point with its seals and great terraces of flat rock stood the Pier Hotel, whose public bar had the best view in all New Zealand, if not the entire world. From here I could stand, later, at a leaner with a glass of beer, look over the fishing boats moored in the deep blue bay to the snowy Kaikouras, and tell myself that Queenstown was for beginners.

Kaikoura was the main reason Christchurch thronged SH One then. It was as far north as anyone could wish to go. People pulled crayfish from the pools and dreamed of little baches in South Bay.

A little to the north lay Mangamaunu, where the great Australian bush poet Henry Lawson once taught Maori kids. It later became a mecca for surfers (who would have got along with Lawson very well). To the north, the flanks of the seaward Kaikouras hid a secret history of old farms and falling fences and buildings rotting back into the bush. But unless you were a tramper, you weren't looking on that side of the road, you were looking at the sea, and the blue, and the white foam lapping the rocks, and the brown kelp swirling, and the seal flippers standing up like sails. And you stopped, and got out of the car, and stood wedged between the mountains and the sea, and you could taste the great ocean and feel the strength of the land.

What stood between you and lunchtime, however, was a series of little bays with caravans for baches and crayfish for sale. A crayfish and a smooth rock and the sea serenade made the perfect picnic. Under the sun, of course. It was always shining.

You reached Ohau Point, where the road was notched into the rock. Even a stranger knew this must be Ohau Point. The side of the road was crowded with cars and campervans and people leaned over the precipice looking at the seals below. The seals were languid stars. They rolled, and yawned, but mostly they slept. Their smell rose up in clouds.

A seal pup nursery lay just beyond. You ducked under the railway lines and walked up a short path through the bush. It ran beside a stream and ended at a pool fed by a waterfall dropping over a black cliff from far above. Seal pups frolicked in the spray. They slid through the water, under each other and over, curving into furry knots. They were magical, entrancing.

And beyond them, before the road rose up and over the hills and through the hot dry towns of Ward and Seddon and Blenheim, Kekerengu lay at the foot of its reef. I used to think Kekerengu was just a tearoom that served the best afghan biscuits ever baked. But the tearoom gave way to a wonderful place called The Store, full of sculpture and old beams and a big open fire for the winter and wide wooden steps where you could sit and watch the reef.

This was where the errant chief Kekerengu was said to have met his end.

Most people did not know of an old settlement running up the valley. You drove up a side road, passed a few houses and came across St George's, a tiny jewel of a place. It is said to be the smallest church in New Zealand, and it would be hard to imagine one tinier: it is about the size of a bus, its tiny pews and absolute simplicity giving an instant peace. The little cemetery told of ancient disasters, shipwrecks, drownings. The Kekerengu community lay beyond, invisible, unknown to all but the curious.

***

All of this made State Highway One far more than a road. It was a gallery, pathway, arcade, experience, excursion, pilgrimage, odyssey. If you knew it, you understood New Zealand.

It changed in a flash, just after midnight on 14 November 2016. A huge earthquake hit this coast and, just as the previous Christchurch earthquakes had done, shifted lives forever. In a web of fault lines, one ruptured. It set off other ruptures on other fault lines, the sequence growing bigger and more damaging as it raced northwards through the network, killing a woman in the little ski settlement at Mount Lyford, crushing a man under a big old house on the coast. It shoved Kaikoura a metre northwards, and left the coastal seabed high and dry, crayfish, paua and all. It heaved Christchurch southwards and Wellington northwards. Slip after slip blocked the main highway, wrecked the railway lines beside.

It also closed the only other way into Kaikoura, a narrow, meandering route passing through Waiau and called the Inland Kaikoura Road.

Months passed.

Kaikoura, clinging to its narrow shelf, was marooned until road crews pushed a way through the fifty slips on the Inland Kaikoura Road, now renamed the 'Kaikoura Emergency Access Road'.

People did what people do in a disaster. They got through it as best they could.

They slowly cleaned up. Some of their town was gone forever. Many of their houses were severely damaged. The old Adelphi vanished. The New Commercial Hotel was first ruined, then burned. The wooden Pier Hotel, so fortunately placed, now housed a restaurant. It survived.

Buildings can be replaced, but the ecosystem takes a little longer. No one knew when Kaikoura's would recover, or what it would be like. Some people rescued the crayfish the town had been named after, for the seabed had been raised so high that now a great apron of rocks ran out to the water. Its reefs and caves and underwater alleyways and sealife lay open to the sky, drying and dying. Kaikoura's foreshore, a difficult, rocky affair where only the determined swam, was transformed into a broad, enticing beach.

A vast avalanche of mud and sand and rock poured down the sides of the deep canyon where whales fed, then flowed 700 kilometres north along the Hikurangi Trough to the Wairarapa. Astonishingly, the whales returned only a couple of weeks later. But Kaikoura lost its lifeline: State Highway One.

In the meantime, we were given a graphic demonstration of what was at stake here. The official route between Picton and Christchurch was diverted through remote territory: Wairau Valley, St Arnaud, Murchison, the Shenandoah, Lewis Pass. The officially estimated driving time expanded to seven and a half hours, three hours longer than the coastal route.

I'd driven through the Wairau Valley only once or twice. It was beautiful, but it didn't go anywhere that couldn't be reached more easily. Now there was no alternative.

But some of those roads just weren't built for the loads they now carried. They became full-scale adventures. Potholes scarred the tarmac. Trucks crashed. Cars expired. The roads were repaired, then the repairs were repaired. Then the repairs to the repairs had to be fixed.

The New Zealand Transport Agency, which is responsible for roads, complained it was running out of money and, to the great disgust of locals, put parts of the road on hold until later. New Zealand's critical-roads strategy came down to this: fingers crossed.

Even the diversion had to be diverted, once through Reefton, once even back to the precarious SH One.

The official journey time between Christchurch and Picton grew, and grew, and with that came all sorts of complications. A young shearer from Cheviot had to drive five hours, double the usual time, to reach the shearing competition at the Marlborough A&P show in Blenheim. He won.

Truck drivers dubbed the road the 'white-knuckle highway' and began quitting their jobs for safer ones. Roads and bridges started collapsing under the strain. The road toll rose alarmingly.

Some of the uninhabited part of the route was so remote and dangerous that NZTA had to extend cellphone coverage specially, along with an emergency phone — and a toilet, which probably came in handy for nervous drivers.

How often does the main road through a country, its most important arterial, the very life-course of the nation, get jiggled around? So I took the diversion one spring morning in September, its easy, comforting familiarity as close to the joy of the open road as I ever get. I dream of road trips, but the dream usually gets a bit damp after the first hour or so of queues, and the inevitable discovery that your favourite café has changed hands and is, by some mysterious rule of the hospitality industry, no longer as good.

I left Christchurch on a drizzling, grey Saturday morning. Spirits were damp despite the usual brisk Saturday-morning traffic, shoppers, sporty carloads, people with that air of urgency that comes with either trying to get to work or celebrating *not* having to get to work.

I tripped into a desert, where I was thoroughly lost. The landmarks had gone. The *houses* had gone. Whole housing developments, great chunks of suburbs had just vanished into the huge debris dumps to the north. The earthquakes had done for them. I was deep in the Red Zone.

Riverside suburbs had disappeared. Just the odd garden feature or fireplace remained as gravestones. I drove through what was left of Burwood, or so I guessed, and onto Marshland Road, previously the main north road from the city's eastern suburbs. It was once a swamp, of course, and the earthquakes did their best to turn it back into one. In fact, part of the road was originally to have been a canal, and the earthquakes tried to restore that plan too.

I imagined pulling off onto a side road, perhaps to change a tyre, and upon getting back in the car becoming disoriented. The grey closing in around us. Lost at sea. I might be trapped for weeks in the maze before someone noticed a muddy Subaru Outback shuttling back and forth, for I stuck to the New Zealand male driving rule and never asked directions.

Signs along this route pointed resolutely to Picton, until they did not. They took their business elsewhere, leaving traffic on anonymous grey tarmac somewhere on the marshy flats of northern Christchurch.

But this Saturday morning the land felt firm enough, and I turned off onto the motorway and was immediately stuck between a huge yellow earthmover riding on an even bigger green truck, earthquake bric-a-brac, and an orange party bus going god-knew-where on this grey morning.

This was once dry Canterbury. Now vineyards crowded the landscape and here was a whole new town, Pegasus, whose developers boasted that 6000 people would one day call it home. It was as if the huge fist of the earthquake had knocked everything out of the pond, and little puddles of Christchurch had formed all around.

But now, at Waipara, a bright orange sign told Picton traffic not to go straight ahead, as it had done since long before Europeans settled in this country, but to turn left, through the limey soils of the Waipara vineyards to pass beneath the famous Frog Rock hanging over the road in the Weka Pass, flash past ancient Maori drawings in limestone shelters, and go by the moa-bone troves of the Pyramid Valley.

We pulled in behind a tourist bus. It had a learner sign in the back window. The driver hadn't practised pulling over. A growing number of cars formed a queue behind. A whole funeral procession.

It was 422 kilometres to Picton, which could take an awfully long time. Perhaps I should stop in Hanmer and loll in the hot springs instead? Two hours had brought only the old Hurunui Hotel into view, and that looked inviting too. But no, I was on a mission. Spray from passing trucks coated the windscreen. The wide forests were being cut down to make way for dairy farms. An end-of-the-world feeling seeped into the car.

Over the Lewis Pass. Into the forests, huge raindrops gobbing from the tall trees like cricket balls. It was as dark and cold as the Kaikoura route was full of light. Past Springs Junction, where the tourist bus forked off. Our loss would be Reefton's gain.

Huge trucks created their own weather systems: torrential rain, gales, their headlights like lightning, their sides flashing strings of lights. Every now and then one pulled off the road and sat there like a town taking a rest. The procession behind it passed and honked thanks, politely. The road just wasn't designed for this kind of traffic.

We trundled over the Shenandoah, such a hurdle in the old days and now revisiting its former reputation. Over Pea Soup Creek, past the 'View of Old Man Range' sign. No view, no range, just the grey.

We rolled into Murchison, which must have hoped SH One would never reopen. The little town was throbbing. The old general store, an endangered species in this country, was open for business. The junk shop was crammed with treasure. The butchery boasted of its gold medals. The French bakery smelled delicious.

On to Kawatiri Junction, where the default SH One turned and headed through Nelson Lakes National Park for the coast. Now the road, all but terminally ill, took a turn for the worse.

Road crews toiled like cleaners. The heavy traffic rolled through, road workers mopped up. The carriageway was stitched and patched, except where it no longer existed, and forlorn men in wet-weather gear presided over one-way stretches. It passed through St Arnaud, the national park's capital, which succeeded in looking even lonelier than usual. From this end the old stock route between Nelson and Canterbury looked quite enticing as an alternative main road. Mountains, gorges, rivers? Didn't worry the drovers.

The terrain flared out into the wide and beautiful Wairau Valley with its cliffs and peaks and superb river. I passed a woman in a lonely caravan offering bacon butties and chicken curry. In this café desert, never had a menu been more popular. The road rejoined SH One at Blenheim, and the procession rolled on to Picton on a highway that felt soft as carpet.

The journey had taken eight and a half hours, almost double the usual time.

***

By now, Kaikoura had been relieved. The Inland Kaikoura route had been opened to traffic, in fits and starts.

That route turned off the Lewis Pass road just before Hanmer and ran through the little village of Waiau, nicely preserved right down to its jail. It had been left alone in its corner and was free of supermarkets and fast-food chains. Its two churches seemed to complement the old pub.

The Inland Kaikoura route ran through the town rather than over it, then through farmland and canyons until it joined SH One just south of Kaikoura, avoiding the slips blocking the main road. Its main attraction, for me, was a single, tiny grave above the road, the last resting place of tiny Alice George. The daughter of a road-builders' cook, Alice was one year and ten months old when she fell ill in 1887. A doctor rode his horse for hours to save her. He failed. She died, and a clergyman had to ride just as long to bury her.

That little grave seemed to carry the country's hard lonely soul within its railings. But now, more traffic than Alice had ever seen rolled past. Five weeks after the earthquakes, this road had become Kaikoura's lifeline.

A wider pessimism remained. Some had wanted to abandon Christchurch after the earthquakes there, arguing that the city was too badly damaged, too expensive and too badly sited to repair. The same chorus was now rising over Kaikoura.

The coast was too precipitous. The rock could never be held back. They'd have to find another route for State Highway One, a detour around Kaikoura. Why not the old Molesworth Road? It circled around the treacherous coast. It started at Hanmer Springs and ran inside the Inland Kaikouras pretty much in a straight line all the way to Dashwood on One.

Well, not many people used that road, for good reason. It dated from a time when huge sheep stations covered the land and drovers dictated the routes.

It was guarded by Tapuaenuku, the beautiful giant at the northern end of the Inland Kaikouras, beckoning, showing envious North Islanders across the Strait what real country looked like. At its southern end the road started at Hanmer, the kindly face of what lay beyond. You drove up the Clarence Valley Road and over Jacks Pass and in that short time you were, again, in another world. The thermal pools and the cafés and the motels became a dry golden country so lonely you immediately checked all your car's vital signs, and your own.

Yet another route forked off this road here. It was the Rainbow Road, whose qualities were summed up by its hours:

open in summer during daylight, closed in winter. Part of it was the old drovers' route between Nelson and Canterbury. It ran through the mountains to Tophouse beyond the Nelson Lakes National Park. It was spectacular, narrow, slippery, slimy and for enthusiasts only. Yet some suggested this too as an alternative route for the damaged SH One.

Those who loved the back country prayed that the main road would be restored unto the nation, and soon.

Back in the real world, or perhaps the ethereal one, the road we were on became the Acheron Road, at first following the Acheron River. It was crowded by hills but the country felt open, for there was no bush, only a few trees and vast patches of yellow broom like sunlight through clouds.

It was an ancient land and felt no younger even when you reached the outlier of this sparse civilisation, the Acheron Accommodation House, one of a chain of thick-walled, graceful cob houses built for drovers within a day's trek of each other and reaching all the way from Hurunui to Nelson following a Maori trail: Te Rauparaha and his allies sneaked through this country in 1831 to attack Ngai Tahu in their fortresses. The accommodation house was a palace in the wilderness. Travellers and drovers rested in its small rooms for seventy years until 1932.

Further down the road lay the main buildings of Molesworth Station, best-known of all high-country stations, biggest of them all, larger than Stewart Island. The station was part of our folklore and still publicly owned.

The road here was stony and dusty and you drove carefully over its length. It crossed Isolated Flat, hurdled Wards Pass and dropped to the flats beyond.

The Molesworth homestead settlement was not far from here. The road now circled around the settlement. Instead of driving through it, as they once did, visitors were directed up a side road to a vantage point above. The sixty-kilometre, two-hour drive through the station was scarcely built-up. Now that it detoured past the station buildings, you passed only two houses on the road. The first was the Accommodation House. The second lay at the other end of the station, another fine old cob house where the station manager once lived.

The road then climbed, clung to the side of a steep gorge, dropped, became paved, then unpaved, repeated this pattern for a while as if uncertain of the permanence of the people it served, then took hold, boasted a white centre line, and you knew you were getting close to somewhere that actually appeared on a map, which here is Dashwood.

It was not a dangerous drive, nor even a hard one, in good weather at least. In winter, when the road was closed, it became treacherous. Winters here were truly icy. Long vehicles were not allowed, nor boats or caravans.

Yet some now suggested it as an alternative route between Christchurch and Picton. It was shorter, at 207 kilometres, but not quicker. Some tried it and ran out of petrol. Many ran out of patience. Neighbouring farmers ran out of goodwill. They longed for autumn, when the road was closed. A few drivers ran out of nerve, some complaining bitterly that road workers had suggested the road as a detour, when no sane and sensible driver would ever go there.

But an alternative to SH One? What a shame that would be. First, we'd lose the most enchanting stretch of our prime highway. Second, we'd spoil the superb desolation of the Acheron country.

A highway, passing lanes, the clutter of signs, rest stops, petrol stations, cafés? What a disaster. Third, Kaikoura would still be isolated.

***

But with Kaikoura sitting in fault lines as webbed as the veins of a very old person, and its road whittled from rock and an even harder place, the sea, who knew?

Why, those sterling fellows from the New Zealand Transport Agency did. They never lost faith. Great earthmoving machines toiled. Engineers moved mountains. An army of abseilers stabilised them. And one wonderful day, they announced success: the second-class version of SH One along the Kaikoura Coast opened for part of each day from just before Christmas 2017.

I had to give it a go, of course. How many times in a lifetime do you get a front-row seat as the state moves mountains and conquers not one, but two mighty earthquakes? So on Waitangi weekend 2018 I set off from Christchurch again. My heart was full. The road was too. These were the weekends of my youth returning, long queues of cars and caravans carrying cheerful people off for a holiday.

Signposts said that State Highway One through Kaikoura was open between 7 a.m. and 8.30 p.m. The cavalcade took on a pioneer hue. Kaikoura had been suffering, withering, without its visitors, its arteries blocked by mud and rock. We were the rescue column, the relief force, the liberators!

We poured through Parnassus and over the Hundalees and on the other side was the sea, the sea, the sea. Where the sperm whales cavorted and the dolphins flew and the crayfish crawled deep into the cracks and crevices of their new habitat, the old one being hoist into the frame of every passing mobile-phone camera by the great uprising months before. Little white horses galloped across the blue and it looked like the Kaikoura of old, the happiest place in the world.

Couldn't get away from the earthquake, of course. We soon ran into its rubble. The traffic slowed, then stopped, then jerked forward in a single lane.

The people controlling the flow were housed in little huts beside the road. The huts were the size of outhouses and looked like sentry-boxes. These people were the palace guards. From the corner of my eye I noticed something else odd about them, without it registering.

A couple of stops and starts later I realised ... They were waving at the passing parade with what seemed to be genuine affection. We flapped our hands. They waved the harder, called words of encouragement, leaned through a few open windows for a chat. Some threw in a little dance for good measure. Perhaps they had performance criteria to meet, in the more literal sense. Possibly they were as delighted as we were that after so many months of work they were triumphant. They were the cheeriest, most entertaining stop-go people on the face of the earth, especially *this* earth, which recently had been wobbling so frantically.

When I saw what they'd done, I got it. They were celebrating, saluting the successful outcome of the greatest road-building effort ever seen in this country, men and women and machines working day and night in every kind of weather to repair a vital link in the nation's affair. They were proud of themselves, and we were proud of *them*. Many of us clapped.

We passed the settlements of tents and caravans on the thin reserves between the highway and the sea. I recognised the scene from my childhood: men wearing singlets and determined looks, women in gumboots. They gutted fish for tea and laughed.

The seascape *had* changed. The seabed had been lifted and thrust into view. It lay white and odd. Was that reef out there before? That rock standing alone like an obelisk?

But here were the first two road tunnels, then the second pair, although only one of them was being used. They were reassuring. Still, it didn't seem right to honk the horn. Over there was the concrete-sided railway tunnel with the slits.

Above, the cliffs and hillsides had been scraped to their bones, first being shaken like pups by the earthquakes then cleaned of hanging rocks and debris by men and women dangling from ropes.

The road squeezed around rocks and poked into bays, the cliffs and buttresses above them pegged up, studded, wrapped in steel. I'd always taken the road north and south of Kaikoura for granted. Now it was easy to see how it had been chipped from the edge of the world.

Kaikoura town was bustling. Some of the shop verandas were propped up but the shops themselves were busy. The smile had lost some of its teeth: the graceful old Adelphi Hotel was just an empty space, the New Commercial around the corner a charred ruin.

The town's lovely old cinema was fenced off but most prizes were still in place, even James Mackay's rocky stool in South Bay where the agent sat bargaining the Ngai Tahu out of their land. The pointed rock must have given him piles. But the town's beach was even more beautiful, lifted from the sea and strung with rocks and reefs.

Ohau Point lay on the north side of town. I had to search for the place where SH One had been widened to accommodate the throngs of visitors who stopped and watched the seals on the rocks below. The point lay like a long finger above them. Now it was stripped, skinned. Nothing recognisable was left. I'd passed by this place hundreds of times, but now I had to check my phone to make sure I was there.

Tucked in the bay around its tip lay the stream where once tumbled baby seals, the waterfall pouring onto their heads. Even the track had vanished. I saw a hole in the bush that might have been the entrance but it was blocked by road crews. The pups were long gone, and probably the waterfall too. But what had been sea floor now lay white in the sun, strewn with black seals, as fine as ever.

Ohau Point was the place where everything became apparent, where the monster showed its hand, where all its forces had seized the land. What a mighty construction, what effort and courage and skill had gone into rebuilding a road and railway line when not very much of either remained.

Mountainsides, shorn, bolstered, corseted, hung over the void. Stopping for a closer look was banned, should some fool even think of pausing beneath those creaky cliffs. (One did. He crashed the road cordon in a 4WD, dodged a digger trying to block his way and fled north.) At the other end of the danger zone, Goose Bay, schoolchildren at a camp had been led through a rail tunnel when the trains were running. Perhaps earthquakes inured people to risk.

I'd had enough of living dangerously. I turned around and joined the queue for Christchurch. A stop-go man did a little jig as I passed.

6

Finding God

I never spent so much effort getting to church as I did on the elusive Serpentine. The church there isn't much as old stone churches go. It is tiny, completely unadorned. Its only architectural feature is its simplicity: four walls and a roof. It doesn't even have a steeple. Yet if God awarded marks for attendance, you'd score highly for this one, for the Serpentine church is very hard to reach. It stands in wild, remote country which freezes in winter, scorches in summer and in between is just vast and windy.

The church is the loftiest in the land: that is, it stands at the highest altitude. Churchgoers elsewhere raise their eyes to heaven from much lower levels. Altitude being one prime aspect of godliness, I determined to reach this minster.

My first attempt failed. I set out from Outram in the dawn mist of an early December day, taking the road that runs through country looking from above like the creased grey matter of a human brain. The road goes to Middlemarch then to the

Maniototo. At the old, pink Clarks Junction Hotel, I turned left and headed for the Old Dunstan Road.

It was built by gold miners. They had no time to waste. They were in a gold rush. Two miners from California, Horatio Hartley and Christopher Reilly, had struck gold near what is now Clyde, in an area called the Dunstan in Central Otago. Fabulous quantities of the precious metal lay there for the taking, and 40,000 gold miners rushed in. They wanted the most direct route between Dunedin and the Dunstan goldfields. In the summer of 1862–63 they followed a faint dray track from Clarks Junction, found a place on the Rock and Pillar Range to cross into the Taieri River valley above Patearoa, then headed for Rough Ridge on the other side. Rock and Pillar? Rough Ridge? These men didn't muck around. They called the country as they saw it, although they showed a little style with the Serpentine.

They carved a road crossing four mountain ranges. It was sometimes called the Mountain Track. The route was so tough it took five days to traverse its forty-six kilometres, if the weather was good. Much of it was covered by snow and ice in winter, when it became dangerous and desperate and often impassable. Some of those early miners simply disappeared, snap-frozen somewhere in the rocks.

The track was used for only a few years before a route from Palmerston through the Maniototo became the main road. Miners called the new road the Pigroot, the name it carries to this day. Its only explanation comes from A.W. Reed's *Place Names of New Zealand*, which reports an incident during John Turnbull Thomson's survey of the area (Thomson also named the Dunstan). Wild pigs were so common that Thomson watched a huge boar approach and rub noses with his horse.

The Pigroot was longer, but easier. The Old Dunstan Road became much less used but, surprisingly, it survived the next century and a half.

Today the drive over the Old Dunstan Road isn't as long as it used to be, but it still takes a few hours in a tough vehicle. The track is as raw, the rocks as hard, the mountains as high — and the weather just as vicious. The road is still closed in winter.

Those early miners would have no trouble finding their way, even now. The country they traversed remains pretty much unchanged.

The road is a registered historic place. It was recognised by Heritage New Zealand 'by virtue of its historic importance and association with the very early days of Central Otago gold mining, its rarity as one of the country's oldest extant roads, and its length, which is far in excess of any other recognised heritage road in the country'.

The local guidebook told me that I would 'experience solitude and beauty on this desolate but ethereal route'. Solitude, beauty, desolation, yes, but ethereal? Mmm.

Rocks, and pillars, and temples and statues and stacks adorn the landscape: no one lives outside the valleys. It comes to life once a year when a cavalcade of horses, wagons and people on foot retrace the miners' track. Otherwise it is far too cold, too windy, too lonely, too remote. Big mountain hares lope between the rocks.

I bumped and ground across this unyielding land until I descended into the wide green Upper Maniototo Valley of the upper Taieri and travelled past the old stone Styx Hotel, once an overnight coach stop. A gaol house beside it was used for storing gold, and stables still stand alongside.

In this green settled country my brother once worked on a farm. He lived in a stone house that soon made you forget quaint notions of charm: its most outstanding feature was an ambient temperature that would have even a hardy Dunstan goldminer reaching for his blanket.

The Dunstan Road climbs back into character on the other side of the valley. My map showed two routes to the Serpentine: one was the Old Dunstan Road, the other a track that took a more direct line to the old goldmining town. Both climbed Rough Ridge.

One of them followed Waimonga Creek. The creek wound in such a way that the miners decided a better name for their settlement would be Serpentine. Besides, they were not much given to Maori names. Maori may have passed through this place, but they left no sign. Archaeologists have found moa-hunters' sites a little further south, but they seem to have given the Serpentine a miss, probably wisely. That was the way I wanted to go, and I was searching for the way into it when a local farmer bent a steely eye on my rented Toyota Surf. I wasn't going to make it in that, he said.

Well, I quite liked the truck. It felt rough and ready, compared with my more urban Subaru Outback.

'Nope,' the farmer said. 'Take the Old Dunstan Road.' That wasn't too good either, but if I turned off at the top and headed for the Serpentine by that route, I might make it. He surveyed my truck again and rubbed his chin in a doubtful sort of way. Authorities here recommend that if you're fool enough to try for the Serpentine, a much rougher route than the Old Dunstan Trail, you should travel in convoy with another vehicle. Passengers would be good too. If you got stuck, somebody would need to get out and push. I was a bloke on his own, in a townie tractor, and the farmer wasn't keen on any part of it.

Rough Ridge was certainly rough. The rocks were sharp and numerous. The road curled through them and, as often, over them. The truck bounced and grizzled. I bounced and grizzled.

An intersection lay at the top. Not the kind of intersection townies are used to, where two roads cross and conduct traffic in an orderly fashion. It didn't even seem like the top, more a flattish sort of place which might go back downhill, eventually. A pub called the Black Ball Hotel once stood there, but it was long gone and you had to guess this was the right place to turn, open a gate, and head along a track grandly called the Long Valley Ridge Road. It didn't look like a road, more a confusion of ruts. It didn't really seem like a ridge either, just another bump in a ridgy landscape.

Long Valley Ridge Road soon came clean. Yes, it was not so much a road, it announced, as a track. Well, not so much a track as grooves in the ground, where the ground could find a place for them between rocks.

The round trip was some twenty-five kilometres from the Black Ball Hotel site. I ground along it, kilometre after kilometre, through tussock and spaniard. The road is covered in snow in the winter, and even in spring patches of snow still lay around. I was headed for sites said to be rich in gold-mining history. The remnants of the old Serpentine village, mine shafts, stamping battery, water wheel and ruins were reputed to lie around.

I missed them all, only partly because I was never still enough to see anything clearly. Eventually, I stopped. Did I imagine I saw the church far ahead? Oh, the hell with this heavenly pursuit. I felt lonely. Did the AA come this far? If something went wrong, it might be a very long time before anyone came along. I'd be frozen solid: they'd have to chip me out of the driver's seat.

I turned the truck around, with difficulty because the difference between being on the track and off it was that while the track was rocky and rutted, the ground beside it made up for its lack of ruts with many more rocks. And that was that.

But the church preyed on my mind. Why go to all that trouble, all that distance, and give up? So here I am, a couple of years later, having another crack at it.

I hire a Toyota Hilux. It is more brutal than the previous Surf, but also more refined. It gives out a kind of purring growly chatter. I don't get into its black-leather interior, I ascend. I am truly king of the road! I look down on other cars. Oh, confined creatures of tarmac, out of my way! For I am now lord of the back roads, the Toad of the South:

All those wasted years that lie behind me, I never knew, never even dreamt! But now — but now that I know, now that I fully realise! O what a flowery track lies spread before me, henceforth! What dust-clouds shall spring up behind me as I speed on my reckless way!

Perhaps not so much reckless as fifty kilometres per hour for a start, and not so many dust-clouds in those refined reaches of the South. I am in a truck once driven (by Jeremy Clarkson, but nevertheless) to the North Pole. The Serpentine should be a pushover. *Poop poop!*

This time I go in from the other end, past the old Moa Creek Hotel. Nor am I alone. My wife Sally is in the passenger's seat.

Of course, this may mean only that two of us might need to be rescued rather than one. But it feels better.

Moa Creek was a village once, sheltering in its little valley under the Raggedy Range. The old school closed down in 1991, but the teacher's house is still there, and the old grocery store. Everything here is prefixed by the word 'old'.

Moa Creek once stood a day's travel away from Alexandra, and from the other direction it must have been a wonderful sight for diggers nearing the end of their long trek over the Dunstan trail. An advertisement in the *Dunstan Times* proclaimed the hotel a 'popular and well-appointed house' offering superior accommodation to travellers; also, 'A new and commodious hall to let for meetings, pictures, socials etc.'

I stop at a farm to ask directions. The farmer is civil but distant. I call it the Old Dunstan Road. He corrects me. '*Track*.' Perhaps he is thinking about something that happened many years before, for this is a small place, where stories about strangers never go away.

They still talk about one of New Zealand's most mysterious unsolved murders here. William Peter McIntosh, aged sixty-two, was found dead in his woolshed at Moa Creek on 28 September 1949. He'd gone out to work on his farm, telling his wife he'd be back mid-afternoon to listen to the rugby on the radio. He never returned. A search party found his body that night. He had been bashed to death, probably with an axe. Suspicion centred on a stranger who'd called at the McIntosh house to ask directions and then disappeared. The murderer was never found.

At the old Moa Creek Hotel two women are sitting on the veranda in the sun, sipping from mugs. For one brief, delighted moment I imagine the pub might once more be open for business and I pull alongside. No, they say, just catching up, having a chat. Oh well.

I leave the green valley and take to the tawny track.

The Dunstan Trail with its warning signs ends, or begins, not far from the pub. It runs past the Poolburn Reservoir, a rather dull name for a lake with inlets and islands and points and peninsulas. Peter Jackson loved it.

The Poolburn Dam was built by Depression labour and finished in 1931. The plan was both to irrigate the Ida Valley, the valley running beside the Raggedy Range where Moa Creek sits, and to give jobs to some of the men thrown out of work by the Depression. Work started late in 1929 and finished in 1931: even by today's standards a nippy project, especially for men with picks and shovels. Seven of them were hurt, some badly, when scaffolding collapsed. One man died in a fall. Apart from that, their main problem was the cold. The winter snow was bad enough, but the wind brawls through here with cudgels. Yet the result, unusually for an irrigation project, was a thing of beauty. A lake formed behind the new dam, its archipelagos making it intricate and mysterious.

Once, five hotels lined the road here. The one most often remembered is the Drunken Woman Inn. The pubs have all gone now, but the Drunken Woman lives on: a bay on the reservoir is named after it.

A new civilisation has grown up around the lake edge. Baches sit on flats among the rocks and tussock, or wedged into the rocky towers. They are highly individual, eccentric even, but they have one common feature: they're very pretty. Jackson thought so too. He used some of them for the Rohan Village in *Lord of the Rings*.

Most of them are well kept, but there are a few doer-uppers. I head for one of them, almost hidden behind sculpted rock. Why, some new weatherboards there, fix that window here, maybe a porch ... I can feel the hammer in my soul, see myself sitting on the new deck looking over the water to those superb ranges beyond.

Alas. The authorities know a thing or two about blokes with ladders. Signs forbid resurrecting old baches. A few years previously an Aucklander was so entranced by the serenity of the place that he proposed improving it with a subdivision. He wanted to carve up 902 hectares for houses. Hundreds opposed the plan. So did the Central Otago District Council. A hearing was scheduled, but just before it began the budding developer withdrew his application. Tranquillity again descended.

I stop at a handsome hut where a couple of utes and a car are parked. A man is outside, putting away fishing gear. He hasn't had a good day. In fact, he says, he isn't much of a fisherman but — an arm curves over the still water, the tussock, the last of the snow on the tops — who cares?

Trout, rainbow and brown, have been released into the reservoir, but they fish for only brown trout now: the last rainbow has faded into history. When the weather warms up the fish rise too, but this is early spring and it's cold. The men inside the bach don't care much. It's only the second day of the season and they've caught a few but no keepers, yet. They're having some beers and frying up lunch and talking about old times. The table is covered in bottles. They're old friends and this, they reckon, is as good as it gets. 'It'll blow you away up there,' one of them says. He's dead right, if in a more literal sense.

The Old Dunstan Road is closed from June until the end of September, and it has only just reopened after the winter. It feels lonely. It *is* lonely. But as you climb, it becomes peopled by stony figures. Here are two trolls playing chess. There's a tin can with the lid half off. A motorhome is parked beside the road. It turns out to be a real one, not a rock. The couple inside are going to have a crack at Rough Ridge. They've heard the stories but still, the driver says, 'It costs nothing to have a look, does it?'

Perhaps they're up there still and people like me are driving past the rock formations and saying, 'Look, there's a seal on a rock, and a dancing whale, and a tyrannosaurus, and a crowd of people, and doesn't that one over there look just like a motorhome?'

We reach the site of the old hotel. I get out and open the gate. The wind is slight, more of a breeze, but it has the strength and stamina of a scimitar. Only remotely ethereal. I have leather seats and air-conditioning. Surreal.

The truck sinks hub-deep into ruts. It kicks up skirls of dust which dance wraith-like around us. Struggling vehicles have created canyons, gulches, ditches, valleys in the mud. The truck bounces. I bounce too. The tussock doesn't so much wave as applaud.

So we make our cheery way along Rough Ridge and soon reach an outpost of civilisation. It is called the Oliverburn Hut, and it is the size and colour of a fridge. It is roughcast white and so perfectly arranged inside it would entrance those architects pursuing the craze for small houses. Rabbiters and musterers use it.

Inside this hut, which is about the length of a tall man, are two bunks, a kitchen and a cunning little table, as welcome a refuge up here as anyone could hope for. I'm tempted to stay for a while, reluctant to leave this unlikely oasis, but I hear the siren call of the Serpentine.

We clunk and bump along the track, skirting bogs, trying not to damage the tussock, splashing through the occasional stream. Much of this was once a dray track used by miners. Now it has the sinuous, blasted quality of a World War I trench. It winds along ridges and into gullies and every time you think you must see where you're going when you're around the next bend, you can't. We reach the point where I turned back the last time I was here. A little further on a sign points down another track to the old stamper battery and water wheel, both of them restored.

The battery was built to crush ore from the mines. It was first set up at German Jacks fifteen kilometres to the north, then moved to another mining area 7.5 kilometres to the south, doubled in size, and shifted again in 1890 to its final resting place at Serpentine. Easy to say, or to write. But look at the thing! It is huge, and very, very heavy. After all, it was built to smash rocks. Look at the terrain it was commuting over. This is a mountain range. Oh, the work, the effort! And all for nothing. It was used for only a year or so before it was abandoned as a bad job. Now both it and the water wheel look ready to go again. All they need are a few desperate miners and a sniff of gold.

When you look closely you can see a working mine: the water-wheel race, traces of the railway which carted rock to the stamper battery, the main mine tunnel. Then, piles of rock move into focus. It is like waking up in a dark room and from the confusion picking out furniture, chairs, a table in the corner.

Why, they're not just eccentric rock stacks. They have walls. They're old miners' huts and over there is something said to have once been a store.

Gold was found in the Waimonga Creek in 1863 and Serpentine sprang into being, the highest goldfields township in the land, an instant town of 500 people with two stores that doubled as hotels, a blacksmith, huts for the miners. Somewhere in the tussock is a cemetery and a racecourse. The town reached its peak ten years later in 1873.

The Millers Flat Correspondent of the *Tuapeka Times* came the same way as we did but more than a century before, in 1898. He described his first view of the Serpentine like this:

> ... a scene of oppressive desolation ... Never did I witness a more forbidding habitation ... Lindburn Township [Serpentine] is a combination of store, butcher's shop, post office and hotel, all amalgamated into one business, but which was which I could not say ... Behind the store was a rickety billiard room and table with a mixture of European and Chinese players and lookers-on. They were an unwashed and uncombed lot; the debris of ages seemed to have accumulated on their hands, faces and clothes.

A little further along the track I see it. The survivor. The church! We bounce over a last bump or two, splash through a muddy little creek. Unlikely as it may seem, this town was built on swampy ground, but the church is high and dry, for the wise man builds his house on rock.

It's a beautifully simple little building, no steeple, a couple of posts and a sheet of iron for a porch. The roof's pitch is perfect, its angles exactly right. Wire cables run from its ridge flashing and down its walls to hold down the roof. They are either tethered to the ground or attached to large rocks that hang around the church like the corks on an Australian bushman's hat. In some places they've cut a groove in the ground as they sway. The wind up here at 1000 metres must rocket across this flat. Even now it clangs the roofing iron. Clouds zoom above us like spaceships.

The door scrapes open. The roof is thatched, the iron covering the thatch. A beautiful little cupboard stands inside the door. There's old china and mysterious pieces of iron. A couple of rough beds with fencing-wire springs.

The church's history has been burned laboriously into the hymn board. It was built for £100, all contributed by miners. This country is alien, spartan, and the work was truly dreadful. Miners must have looked for some kind of meaning — other than gold, of course. It's unlikely they subscribed to the biblical view about how much better it was to get wisdom than gold.

Back to the hymn board. It says of the very first service in the new church: 'The Minister being late, the congregation of miners after waiting for some time went down to the hotel for refreshments and drank deeply to keep out the mean July air, keener than ever at this altitude.' When the preacher finally arrived, he was not well pleased. After they sang the first hymn the miners demanded an encore: 'The preacher, after expressing very strong disapproval, went on with the service which was however abbreviated.'

Not many services were held 'because of the small number of inhabitants and the difficulty of access', which seems a concise enough description of Serpentine. Soon it was an impossible church. Not only did it have no vicar, it had no congregation either.

After only a few years the church was redundant. It became the property of its largest subscriber, who sold it to a Mr Wilson in 1889. At the time the historian was searing his text into the hymn board, it was owned by a Mr Greer. It became a 'residence', although it can have been only slightly bigger than the miners' huts. An old iron Shacklock stove still marks the kitchen. It would have come in handy. Even now, in a chilly September, it is colder inside than out.

The brown tussock whispers and a congregation of rock gargoyles sings a lonely song. It feel precarious here. No birds, not even a hare. I haven't seen anyone since the Poolburn Reservoir. I want to go. We climb into the Toyota, the real sanctuary here. We drive back through the creek, past the relics and the ghosts, and leave.

Much later, I come across an article in the *Otago Witness* of 24 October 1895. Its headline was 'The Missing Chinaman', its subtitle 'A Senseless Hoax', and it was reprinted in newspapers all over the country. It concerned the disappearance of Kong Wah Jun, who had made a considerable sum on the Serpentine goldfield. He left Serpentine to go home to China, visited his brother in Alexandra, left his money there and proceeded towards Butchers Gully to see some friends who, incidentally, owed him money. Butchers Gully was a rich goldfield between Alexandra and Roxburgh, now submerged under Butchers Dam on Flat Top Hill. He never arrived at Butchers Gully. He simply disappeared.

A little later, police found a body, apparently that of Wah Jun, on the river bank below Alexandra. His hands and feet were tied tightly together and a huge stone was tied around his neck.

The body was taken into Alexandra for identification. Jurors were summoned to attend, along with the coroner and two doctors. A crowd of small boys collected outside the temporary morgue and was kept back by constables.

The body had to be viewed by the jurymen:

> and for this purpose the jury ... stood around with wry
> faces and highly perfumed pocket handkerchiefs. On the
> cloth covering the face of the deceased being withdrawn the
> brother failed to identify the features as being those of his
> brother Wah Jun.

Luckily, as it turned out.

> One juryman found voice to expatiate upon the cash-paying
> virtues of the deceased, but reluctantly asked the coroner to
> have the cloth redrawn over the features as he (the juryman)
> could not bear the stony rigidity of that stare from the left
> eye of the deceased.

The examination continued, the police objecting to the loosening
of the knots, as they could be material evidence in detecting the
crime of foul murder. On taking off the trousers, 'a strange and
gruesome sight presented itself ... for, strange as it may appear,
there was no human body there, nothing but a sheepskin, the
entrails of some other beast, a few pig bones, a kidney and a set
of goat's teeth'. The article dwelt on the detail:

> The sheepskin, nicely tanned and turned inside out, formed
> the head and face, and in this a slit was made for the mouth,
> the edges being drawn back to form the lips, between which
> a faultless set of goat's teeth gleamed with pearly whiteness.
> The features were complete, nor was the pigtail forgotten.

No one, apparently, knew quite where to look. Eventually:

> The jurymen walked home, and so did the medicos, and
> so did the coroner, and so too did the police, but the latter
> in quite a different mood than the former. The little boys
> went to play marbles or some such harmless game, and so
> ended one of the most remarkable inquests of the nineteenth
> century.

What of poor Kong Wah Jun? I could find no further reference.
Like Serpentine, he vanished.

7

Strutting stuff

Queen Street, New Zealand's best-known street, has a double life. In one it is a thoroughfare. Buses and cars jostle on the roadway, pedestrians on the footpath, shops and tall buildings line its route. In the other, it chucks the suits, climbs into its jeans and screams. It mutates from a city walk to a wild journey. It becomes a stage. It turns into New Zealand's Trafalgar Square, National Mall, Central Park, Place de la Bastille. If you need to say something, protest against anything, even celebrate a win, then off you go down Queen Street.

This is the most crowded street in New Zealand, yet there's always room to move on its broad pavements. Sometimes people change places with the traffic, for on Queen Street nothing stays the same for very long. Pedestrians burst onto the roadway, dodging the mysterious construction choreography that is a constant part of Queen Street theatre. People in hard hats and hi-viz vests are always directing traffic to, well, somewhere else.

In the first decade of the new millennium Queen Street was upgraded, and everyone — cars, buses, trucks, pedestrians — was subjected to years of torment. Adding injury to insult, the cost of the upgrade doubled. Queen Street claimed another victim: the work took some of the blame for unseating the mayor, Dick Hubbard. A new mayor, Len Brown, promoted an even bigger project, the underground city rail link. Queen Street choked again. Brown went too, but for other reasons.

Through all of it Queen Street emerges with panache as a fine piece of Auckland theatre. Now people dance around traffic which runs lights and hops lanes, for on Queen Street progress depends not so much on driving as creativity.

The same applies to its other life. Queen Street's alter ego is, in fact, a public megaphone. An amphitheatre for popular opinion. New Zealand's Circus Maximus.

Sometimes Queen Street has changed our world. In 1981, an anti-union march named 'Kiwis Care' attracted 50,000 people to Queen Street. Flags flew; the national anthem evoked the sanctimony of a test match. The young organiser, Tania Harris, became an instant celebrity. Trade unions, whose own march along Queen Street attracted just 4000 marchers and an awful lot of abuse, were excoriated. The wounds never healed.

Sometimes the street hasn't changed anything. Some 10,000 people marched on Aotea Square in 2001 opposing genetic engineering. Helen Clark's Labour government took no notice, allowing GE experiments to continue.

Win or lose, the wild journeys along Queen Street have a life of their own.

In 2010 Queen Street accommodated one of the biggest protests in our history. It blocked Queen Street from top to bottom, opposing the newly elected National government's decision to allow mining on conservation land. The government had promised to consult the public, and here on Queen Street were plenty of public to consult. Some said the government backed down as a result, but history has shown they simply made the changes more subtle.

Usually, no one dies on Queen Street, although egos and dignity may suffer grievously.

It is the place where causes wither or bloom, the stage upon which the citizenry treads the boards. Excellent, you say. The street has a vivid reputation. Excitement. Public mayhem.

I've been on several of these performances both up and down Queen Street. The first was soon after I moved to Auckland, in 2012. Television New Zealand had delivered the chop to its Channel 7, a commercial-free channel strong on the arts. The government had pulled the plug on the channel's funding, and the last vestige of public television broadcasting was to shut down at midnight that night. Given the choice between a remarkably small amount of money and some 1.6 million viewers, the government took the simple view: cut the viewers loose, the subtext being they were unlikely to be National voters anyway.

The idea was to have a funeral procession along Queen Street, in the forlorn hope that it might save the channel. As only a few hundred people turned up, it probably had the opposite effect.

As we all marched up the street, it soon became clear that, news-wise, the focus had shifted. Closing New Zealand's only public broadcasting television channel had taken second place to a large, rich immigrant who called himself Kim Dotcom.

Dotcom's famous mansion had been raided by the police not long before, ineptly. Now he saw Channel 7 as a symbol of the internet freedom upon which his fortune depended. People who were not interested in internet freedom, still less Channel 7, saw only Kim Dotcom.

I was right behind him. In both senses. The enemy of my enemy was my friend. Besides, he was a large man, it was a rather cold evening, and he was a mobile shelter belt.

We marched past Britomart, disguised as the old Chief Post Office and soon to become, yes, another construction obstacle as somewhere far below workers cut through the sediment of centuries to build more underground rail and carry the Queen City a little further into the twentieth century, with the twenty-first still to be tackled. We went past the expensive stores — Dior, Prada, Hugo Boss, Louis Vuitton, Gucci — where mysterious queues sometimes form at some unseen signal and, kept in line by uniformed attendants, are let into the store a few at a time without unseemly rush.

Up the street we went, past the barely discernible bend that shows the course of the Waihorotiu Stream, which Queen Street was built along, following what was once a bushy gully. Past Vulcan Lane, enticing faint-hearted protesters to abandon their futile quest for beauty, and instead, pop into one of its narrow pubs for a beer.

The Front Lawn sang of Vulcan Lane, of seeing themselves in a cafe window as if they were in colour and everyone else was in black and gray. Now that was reversed. I thought I was in black and gray and everything else was in colour. It was quite clear that Channel 7 was going to go out with a whimper rather than a bang.

We passed the 1865 Bank of New Zealand building, which is the only survivor of Queen Street's mid-ninetheenth-century roots, now in true Auckland fashion just a silly façade for the high-rise now occupying the site. I felt a bit of a silly façade myself.

When you start checking the architecture, you might say you've lost momentum. When you investigate its history, likewise. This was a timid affair. A century before, people knew how to stage a *decent* protest. In 1913 hundreds of strikers, shouting and throwing stones, tried to prevent ships being loaded on the wharves. Large numbers of armed and mounted strike-breakers, supported by hundreds of police and a naval warship, were put on duty at the Auckland docks to protect strike-breakers, or scabs.

The *Weekly News* reported that as the clock struck 5 a.m. on 10 November:

Every unit in the defence of the waterfront, comprising fully 1000 'irregulars' and regular police, was stationed in the position selected for it. As the day advanced, a very angry crowd of strikers and their sympathisers congregated in Little Queen Street, which was guarded by farmers from Cambridge, and towards ten o'clock it looked as if there would be trouble. The mass of excited men forced itself nearer to the double row of mounted country men and shouted the most offensive epithets in its vocabulary, varying the theme occasionally with a chorus of howls and hoots.

The Cambridge farmers sat quiet, calm and outwardly unmoved; but their batons never left their hands, and their gaze was fixed very steadily on the seething, raging crowd in front. 'We don't want to start fighting', said the commander of the troop, when a particularly vile invective was flung at them, 'we are here to protect our port and not to fight'.

Violence broke out all over the place, of course, but the strikers lost.

This day, in 2012, a century later, my body may have been intact but my head was so bored it might even have welcomed a knock from a cockie's stick.

Where was the spirit of, say, 1932, when 15,000 angry unemployed marched up to a Town Hall meeting, fought police and, enraged when one of their leaders was struck down with a police baton as he rose to plead for calm, ricocheted down Queen Street, smashing shop windows? They took one chemist shop's entire stock of contraceptives and vandalised all the wax dummies in a department store. That's picturesque looting.

Well, many of those people lost their livelihoods, and their pride, and their future. We were only losing an arts channel.

On the other hand, a mere power cut was enough to set off a riot at a concert in Queen Street's Aotea Square in December 1984. The concert, 'Thank God It's Over', celebrated the end of the academic year but when the power went off and the music stopped and people started throwing bottles, the riot police arrived. Damage in the end came to more than a million dollars and everyone went home that night with a common thought: 'Thank God, it's over.'

The Queen Street protest against the Trans-Pacific Partnership Agreement (TPPA) in 2016 showed more fire. Thousands of us turned up at Aotea Square and marched down the street, 'shutting down central Auckland', according to some reports. We felt the proposed agreement didn't just stink, it reeked to high heaven.

John Key, the Prime Minister, smelled only roses. Around the corner, choosing the casino for his own stage, he signed the agreement with a flourish. Outside, protesters capered and howled. This was more like it.

I marched sedately behind a group of Maori who believed their sovereignty was about to be signed over to the Las Vegas Roundtable, or Philip Morris. They thought they stood a much better chance with Queen Victoria's descendants.

We all argued that banks would rule the world, that multinationals would roll right over us, and that the environment would be ruined, as if the TPPA would make any of that worse. We shouted so loudly that even John Key might have heard us above the clinking of glasses and chinking of pokies. He emerged from among the high-rollers to declare that Aucklanders were pretty disappointed and a bit confused by the protest, that we were left-wing rent-a-protesters and that anyway there were only a few thousand of us. The media reckoned there were 10,000. The organisers guessed more like 15,000.

Academics argue that big street protests are effective not so much for their cause but for the way they activate the participants politically: they inspire political movement. Later that year Key quit as Prime Minister. Did he detect a flutter in the chorus, a tic in the corner of the nation's smile? But in the end the TPPA was scuppered not by the left in Queen Street but by the right in the United States, in the form of its new president, Donald Trump.

A few months later I was again strutting the tarmac. This time the march was part of a Week of Peace, whose object was to poop the Royal New Zealand Navy's birthday party on the Waitemata. The harbour wasn't exactly crowded with visiting warships, for New Zealand is not only near the bottom of the world but a very long way from any tactical territory: both factors are probably more useful in protecting us than the Navy.

It was a particularly forlorn day, and the warships strung along the harbour looked as if they could think of much better places for a party. So did the matelots wearing short sleeves and lining the decks and probably thinking that if they'd joined the Navy to see the world, sometimes the world just wasn't worth it.

A few protest boats lurched back and forth in the choppy water, none of them threatening but all of them attended by police, who apparently had more boats on hand than the Navy.

We congregated at Aotea Square and listened to speeches so boring even the speakers seemed to be nodding off. This time the group of Maori under their sovereignty banner was all set to go when a group accompanying two elderly ladies, one in a wheelchair, made their way to the front. The two were truly veteran protestors. One or both had been at Greenham Common in the UK, when tens of thousands of women protested against nuclear weapons outside an Air Force base. That protest went on for years, and even after it ended and the authorities announced there was nothing left to protest about, groups of women cut holes in the fence for a week.

So these women had earned their place at the head of the parade, even if, not far away at the Viaduct, arms dealers including the world's largest nuclear arms manufacturer, Lockheed Martin, were signing orders for weapons which would make those Greenham Common missiles look like popguns.

Around 2000 of us set off down Queen Street. We hadn't gone far before I was admiring the Smith and Caughey building and thinking about the remarkable Marianne Caughey, who founded the business and proved it wasn't just the road to hell that was paved with good intentions but Queen Street too.

The upper storeys of the department store, containing all manner of staff amenities — library, sitting rooms, women's rooms, and ... well, once you start thinking about architecture and history *and* mourning the good intentions of a bygone age, all the while marching down the street in protest at the intentions of the current one, then you might as well give it away. So I did. The proper thing to do, I felt, was to abandon the parade and let the others deliver tribute to the barbarians.

In 2017 Emirates Team New Zealand won the America's Cup. The triumphant sailors were to parade down Queen Street. The day was wintery-cold, but flashes of sunlight fell upon the young mariners, raising the god quotient. The parade started just off the top end of Queen Street, every carload of yachties hosted regally by an Emirates flight attendant. All the brass bands in the land seemed to have been summoned for the event, and pipe bands too. Drums thumped, pipes howled and euphoniums honked. The light bounced off instruments big as suns. If there'd been a lesser event this day, say a coronation, or a state funeral, it would have been grievously short of musical instruments.

Marching girls strutted, people dressed as sailors danced hornpipes, gymnasts cavorted, flags waved everywhere and, as car horns howled, our heroes set forth amid a forest of uplifted phones and a thousand, ten thousand, selfies jammed the ether.

Leading the parade were Peter Burling and Glenn Ashby. Ashby, to the great confusion of the non-sailing crowd, since he never took the wheel, was skipper. Burling, whom most people thought was skipper, was in fact helmsman.

A mere technicality. Burling was a hero in the Hillary mould: tall, angular, long lean face split by a crevasse of a grin. The two of them, and Grant Dalton, the boss, took turns hoisting the cup aloft, and they needed all their fitness training to do it. The rich boys, the men who made the whole thing possible, waved too, and I daresay they deserved their share of the glory given the Olympian nature of the cheques they'd written.

Down Queen Street they went, the crowd growing by the minute: 50,000, 100,000, who was counting? 'Woo-woo-woo,' they went.

A woman dressed in a flag strutted a matching poodle. Even the Queen Street homeless looked elated. On to the Viaduct, the rain pouring down now, everyone drenched and no one caring, waka lined up stern as a naval parade, warriors bailing. A fleet of pleasure boats clustered outside, more than were ever seen at the Bermuda contest, according to one commentator. I had no reliable count, but my impression was that more police turned out for the yachties than the trade protest. Certainly they looked happier.

The old *KZ1* hung over the affair like an artefact, although its story was just as dramatic. That yacht challenged for the 1988 America's Cup. The Americans responded with a catamaran. It won the races *and* the court battle which followed. Ah, those were the days. *KZ1* was made of carbon fibre and Kevlar sandwich. It was state of the art. Now it was a dinosaur, a relic of this rich man's sport. But who'd say anything like that, on this day of days?

I abandoned the cyclors for the commutors. I wrung a gallon or two of rainwater from my heavy woollen coat and caught the ferry back home.

Now, that was a demonstration. Of what, I'm still not sure. The age of dissent has its followers; evidently the age of consent has many more.

8

Hunting ghosts

One fine weekend I arrange to meet Rhys Buckingham in South Westland to search for the country's most elusive bird.

It seems simple enough, except that phrases such as 'fine weekend' and 'South Westland' do not sit easily with each other. The weather office might think the weekend will be fine, but South Westland has other ideas. Or vice versa.

Worse, the 'country's most elusive bird' has eluded its putative hunters for years and is unlikely to make an exception for a visiting writer. Does the bird exist? Am I instead searching for Rhys Buckingham, who is almost as cryptic as his bird?

Cryptic. My dictionary defines it as 'secret, mystic, mysterious'. Zoologists use it to describe an animal so anonymous in its colourings, so careful in its proceedings, that it is all but invisible. Ghost-like, in other words.

All of this describes the South Island kokako, as much as it can be described, for the bird is usually no more than a shadow, a wish in the deep green bush. It has earned the title 'Grey Ghost'.

The list of extinct New Zealand birds is long and ignoble. It runs from the huia to the Haast's eagle, from false-toothed pelicans to the New Zealand lake-wanderer, from nineteen species of penguins to all nine species of moa. We are not good with birds.

The South Island kokako was another victim of habitat loss and predators. It was declared extinct too, for a few years, until the various bird authorities decided they might have been a little fast off the mark and improved its official status, marginally.

Everyone has heard the kokako's call, although they may not know it. It is that deep, melodic, lonely, haunting note that so often introduces a tale of the New Zealand bush. Without it the song of the forest is lighter, like an orchestra missing its bassoon.

Rhys Buckingham heard it first forty years before, in the 1970s. This is what he says about that: 'I heard the most amazing call, at the head of Lake Monowai. It was right on nightfall. It was the most beautiful, bell-like tolling. It has never gone out of my mind. It went for some time and then it stopped and after it stopped I could hear it still in my ear.'

In his soul too, I suspect.

I listen on *NZ Birds Online* to the kokako's calls he has recorded over the years (listed as 'possible calls'), then to recordings of the North Island kokako: a long clear pipe, an organ-like *mwonngg*; joyous, tragic, tremendously moving, the magical calls of sirens luring voyagers onto the rocks.

The nineteenth-century South Westland adventurer Charlie 'Mr Explorer' Douglas, who called the kokako the 'New Zealand crow' and wrote of them running around his camp in dozens, found the call 'indiscribably mournfull' [*sic*]:

The wail of the wind through a leafless forest is cheerful
compared to it ... sadly suggestive of departed spirits ...
It is only in the depths of the forest they can be heard to
perfection. Their notes are very few, but are the sweetest and
most mellow toned I have ever heard a bird produce. When
singing they cast their eyes upwards like a street musician
expecting coppers from a fourth story window, and pour
forth three or four notes, softer and sweeter than an acolian
harp or a well-toned clarionet.

The voyage hasn't wrecked Rhys Buckingham, yet. I think of him
more as a knight-errant on a quest that began a very long time
ago.

He calls himself an ecologist, primarily. He has worked, often
on threatened species, for the old Wildlife Service, the former
Forest Service, early versions of the Department of Conservation.
Now he works with clients who need resource consents. That's
his job, he says, although I suspect that if he could bill someone
for all the hours he has put into the South Island kokako he'd be
a very rich man.

He is seventy. He wears a pair of shorts he calls lichen-coloured;
to my mind they're baggy khaki, without the pith helmet. I
haven't seen him for more than a decade, but he certainly doesn't
look ten years older. He is charitable about my own advancing
years but tells me with just a hint of glee that buying petrol the
other day he produced his SuperGold card for a discount and the
cashier asked him for additional proof of identity.

I think of him as Tantalus, who in Greek mythology stood
in a pool forever, fruit dangling over his head but always out of
reach, the water below running away before he could drink it.

But he isn't simply tantalised by the kokako — he is tormented by it. He is part of an ornithological galaxy but in an orbit of his own.

In 1980 he was working for what was then the Forest Service on Stewart Island. His boss was a senior protection ranger, Max Kershaw. (He has a thicket of names, ornithologists, environmentalists, supporters. Some he approves of; some — for the same arguments and jealousies seethe here as in any ardent group — he puts in the same category as, say, a bush lawyer.)

'He was a wonderful man,' Rhys says of Kershaw. 'He leaked to me one day that he'd found a population of kokako, at least a dozen of them, on Stewart Island and he wasn't telling anybody. He thought Lands and Survey and the Wildlife Service [whose conservation duties were later subsumed by the Department of Conservation] were destroying our wildlife. That's how it started.'

The South Island kokako was then officially extinct and had been since 1967, the last confirmed sighting.

Kershaw never said where he'd found the birds but hinted at the Ruggedy Range running along the north-western rim of Stewart Island, around the upper reaches of the Freshwater River. Or they might be somewhere else. He wouldn't be exact.

Rhys determined to find them. He knew it would be hard. He took with him recorded contact calls of the North Island kokako to play in the hope that the kokako would respond. But here's something else about kokako: they have their own accents. Their dialects change. They can tell the difference, just as a Coaster can pick someone from Queen Street (or vice versa). They won't answer unless they're spoken to in their own vernacular, just like a Coaster. The North Island bird's call ticks up at the end, while the southern kokako's continues its melancholy glide.

Rhys has put much effort into understanding the complex encyclopaedia of sound within the forest. After thirty-eight years, he says, he has managed to interpret a very small facet of it.

He searched the river, the range, the Rakeahua River running around the base of Mount Rakeahua into South West Arm. He found a valley where he thought, or believed, there were at least three birds, hearing birds without seeing them, and realising their nature: South Island kokako were ethereal. The legend of the Grey Ghost took flight.

He and a companion were up at four in the morning, squirming through the bush and the undergrowth, working through streams and ravines to their sites, right through to eleven at night. 'Oh,' he says, 'we worked so hard, we'd get up in the morning after we'd been there for a week and we could hardly walk, we were falling over, because we were hypnotised by this amazing bird.'

He made a discovery that was to become a mainstay of his quest for the next four decades: in the Mount Anglem branch of the Freshwater River he found a peculiar kind of moss-grubbing — chunks of moss dug out in definite shapes and left intact. As his search developed he was to recognise moss-grubbing as a prime clue to the existence of kokako in the area.

Something else was needed to fire such a long passion, and he found that too. He describes the terrain quite nonchalantly, but this is terribly difficult country, untracked except for the kokako hunters' paths, inaccessible to all but the experienced, or rather, the truly inspired. Perfect kokako country. Even he was wary: 'It was deceptive,' he tells me, 'easy to get lost in. I felt, if there is kokako, this has got to be the spot. But there was nothing at all, until I walked out. Then something amazing happened. I was a bit confused about the exact location of my base camp. I knew I was getting very close to it. I got out my compass and started working out how far it would be. I moved a few metres to a good spot to have a look, use my compass.

'And suddenly behind me I heard this wonderful kokako call, the full organ song. It was exactly the same dialect I'd been using [for the playback call]. I thought for some reason my tape was playing. But it didn't sound as if it was coming from my pack. It repeated. I checked. It seemed to be coming from a tree, very close. I turned off my recorder just in case. Oh, this amazing call. I never saw the bird.'

And that set the pattern. Heard, felt (the *whap* of its wings), even seen, never filmed.

Rhys was confused. Why the same call as his recording? As his search progressed, he realised the answer: kokako are good mimics, like tui, kaka or bellbirds. They can even imitate the alarm bark of a deer, he tells me. 'You cannot be 100 per cent certain that what you hear isn't a clever tui, or a clever kaka. This could not have been a tui because of its clarity, its nuance of call. A kaka, perhaps. I've experienced a kaka call so close to a kokako's that if I hadn't seen it with my own eyes on a log with its gob open making that call I would not have believed it.'

This is the escape clause in the searchers' unwritten contract: they discount any report that is based on call alone.

The Wildlife Service, as it was then, did not accept his evidence. As far as they were concerned, the bird's existence remained unconfirmed.

Uncluttered by bureaucracy, Rhys's mind was clear. He hadn't seen the bird, but he had heard it, and he left the island believing that, probably, kokako still lived there.

He saw the bird for the first time at Fraser Creek near the Caples Valley with a small team of ornithologists. First he saw that moss-grubbing sign. Then he heard organ calls from the forest edge. One of his companions heard them too, so close they seemed to be coming from the tree above his head. He saw a large, long-legged bird, running up a sloping tree trunk, almost certainly a kokako.

The Forest Service took this report seriously. They gave Rhys three months to search for it.

Already the quest was changing him. He spent those three months alone, sometimes passing the night with trampers in their huts. He became a creature of the forest: 'I became so acute. I could hear the faintest things. I could see tiny movements. I became so tuned-in I could follow kaka and kaka almost accepted me. I became almost one of them.'

He seemed to be a good deal closer to kaka than he was to the Wildlife Service, in fact. They didn't accept his report, even when the Forest Service backed it. Rhys might have been working for the Forest Service, but Wildlife considered him an amateur.

Then he went up the Glenroy River in the mountains south of Murchison, where he was doing some work for Timberlands, the forestry company. First he found that moss-grubbing. He played his recording of a North Island kokako juvenile. To his glee, a kokako responded with a short but beautiful song. He stalked it. An hour passed. Then he saw it!

It was gleaning insects, or perhaps honeydew, from the bough of a big beech tree. It flipped upside down and continued feeding. Then righted itself.

Oh, the moment of clarity! He could see its sturdy, unmistakeable bill. A wattle on the left side of its face, pale-straw coloured, neither orange nor red. It was the only time he would ever see the bird's trademark at such close range.

**

On 19 November 1984 Rhys was back in the Mount Anglem area on Stewart Island and this time he saw his bird, again. He'd been tramping for three hours in pouring rain through truly difficult country even by Stewart Island standards. He crossed a saddle, pitched his tent. He was soaking wet. A tramper would have changed his clothes, dried out, cooked a meal, sat in his tent wondering whether he was having fun yet. Rhys went for a nostalgic walk in the rain.

That's the thing about a quest. This was terraced country, gouged by ravines, lonely, easy to get lost in. He'd had no luck here earlier, but if there really were kokako — so cautious, so cryptic, so furtive — this was where they'd be.

He circled, got back to a stream which he knew would lead to his tent site, heard what he thought was a tui. Funny, he thought, tui don't call in the rain.

He reached the base of a rimu where the call seemed to come from, looked up.

A bird took off. A grey bird, silvery-grey, shining white on its underparts. A slow take-off. He's a good ornithologist: even if he hadn't seen its colours, that take-off ruled out tui or kaka. He can see that bird today just as clearly.

He heard it again, singing from the next rimu along, perhaps sixty metres away. He went to the base of that tree. It was singing its head off, switching between notes, tui-like then bellbird-like, and Rhys wondered if he was mistaken.

Then it flew. Right above his head, a grey bird with a long tail and an even, determined flight. It landed on another tree. Charlie Douglas described its flight as both short and awkward: 'They prefer to run about the limbs and trunks of the low scrub, they never actually walk but run with a strolling sort of gait that is very funny.'

Oh god, Rhys thought, why did I leave my camera behind? He had his binoculars but the rain was blurring their lenses. The bird sat in the tree, its head up, distinctively kokako.

Oh, it was a kokako all right. Rhys knew it. But he had no standing then, and not all that much experience either. He was a volunteer. His sighting was not officially accepted.

All told, he counts seven sightings, four of them either certain or close to it. Not many for four decades' work, perhaps, but definitive.

***

At the turn of the new millennium Rhys and the loose consortium of kokako-watchers decided on a massive search, financed mainly by the then-ascendant Maruia Nature Catalogue and Ecologic Foundation. The search immediately threw up two leads.

A Westport bushman called Dan McKinnon reported hearing, and seeing, kokako in the Charleston area in 2000. No kaka, no tui could have imitated it. The call was more than twenty seconds long — full organ song, clear, perfect — and Dan's descriptions were foolproof enough to be unofficially accepted by experts. He recorded the call. The recording was lost in a house fire.

The search was running true to form.

I first met Rhys in those Charleston forests in 2004. He was working deep in craggy territory with two fellow kokako-hunters. They had heard the calls of three birds. No question, Rhys said.

We had breakfast at the Charleston pub, eventually, for the only other diner that morning proved to be the owner, who was also cook, waiter and sole occupant, and he wanted to read his newspaper and finish his coffee first.

I had visited this place as a child with my father, when the pub was the ancient European. He knew the publican, who showed me artefacts including a jar of gold nuggets and a beetle trapped in 'local' kauri gum. Much later I realised the gum could not have been local and I wondered about the gold too. Even the town's history seemed negotiable, a goldmining place once fabulously rich and said to have had ninety-nine hotels. The European was the sole survivor, and it didn't last much longer.

Tourism is the new gold. Visitors climb through limestone caves, through pits and tunnels. So did we. We drove into the Paparoa mountains to where Rhys's two companions, Peter Rudolf and his wife, Mon, hunched on a track eating their breakfast (nowhere near as a good as ours, but much healthier). Then off up the side of a valley we went. It was tricky going, and our silence was broken by yelps of anguish as we tried unsuccessfully to negotiate fallen trees and avoid the deep fissures and pits in this limestone country, all the while scanning the treetops in case the kokako, Madonna-like, should decide to reveal itself to its most recent converts.

We hadn't gone very far before I was completely lost, unable even to say with any conviction which way was down. I realised what a fine bushman Rhys must be, for he was at home in far more remote and difficult country than this, often alone.

Rhys played a flute-like, melancholy recording of a kokako as a contact call. We heard a riroriro, a tui, a bellbird. Otherwise the forest was quiet until Rhys and his companions froze like pointing dogs, their noses aimed at the canopy. 'Hear that?'

Perhaps it was, perhaps not. Fourteen years on, the memory has gelled into a call, the music lodged in my mind.

I talked to Dan McKinnon then. The old bushman was absolutely clear. 'I was walking through the bush in 1998 and I heard this call. In all my time in the bush I'd never heard anything like it. Next day I heard it again. So I recorded it. And I saw two of them on the same day, big birds, bigger than tui, very sneaky in the bush.'

He was exact, and convincing. The wattles were a different colour on each bird. Their flights were short. They hopped. They could only have been kokako.

I talked to the Department of Conservation, which was officially dismissive of Rhys's work. The kokako-watchers had come up with nothing convincing, they said. It was unlikely that any of the sightings were real.

Not long after that the DoC declared the South Island kokako extinct.

Well, the hunt for the bird is littered with lost recordings, forgotten cameras, missed opportunities. Yet it has been going on for so long, the calls are so rare and sightings so fleeting, that in the end, you have to judge an observer's worth, his or her experience and reliability and take their word for it.

***

The second lead came from a pounamu carver in Greymouth, Mick Collins. He reported kokako in South Westland. He gave a very detailed account of finding seventeen kokako with two kaka in the Lake Moeraki area in the 1970s.

Lake Moeraki lies near the coast, a little north of Haast. Rhys followed his track along a small creek, Venture Creek, to a ravine which usually had a dry creek bed. He bashed through thick wet undergrowth, played a recording, his kokako contact call. Got an instant response from perhaps 300 metres away.

He headed for it, through the heavy understory, played his tape again when he reached a rise, a small spur. *Boop boop boop* came the answering call from right above his head, an unmistakable kokako call. 'So here I am, dead still, binoculars, camera, everything focused. Nothing more. Silence. After a while I quietly move on. You never know. I move a few metres and suddenly here it is, exactly as Mick Collins had told me, this dry creekbed, steep ravine.'

The kokako fell silent. But Rhys remained certain there was something in that forest.

**

We arrange to meet there in November 2017. The trip falls through. I miss my shot for the first time, but not the last; and this would have been the most promising of meetings, for he had three brief glimpses of birds which looked exactly like kokako.

Two months later he goes to the same spot. Nothing. He is despondent: 'This is an area which was so exciting in November. I miss that slot and go in two months later. There's absolutely nothing. How am I ever going to resolve this enigma? This is impossible. I'm giving up.'

I cannot believe it. After a silence of perhaps two seconds, he adds, 'Of course, I won't give up, as you know.'

Still, this is ominous. Few things can be more heart-breaking than declaring a lifetime's work a failure.

We make new arrangements. I'm to fly to Christchurch, drive to the West Coast, travel to the south of South Westland, leave my car at the Whakapohai River bridge, ignore a more recent track and take another one along the river to a small clearing in the forest where Rhys has set up a fly camp.

The weather forecast goes from threatening to truly awful. We call it off.

I have an argument with Air New Zealand over rebookings and flight insurance, which, to my great surprise, I win. Meanwhile the forecast storm simply doesn't appear. The weather turns out to be quite good. Damn.

I hear a defeated note in Rhys's voice when I next talk to him. It's so unusual that I cannot miss it. Usually he is cheerful. He has to be, to sustain hope and enthusiasm for so long.

We set a new date and I make new bookings. The weather forecast goes from ominous to truly awful. Rhys calls. It's a weather bomb, he says. It's going to strike first exactly at the spot where we're going into the bush to pitch our feeble tents. They'd be blown over the mountains all the way to Dunedin probably. Either that or they'd be flattened by falling trees, even if we got there, for he is certain that a bridge or two will be down and roads washed away or blocked by slips.

The heck with it, I say, it all came to nothing last time, let's take the chance.

The lesson I should have learned, even if not from long experience of the Coast then from our experience a few weeks earlier was: never bet on West Coast weather.

***

A fierce nor'-wester is blowing hard as a blacksmith's bellows as I fly in. The Canterbury Plains have the bony look of a bare-knuckle fight.

The day before, temperatures in Central Otago reached 37.6 degrees, the hottest January in fourteen years. Today severe gales and horrid rain are forecast for, well, right where I'm going. I'm starting to believe.

Leaves, small branches fly onto the road and smack into the car windows like bullets. The air goes cloudy with a grey glaze like an old bathroom window. The mountains are black with menace.

I pass through the Plains towns — Kirwee, Darfield, Springfield — and the tussocks lie down like whipped dogs. Shingle slides trickle down the mountainsides as if the iron clouds above are leaking metal. The first raindrops hit the windscreen like hailstones and suddenly I'm inside that Canterbury nor'-wester phenomenon, fiery hot to wild to storm in half an hour.

Over Porters Pass where the wind turns gullies into blowpipes, whipping rocks off the cliff-sides, sniping at the car. Up the Waimakariri River, whose vast reaches seem to be on fire, clouds of spray whipped off the water and blown into the air like smoke.

Into the dark, deep tunnel of Arthur's Pass and over the Alps I go, the mountains spectres in the grey. The heat is just a memory. The rain is beating on the roof and I need a jacket.

Hokitika seems quiet. It *is* quiet. People at the petrol station tell me power to the town has been cut off, right down the Coast too, and it is likely to stay that way for forty-eight hours.

Things are getting worse. I head south, but only for a few kilometres. A friendly man stands at a roadblock. The road south has been blocked, he says. The good news is that it's now open. The bad news is that it's only open as far as Hari Hari.

I go through anyway and it's not long before I see why the road has been closed. Trees, some of them giants perhaps a century or two centuries old have been plucked at random and thrown across the road. Why would the cyclone pick *that* tree, and not its neighbour? Heaven knows what it's like inside the forest. I think of the fly tents where we planned to spend the night and shudder. Rhys was right.

Tree trunks have been chainsawed to allow the trickle of traffic through. A giant fully two storeys high almost blocks the road completely. It's an upturned tree viewed from the bottom, its roots gesticulating in the air. I sneak around its edge, zig-zag along the highway, past, around, sometimes even over the debris and reach Hari Hari.

It is growing dark, and it is clear that this is the biggest thing to happen to Hari Hari since Guy Menzies crash-landed his biplane in a nearby swamp and tried to convince disbelieving locals that he'd just made the first solo trans-Tasman flight.

The hotel is full, of drivers and drinkers, many of them hoping to be guests. There's no room at the inn. The owner tells me he could have filled his hotel twenty times over. It looks as if it *has* been filled twenty times over. People pack the the hallways, the reception office, the bars, the dining room. 'Try down the road,' he says wearily.

A set of motels or cabins stands beside the road. The owner is talking to tourists and I can see his body language from afar. He comes down the drive. 'We're full,' he says, unnecessarily.

'Oh well,' I say, 'it's an ill wind ...'

He laughs. 'Certainly is.'

I drive back along the road, past the lovely Lake Ianthe and the roots and the wrecks, the rain spurting, until I reach the old bushman's camp at Pukekura. It's dark, of course. I have no cash, I say (stupid of me), and if they have no electricity, there's no Eftpos …

'Well,' says the man, regarding me with bright blue eyes, 'we can't turn you away on a night like this. Where would you go? Do you have a sleeping bag?'

I do. He unlocks the door of a small room in what seems to be an old accommodation lodge, a row of bedrooms each opening onto a veranda, a lavatory and cold shower at one end, kitchen at the other. Even without its glow of refuge, it's a nice room, three walls pale yellow with cabbage trees painted on them, the fourth black like the ceiling, whose gold-painted stars sparkle in the dark.

It has an old dresser with droopy plated brass handles and a mid-century Danish armchair which would fetch a fortune in Ponsonby, and a double bed, very soft. It is paradise in the storm and I stand on the grape-covered veranda and listen to happy voices from the kitchen and don't think about Sky or spa baths.

I leave a message for Rhys, who has taken refuge at Lake Paringa: 'I'll be there in the morning, don't despair.'

Next morning I drive back to Hari Hari, get some cash, return to Pukekura and pay for the room ($25, he says, but I force him up to $40) then drive back to Hari Hari.

Everything is dripping. Beech trees lie everywhere. Huge pieces of earthmoving equipment pass on trucks. I follow them through Hari Hari and on to Whataroa.

This road is supposed to be closed. It's a wobbly course. But past the Mount Hercules bendy bit the road evens out. I reach Whataroa.

Yes!

I celebrate all the way through the little town until the road turns at its end and there's a roadblock. A local has parked his car across the highway in case some dumb tourist or greenie doesn't believe the story. Which is, that the road is blocked, that Franz Josef and Fox Glacier and points south are isolated, that 115 motorists, mainly tourists, have been stranded overnight in their cars and buses on the high road between the two tourist spots, that the road will be closed for at least two days.

A crowd of tourists clusters around a man in a hi-viz jacket. He's explaining to them why they can go no further: huge trees lie across the road, they've brought down power lines and they're now tangled in the branches; one slip in particular is passable if drivers can cling to the wreckage of the road, but they're much more likely to slip into the adjacent lake.

A kind of groan, an amazed chorus, rustles through the crowd. Asian tourists look puzzled, Europeans indignant. 'What do you expect us to *do?*' one demands, in an English accent. The roadman looks as if he might make a suggestion, but desists, although he has the contented look of an official giving bad news. It might be two days, or two hours, but he might as well deliver the worst-case perspective: after all, if it's wrong, who's going to complain?

A few locals hang around. For years tourists have been looking at them. Now they're looking at tourists. They're essential to the local economy but that doesn't mean locals have to *like* them. For many Coasters, tourists are like the Greens, or ratatouille: they might be all right in their place, as long as their place is somewhere else.

Greens? That brings me back. I'm chasing a man who's chasing the South Island kokako, but must be getting very sick of me. I've pursued him around and around the most remote parts of the South Island.

I leave him a message. The road is closed for days. He'll have to go over the Haast Pass and through Wanaka to get to his home in Nelson. Why don't we meet in Christchurch on his way back?

I go back over the Alps to Christchurch. Next day I get a message from him. He's in Hokitika. He got through the slips and the roadblocks no trouble. The road was only closed for a day. But where am I? Evidently our messages to each other have been marooned all over the hills, like tourists.

We give up. He flies up to Auckland and we meet on Waiheke Island, where I guarantee no one has ever spotted a kokako, North Island or South.

***

The North Island kokako has edged back from extinction, not without protest and a great deal of work.

It seems unbelievable now, but government logging of native forest was still thriving in the 1970s. Official policy embraced clear-felling. Native forests, even kauri, were chopped to the ground.

Kauri was saved first. Yet the Forest Service still insisted on 'selective' logging, taking some of the trees but often ruining the forest ecosystem. It took a massive public protest and the Maruia Declaration in 1977 to slow then stop the carnage.

The North Island kokako became a symbol of that movement. Protesters took to the treetops to stop logging in one of its last strongholds, the Pureora State Forest. Now what's left of that forest is the Pureora Forest Park, and the North Island kokako's haunting song can be heard in several carefully managed habitats in the Waikato, Bay of Plenty, the Ureweras, Northland, even South Auckland. They've been fostered in various arks — Little Barrier Island, Tiritiri Matangi, Kapiti, Mount Bruce and other reserves in the northern half of the North Island — so successfully that the breeding population has increased five-fold since 1999.

Can the South Island kokako be saved in the same way? Possibly. But someone has to *find* these ghost-like animals first.

The bird's standing improved a notch — more a mark on a bureaucrat's pad — in 2013. Before that, its last officially accepted sighting was at Mount Aspiring in 1967, and in the void since it had been declared extinct.

But it was seen again in 2007 in the Rainy Creek area south of Reefton and, six years later, the powers-that-be decided that reports of its death might have been exaggerated.

Rainy Creek was one of the places where Rhys heard a kokako, in 2004, when he was working on bird surveys for Oceana Gold. The company later mined for gold near Reefton, closing the mine in 2016. He was walking up a ridge when the kokako called. 'It was a beautiful organ note, but [the bird] had the same characteristics of invisibility. It was right beside me, but I couldn't see it. I was busy trying to get the work done so I didn't spend much time there but I thought, What a good site for kokako. In time one of the people doing predator control work is going to encounter this bird.'

That is exactly what happened. On 21 March 2007 a man employed by the predator-control people saw a kokako.

Len Turner was, in fact, engaged in relieving his bowels at the time, an unusual position from which to make history. He told Rhys he knew no one would believe him, but he also knew what he saw: a big steely-grey bird with a bluish tinge. It looked at him curiously, as well it might, turning its head from side to side and revealing amazing wattles, fleshy orange with a deep matt blue base. That was the clincher, really. The North Island kokako has blue wattles, the South Island a rich orange. But you had to have *seen* the bird to know the nuances of its wattles, the orange turning blue at their base.

The sighting was confirmed by a second person, Peter Rudolf, who had experience with North Island kokako. He accompanied Len to the spot the next day. Peter was startled first to hear the distinctive deep thudding of the kokako's wings then to see the allegedly extinct bird flying away from him in its typical shallow glide. Their report lifted the bird a notch above oblivion. It was only slowly elevated, however. The authority here is the Records Appraisal Committee of Birds New Zealand. The committee was cautious, understandably. The Department of Conservation had declared the bird extinct. The last accepted sighting of the bird had been in 1967, forty years before. That was a big gap, and the wheels ground slowly. Eventually a result emerged, reported to have been a majority call: now the bird was no longer extinct but in a hinterland called 'data-deficient'.

Still, Rhys, the most enduring South Island kokako-hunter in the land, was delighted. Even now, his voice rises in excitement as he talks about it.

But the South Island kokako is still not ready to fly. 'Data-deficient' means too little is known about the bird to be certain one way or the other.

Alec Milne, a long-time kokako-hunter, and a fellow-ornithologist, Richard Stocker, both of them from Golden Bay, compiled and published a list of 241 reports of the bird, both sightings and song, running from January 1990 to June 2012. The most certain of the reports were sightings from within ten metres with the naked eye or fifty metres with binoculars, and especially, those that described the complexities of the bird's wattles, their ultimate identifying mark. That analysis reduced the numbers to thirteen compelling reports of the South Island kokako and and twenty-three likely ones. The eleven most authoritative went to the NZ Birds committee; the one in Reefton was accepted, while two others were attributed to the North Island kokako. In the bird world, becoming non-extinct is evidently as painful as extinction.

To a layperson, 241 reports of a bird, from many different parts of the South Island, would be compelling evidence on its own. Even the cautious analysis of Messrs Milne and Stocker concludes that 'the South Island kokako is extant'; that is, it survives.

And why not? The New Zealand storm petrel was thought to have been extinct since 1850 when one was sighted (and photographed) off Whitianga in 2003, then more on Hauturu, Little Barrier Island.

The takahe was declared long dead, vanished since 1898, gone without trace, before Geoffrey Orbell found a few huddling deep in the Murchison Mountains near Lake Te Anau on 20 November 1948. Careful conservation has increased their numbers to more than 300. Despite their record, New Zealanders *do* care about extinct birds and this Lazarus performance excited them considerably.

It certainly inspired W.J. (Bill) Phillipps, ornithologist at the Dominion Museum in the first half of last century. His particular interest in extinct birds was the huia, the kokako's fellow wattlebird.

The huia was last seen officially in 1907. He looked at the all-but impenetrable gullies and spurs of the heavy bush between Wellington and East Cape, and the many reports and sightings since, and was quite certain the bird would be rediscovered. He was particularly excited by a 1961 sighting near Lake Waikareiti in the Ureweras by an English tourist, and was certain that she'd seen a huia, although after reading his book I'm not at all sure the sighting would have carried much weight with the Records Appraisal Committee. The huia has been 'sighted' spasmodically since — calls in the Ureweras were reported even in 1977 — but the fact of the bird's existence seems to me less important now than the romance of it, like the search for the Peking Man.

**

I think Rhys is becoming tired by his search, although not of it. He seems to be on a wave graph, excited one moment, exhausted by it the next. He's wiry and fit, but he's still edging his way into thick bush in the kind of awful country most trampers would do their best to avoid. Still sleeping in fly tents, eating the sort of food whose best description is 'healthy'. For him it's a way of life and he's nonchalant about it; only people who've been there know how hard it is, how lonely. It seems to me that he is on the edge of his hunt, just as the South Island kokako teeters on the brink of life.

'No, I don't think it's extinct,' he mutters.

But why, after thirty-eight years of searching, is he telling me suddenly the proper term is 'functionally extinct'?

'I could have told you that years ago,' he says. 'People sometimes think we're chasing ghosts, and that is what we're doing. We're chasing a bird that is flesh and blood but behaves so like a ghost that you're best to think of it as that rather than as a reality.'

Well, never have ghost-hunters been so tempted. At the time of writing, the South Island Kokako Charitable Trust has put a $10,000 price on the bird's head, or rather for information leading to confirmation that it is still alive. Several reports have already been received.

What does the nation's leading kokako-hunter, a man who lives frugally, whose resources have very largely gone into this search, think of that? If it works, well and good, is the gist of his reply, but I don't think it makes very much difference to him.

The North Island kokako was saved from extinction. They're cryptic too, but susceptible to recorded calls. They could be caught in fine nets and managed. The Chatham Islands black robin was down to five birds, the world's rarest, when Don Merton and his team devised a way of saving it. It now numbers around 300.

Why not the South Island kokako? After all, the Kokako Trust maps eleven 'most likely' encounters with the bird from 2015, and far more previously, and they range from Nelson and Golden Bay down the West Coast to Fiordland and even Southland.

Rhys thinks there's a meagre possibility of finding a way to lure a bird into some kind of captivity or plan for saving it. The problem is the kokako's incredibly cryptic manner. It will not be reliably attracted by recorded calls, and that, Rhys believes, might be the single reason why it will not be saved from extinction. Kokakos can be managed only in their home forests and only if pairs of both sexes exist: unlikely in South Island forests.

In 1984 Rhys thought he might be able to capture the kokako he heard in that remote branch of the Freshwater. He dubbed the bird 'Titus Groan' after the Mervyn Peake character who is tied to both his lineage and a desire to escape his fate. Titus was his best bird, so well-behaved, so lacking in shyness, except for one thing: it revealed itself only once.

I realise that when Rhys talks of ghosts he's being literal. An element of the supernatural enters the conversation. 'Why am I up and down, why is this so difficult?' he wonders aloud. 'One reason is, the kokako is incredibly rare. The second one, which is really why I'll never give it up but I'll say I'll give it up because it's psychologically draining, is because it behaves like a ghost and how the hell do you prove a ghost? How do you get anywhere close to a ghost? You cannot save a ghost from extinction.'

There's not only a spiritual element here for him: it's a quest in the purest, the most romantic sense. And perhaps it's also a drama like *Romeo and Juliet,* in the sense that it is not going to end well for either side?

'Oh yeah,' Rhys responds. 'It's very, very spiritual. But there's still the scientific reality that there's one or two birds hanging on in there, in flesh and blood. I'll never have any doubt of that. Without the sightings I'd definitely have had that doubt.

'But there are other things too. I never hear, now, that magnificent, cathedral bell-like call that I once heard. There's a graph and it's downwards. It's very sad to me, but it's disappearing. You no longer hear that call and we may never hear it again.

'It is the most beautiful call I've ever heard from any bird here or anywhere else, like the Amazon or Himalayan jungles. It is like a violin being tuned through a whole different range of frequencies, in the most divine spiritually wonderful way imaginable to the human ear. The cathedral bongs, loud, resonant, are truly hypnotising. They can toll for minutes at a time with surreal effects on the listener. I realised, I have to save this bird, because there is no bird in the world with such a remarkable call, even the North Island kokako. So the huge obsession for me was to save this bird from extinction.

'Then I heard the term "functionally extinct", not being able to save the bird for the next generations. It has dwelled with me, and now I've got to give up my obsession because I'm dealing with something that cannot be saved for future generations. It's really, really sad. Such a grand scale of sadness.'

I'm not sure which is more sad, the disappearance of the South Island kokako or the failure of a lifetime's quest.

Then: 'The frustration, the psychological side of it, but you know, it only stops you at a point in time. A few weeks later I'm raring to get back there.'

Where?

'Well, Lake Fraser possibly.'

I look it up. It is a tiny lake beside West Cape, in the deepest, most remote recesses of Fiordland, wedged between Chalky Inlet and Dusky Sound: untracked, dense, difficult country with deeply incised gullies; all but impenetrable; tight, wet vegetation; so rainy the possums won't go in there and eat the mistletoe because they don't like getting their fur wet; no beech mast to attract the rats; out of the reach of earthbound human beings — a fine habitat for kokako.

Rhys seems to put on hold his plan to give up his quest.

A float plane could get in there ...

9

Going south

South Cape is a mystical place. Even when you're there, you're not quite sure where you are. Capes of the imagination have cliffs, rocks, turbulence, storms. Real capes have more. They're fearful. Capes have a desolate feeling, where something ends and something else begins.

South Cape marks the end of mainland New Zealand, and that, as they say, is as far as it goes. There's not much else in those southern latitudes, except for the loneliest bits of Argentina and Chile, such as Cape Horn. Oh, South Cape doesn't lack turbulence and storms. As for the rest, well, we'll come to that.

South Cape is not much visited. Overland it's a long and difficult hike down the length of Stewart Island. It's hardly better by sea, when it's much, much preferable to stay well away from it. South Cape does not entice you to come ashore. North Cape is a positive tourist trap by comparison.

Murphy Island, hardly more than a rock, lies a little to the west and about a hundred metres further south than South Cape, so just as North Cape is not the most northern part of New Zealand, neither is South Cape the furthest south.

Captain Cook rounded it on 9 March 1770, having mapped Stewart Island as a peninsula, although he believed there was probably a passage making it an island and left his chart incomplete. An American sealer sailed through it in 1804, and Foveaux Strait appeared on European maps. Maori, of course, always knew about it. Their ancestor Kiwa tired of walking the isthmus between Rakiura and the mainland, and asked the whale Kewa to chew a channel so he could cross by waka.

Some, although not Cook himself, believed that the coastline the *Endeavour* had been following might be part of the great southern continent Cook had been ordered to find.

The hopes of the continentalists, who included the wealthy botanist Joseph Banks, who accompanied Cook, foundered on South Cape. If New Zealand ended there, it could hardly be part of a continent. That theory, Banks conceded, was demolished.

The ship rounded the southernmost tip of New Zealand and found clear water ahead. New Zealand was a chain of islands, and judging from the huge swell coming up from the south, no significant land lay down there either.

The crew celebrated the turning-point with a Tahitian dog stew, although they might have drunk to a narrow escape, one which could have wrecked the *Endeavour* along with the continental theory.

Cook had his latitude, or his distance to the south right, but his longitude, on those imaginary lines running from Pole to Pole, was more difficult to calculate. In fact, when Cook thought he was a safe distance to the west of that rocky tip, he was just about on it.

So a great deal of mystique cloaked that lonely point. At a certain, restless stage of my writing career I was thinking about parts of New Zealand I'd never been to. I thought of South Cape, and West Cape too. Oh all right, they were hardly places most New Zealanders wanted to tick off their bucket lists. But few people had been to either of them.

The chance to visit South Cape came when photographer Bruce Connew and I decided to charter a boat and steam to the bottom of New Zealand. He was interested in titi, or muttonbirds. I was interested in South Cape.

We contacted Colin Gavan, widely known in the far south as Wobbles, and captain of the steel voyager *Argus*. Certainly he'd take us.

We went down to Riverton, the ancient southern port where the *Argus* was moored. The boat wasn't there.

That was not surprising, because a gale was blowing in Foveaux Strait. I'd fished for crayfish down there in my own boat, the *Nina*, and it seemed to me that a gale was *always* blowing in Foveaux Strait. We found a motel in Riverton, with a view of the sea (although most of Riverton has a view of the sea) and moved in.

Several days passed. We got to know Riverton, aka Aparima, quite well. It's a very old town, whose Maori history goes back centuries and its European one to around 1835, when the whaler captain John Howell set up a whaling station there. The town is Southland's oldest, and one of New Zealand's most venerable too.

Howell smartly married the daughter of a Kati Mamoe chief and his toehold on the place became a foothold, now set in stone in a memorial near the estuary. Remnants of past grandeur lie all around in civic buildings and grand houses, but for me its main attractions were its perfect fishing port, and the Aparimu Tavern.

New Zealand's old fishing ports are dwindling, in size and number. The graceful wooden fishing boats are disappearing, along with some of the ports themselves, as fishing becomes harder and more specialised. The fishing boats were going from Riverton too, one by one. But then, Riverton had that feeling of people who had lived where they worked for all of their lives, and their parents' and grandparents' lives too, the feeling of comfortable belonging, of solidity and respect and care for each other in a climate which was not a common enemy but just part of their lives. All nonsense, of course. For stress, anger, conflict and bloody-mindedness the town is probably the same as any other. But I wandered about, enjoying the fiction. The rest of the time I spent in the Aparimu Tavern, which looked over the red river flats to the hills and was warm and friendly and comforting.

And one morning, when we looked out of the window, beyond the river bar where the wind whipped the tops off waves and threw them high into the air, the *Argus* lay waiting for the tide so it could enter the estuary.

Wobbles didn't mess around. Fuel, water, food, beer. He wanted to go. What about the weather? 'I don't give a damn about it,' he said, with the nonchalance of a man used to the stormy south. We didn't share his calm. But we looked at the gale, and the iron-grey of the strait, and the frowning cloud, and followed him with the faith of disciples.

Back over the bar we went, and headed for the top end of Stewart Island, then a black hulk on the horizon looking nothing like its Maori name, Rakiura, 'isle of the glowing skies'. All that was glowing was the light at the end of the tunnel in our minds.

I fondly believed it would lead us out of the darkness and storm and, yea, unto calm and safety.

The *Argus* ploughed on solidly. Sure enough, the waters calmed into a greasy swell. Near Herekopare Island we stopped and threw cod lines over the side, big hooks with chunks of bait sinking into deep green water mysterious as space. Women's Island lay behind us, Jacky Lee beside. Ruapuke bulked in the dusk.

Not far from here in 2006 the fishing vessel *Kotuku*, returning to Bluff with muttonbirders, was hit by two big waves in quick succession. She rolled, trapping three people in her hull. Another three died too, three more surviving after swimming to Women's Island. Three generations of the Topi whanau were among the dead. I imagined the sense of terror, the panic, the disbelief of betrayal in home waters so familiar.

On that evening all we had on our minds was what to have for dinner. The crew were reluctant to eat fish, because they had a venison stew on the stove, and who wanted plain old blue cod? We did, of course, for the further up the mainland you went, the harder and more expensive it was to get, and blue cod was becoming as much a rare New Zealand delicacy as oysters. Its beautiful white flesh was always the best fish I'd tasted.

The cod didn't know anything about scarcity. They struck the bait as soon as it was down, while the *Argus* idled in the swell and its big engine rumbled. In these latitudes fishermen didn't need patience. If the fish didn't bite immediately, the boat moved on.

In no time at all, we had all the fish we could eat aboard, lying blue-green on the deck, their mouths looking just like several discontented people I knew.

The crew hooked into their venison stew. Bruce and I tucked into a stack of cod fillets. When I was a crayfisherman, we'd eaten crayfish for the first day or two, then got so sick of it we didn't touch it for the rest of the trip. Sometimes a helicopter would arrive overhead and lower a leg of venison. We'd fill a bag with crayfish and send it up. We thought we got the better of the deal. So the *Argus's* crew stuck to their venison stew, while we ate blue cod every way we could think of: fried, battered, curried, chowdered.

We headed south. The long southern dusk cloaked the islands, and golden beaches were conjured for us through the gloom, and reefs, and little peninsulas topped with bush so dark it seemed part of the sea.

The barometer was still falling, but we knew that down here anything could happen and, as the old saying goes, it usually did. Cape petrels followed the boat, and mollymawks with their fierce eyes and precise markings, Mother Carey's chickens, and sometimes even a royal albatross. Darkness gradually covered them, until they were strange shapes appearing in the gleam of the navigation lights then vanishing.

We sailed on, in the dark now, the ship rolling, white crests flashing in the black like phantoms, sometimes a seabird arcing through the lights, passing Chew Tobacco Point, Weka Island, the welcoming mouth of a refuge called Port Adventure.

Some time that night, much later, the murk took on a peculiar quality and the phantoms began leaping so earnestly I realised we were heading straight for a cliff. Mark, the crewman, went up to the bow with a torch. It may have been some comfort to the captain, but not to us, for it played over black rock and the waves became frenzied and surely we were all bound for the bottom the hard way.

Magically (for so much down here had the sorcerer's touch) the cliffs opened. The frenzy slipped behind us, yelling and booing in the gloom. We sailed in calm water into the peace of Port Pegasus and the captain stared ahead, turning this way then that way, without any purpose apparent to the passengers gazing blindly around, until the boat seemed to be copying one of those strange Victorian dances where people wove and stepped and bowed in a choreography that had no purpose other than grace.

And we went to sleep without so much as a wayward ripple to disturb us.

I was woken next morning by the captain murmuring stories and imitating the kaka's rough squawk and telling of a tunnel through the rock, once used by Maori to watch early Europeans anchored in exactly the spot we were in now.

We were deep in Port Pegasus, the water like glass. We were surrounded by islets, and rocks, and the passage into them looked dark as a dream, and forever after (for I've run into Wobbles several times since) I have wondered about the particular kind of necromancy that got us there.

***

In the admirable *New Zealand Railways Magazine*, Rosalind Redwood wrote of Port Pegasus:

> It is so remote that few people other than fishermen ever see
> its glories, and yet its arms of placid waters, shut off from
> the rougher seas by bushy walls of protection, are capable of
> holding the whole of the British fleet with ease … But alas,
> so far out of the way!

Which might have been significant given the date of publication, September 1939, the beginning of World War II.

Sealers and whalers worked out of this harbour, gold miners worked the creeks around it, tin miners tunnelled into its rocks, and Port Pegasus once boasted a hotel.

Now, here's the thing about Stewart Island. The excellent name Rakiura was discarded by the colonists, who preferred to name it after one Captain Stewart. Descriptions of Stewart run from romantic to rat, possibly because several Captain Stewarts were roaming the coast at the time (one of them carrying Te Rauparaha's war party south to massacre Ngai Tahu in Akaroa harbour). This particular Stewart left a party of men in Port Pegasus building a boat in a bay now named Ship-builders Cove while he sailed to Sydney with a cargo of seal skins and oil. One report said he was arrested in Sydney and thrown into jail.

The men he left behind grew desperate. They built a smaller boat and sailed to the mainland. Eventually Stewart *did* return, working on another ship, but too late to do his marooned men any good. Still, he was said to be a good cartographer, drawing accurate charts of the island coast.

We steamed out of Port Pegasus heading for South Cape. This was the objective, and I was keyed up. The end was in sight.

In this strange seascape the Cape would surely be wild, scary, pointing bleakly towards the great wastes of the cold ocean that ran almost uninterrupted all the way to Antarctica. We ran through clouds of sooty shearwaters, muttonbirds, dark on top with slashes of light beneath their thin wings. They'd rise from the sea, wheel a few centimetres above the waves, and land behind us as we passed.

The coast changed too, as we neared the bottom of New Zealand. The dark tupari and turpentine scrub seemed to shrivel, become patchy, so it looked like a homeless person too long in the cold. The rock was smoothed by centuries of southern seas sometimes caressing, more often beating.

'That,' said Wobbles, 'is South Cape.'

What was this awful waypoint? It took me by surprise. This was one of the five great capes of the south, keeping company with Capes Horn, Agulhas, Leeuwin and Tasmania's South East Cape. It had been feared for centuries, lying in early sailors' memories like a caged beast.

It was a simple knob of grey rock. A lump at the end of a low, short promontory, sticking out from a covering of scrub like a fingernail. All around it lay rocks so nearly identical that the Cape itself seemed to have been chosen arbitrarily: why this rock, and not the one beside it?

I wondered at the skill of Cook, the great navigator: how had he calculated that this particular point on a uniform coastline was New Zealand's southernmost? And what if he'd missed his guess and the *Endeavour* had struck? Even had he and his crew been able to clamber up that smooth surface, they would have faced a lonely, hungry old age.

I felt more in tune, for once, with the difficult Banks, who goggled at sun glancing off the polished faces of inland escarpments. They are now called Gog and Magog, the Old Testament crowding out their Maori names, Kakapuri, for the reddish parrot-like streak on Gog's flank, Tupouri for the gloomier Magog. The light winked off them as we passed.

***

Next time I went around South Cape, it was by accident.

I was intent on reaching the Titi Islands, the forbidden islands of the cold southern seas.

I could not land on them. Some of them were 'beneficial', owned by families, whanau of Ngai Tahu, Ngati Mamoe and Waitaha, for centuries. Others were islands that had been returned to Rakiura Maori by the Crown under its Treaty settlement with Ngai Tahu. Either way, you could disembark on those islands only if you were born into the families who had manu, or muttonbirding territories. Those families were bound by webs of rules and customs formed over the ages.

The rules for outsiders were much simpler: they couldn't land and that was that.

We were outsiders. So we hitched a lift on the *Awesome,* a big, fast fishing boat which was taking food and supplies down to the Titi Islands. A few muttonbirders were going down as passengers, but most chose to fly down by helicopter: faster if more expensive.

We left Bluff at midnight. The skipper was Jack Topi, of the spreading Topi whanau with its chiefly status (see Chapter 3, in which Topi shoots the erstwhile raider Te Puoho) and a vastly experienced seaman. That was good to know, because the southern waters were terrifying enough by day. By night they were peopled by phantoms.

The *Awesome* was packed with building materials — wood, plastic, iron, pipes — paint, diesel, food and everything else a family might need if it was going to spend a few months on an island which in its natural state had nothing to contribute to the survival of the human race. Only the titi could live there, for part of the year, by digging burrows in which they laid an egg and hatched a chick whose own survival was seriously limited if a muttonbirder came to visit.

The birders were up at five, gutting, salting, grabbing the grey chicks in their curling burrows, taking them back every couple of buckets-full or so because cold birds are hard to pluck, dressing them in hot wax, breaking open the cold casing, sprinkling the naked birds with salt, putting them in buckets, turning them regularly until they were properly pickled and pink, not brown, because if they were brown they were kippered.

A hard twelve-hour day and early to bed.

Yet every birder I spoke to longed for the titi season to begin, prayed for a good season, loved a feed of muttonbirds, and loved as much the dark difficult life in huts and cribs under the canopies of wind-sculpted scrub. They looked forward to those autumnal days and nights with the fervour of Lions supporters on an international tour, or surfers dreaming of Bali, or foodies in France.

The heavily laden *Awesome* headed out of Bluff Harbour, squeezing past the reefs at its entrance and past the last sign of civilisation, as we knew it at least, we were to see until our return: the Dog Island lighthouse. Its friendly beam shone over sea that anyone north of, say, the Bombay Hills would regard as horrendous but was seen by our crew as just another day in the office: windy with a short sharp swell and spray feathering off the wavetops.

On 15 March 2012, the *Easy Rider* was also steaming south with its cargo of birders and their gear. A wave rolled the boat right over. Eight died; one survived by clinging to a plastic petrol can. These seas had claimed 125 boats since 1831 — at least, for some were not recorded and simply disappeared without trace.

The *Easy Rider* was off Saddle Point, on the north-eastern tip of the island. We were going down the other side, but it made no difference in the dark when logic departs and horrors fill the mind.

Below, some slept in bunks, others in the spacious saloon. In terms of motion it didn't make much difference. The vessel would rise on a wave, hover for a moment, and crash down into the trough behind it. Horizontal passengers were alternately forced into their mattresses or cushions then, at the top of the wave, lost in space for a split second while the bed descended beneath them, coming to the bottom with a thunk.

People started to be sick. I have never been seasick, but almost broke my duck that night. The sea wasn't bad. The smell of vomit, however, was.

I went out on deck and wedged myself between a crate and some roofing iron. Somewhere in the dark lay Codfish Island or, more romantically, Whenua Hou (New Land), the bird sanctuary where the lonely kakapo huddles. I could see nothing in the black night.

The wind was cold, but not freezing. The wake spread into the dark. It was eerie. The boat heaved and, every so often, so did a passenger, squeezing past me in the dark and hanging over the side.

In the bare light of a dawn which some aboard hoped they'd never see, fancying death instead, the boats made a rendezvous in a bleak bay. Then the *Awesome* headed south on its own and began dropping off passengers and supplies at their islands.

The strange, creamy-coloured rock of the southern islands started appearing in the dawn. Jet black then cream, then dull green where the scrub found enough soil to anchor itself against the gales.

I'd looked at the cargo stacked on deck and wondered how it was to be unloaded, for many of the islands were buttressed against the sea: few had beaches or any other of the usual ways of getting ashore.

It must have been a struggle in the past. But this was the twenty-first century. The *Awesome* would pull into a bay, a passenger would be ferried ashore in the ship's dinghy, perform an Olympian leap at the top of a swell, miss the kelp and clamber up the rock with the speed of a Barbary ape before the next wave could suck him back. Then a helicopter would appear overhead. The crew would have the load ready. The chopper would hook onto it and vroom! Off it went to the island.

For most of the year the birders' baches lay empty. Southern gales hammered on their doors. Vicious rainsqualls pummelled their roofs. I caught a glimpse of one occasionally: they looked like huts, but they were, in fact, fortresses.

Beaten-up bastions, though. The birders' first jobs were to fix them up for another year, hence the timber, roofing, paint, tar, cement, rainwater tanks, generator bits and everything else that went ashore in quantities, along with the galvanised buckets which were replacing the works of art known as poha, traditional kelp bags that once carried the preserved muttonbirds back to the mainland.

The *Awesome* slipped into Murderers Cove, Taukihepa, or Big South Cape Island. The refuge lay off a channel between the island and Stewart Island, sheltered from the wild west winds, the wires of the gutbuckets that carried the muttonbird chicks' innards down to the sea lacing the cliffs. In here the water was calm while swells beat the rocks all around.

This was the biggest settlement we'd seen, like a summer bay filled with traditional Kiwi baches, which, apart from the season, it was. Huts of all shapes and sizes clung to the ridges above the water. But the place had a dark past. This was an ancient refuge for Maori, and for early European sailors, and sometimes Taukihepa just wasn't big enough for all of them.

The infamous ship *Sydney Cove* once put into this cove. It was crewed by sealers who'd plundered and murdered their way down the coast. Stories of the *Sydney Cove* are often conflicting: sealers were not best known for literacy nor respect for Maori, and besides, many of them did not live long enough to tell the tale.

The former convict ship is blamed for the Sealers' War, a battle between sealers and Maori. It seems to have started on the Otago Peninsula over a theft by a local chief of items including a knife and a shirt. The chief was killed.

The crew killed another chief at Port Molyneux, a tiny place near present-day Kaka Point, which was made redundant as a harbour when a flood changed the course of the Clutha River and left it high and dry. Maori are said to have retaliated at dangerous Waipapa Point, where they killed a sealing gang.

By the time the *Sydney Cove* reached Taukihepa, Maori were bent on revenge. Under the southern chief Honekai they ambushed a boatload of sealers as they went ashore, killing five of them. Yet one, James Caddell, lived to tell a remarkable tale. Caddell was only sixteen but he too was about to be slaughtered when Tokitoki, the chief's daughter or perhaps his niece, threw her cloak over him, a traditional gesture of protection.

Caddell married her, received a moko as singular as a coat of arms, and became famous as the first Pakeha rangatira.

Taukihepa on a good day might look like a holiday settlement, but it is not. The massacre seems to tint the air. The work is hard and its history is too. I'm always glad to leave, and as we did Captain Topi gave us a choice. We could go straight back to Bluff down Stewart Island's west coast. It was faster, but the west wind was stirring up the sea. Or we could go round South Cape and along the more sheltered east coast, a longer trip but more gentle.

The seasick among us made an instant choice. So we went around South Cape with the etched mollymawks arcing over us like a guard of honour. The Cape hadn't changed at all since my first time round. It didn't even look different from an anti-clockwise direction. It jutted into the sea like a medieval fort, Gog and Magog flashing farewell.

I called in at the Aparima Tavern on my way home. I loved the estuary, the mountains beyond. In 2013 the Tavern burned down. It was 135 years old and flamed like a torch in the night. One of the regulars told the newspapers, 'I don't know what we're going to do now.' Hundreds of kilometres away, I knew how he felt.

A photograph from South Cape, a crowd of muttonbirds banking, diving, scratching the surface of the huge southern swells, every one of the hundreds of birds full of life and action and angles, still hangs on my wall. And once as I sat in an office in Christchurch looking over the Pacific Ocean I got a call from Wobbles. 'Look out your window,' he said.

A dot appeared, far out. The *Argus*, thrashing along the coast. 'I'm on my way to the America's Cup,' he said. He was off to make his fortune taking people out to the races. I don't know how that went, but I guarantee his passengers got something entirely different.

10

Dashing madly

The situation was desperate. I had to get from Waiheke Island to Wanaka. But in the way men do, or *I* do anyway, I'd left bookings to the last minute. Correction, the *very* last. My planning tends to be ad hoc, meaning procrastination then panic. On the other hand, bad planning and adventure often go together: one can lead to the other. It is not a widely approved theory but an interesting one, and this time it came into play.

The rough plan was to fly into Queenstown and hire a car. It turned out that everyone else had the same notion. The nation as a body was packing itself into a plane that week and heading south.

Two choices remained. Giving up was one of them but wasn't really an option. The urgent event in Wanaka was a week's tramping. That might not seem critical to some, but it was for me. I tramp with friends twice a year in the South Island. That trip takes a lot of organising. It cannot be shifted. You either go or you don't, and I was not going to give up half my year's tramping just like that. I'm a South Islander transported to the north, pining for mountains and big skies.

The other choice was to hop in the car and drive. That would take thirty hours including ferries and waiting time. Sixteen hundred kilometres including two ocean cruises, aka car-ferry crossings.

I had to be there on the Saturday. That was when the first complication cut in. By now it was Thursday. The trip would have to be all but non-stop. Oh, what a balls-up. But I almost liked it. The drive might even be fun if so many hours of travelling, some of it over bad roads, counts as adventure.

***

Late that spring afternoon I drive my car to the Waiheke ferry. It's a cheery sort of day, with a clean breeze and little waves hopping over the Gulf. I should have been warned.

My Subaru Outback was a youngster when I bought it. If one year of human life equals seven years of a dog's, what is the ratio for cars, man's second-best friend? Yet it always ran well and gave no trouble until, as is the way with cars, I planned this journey.

The garage serviced the car and noticed it had a slight tremble when they turned the steering wheel. I'd felt that too, but treated it as you do with frailties among old friends and politely ignored it. The garage did not think that was the best policy with cars. They thought it might be something to do with the clutch. There were two ways it might go: expensive, and more expensive. It might be best if I took the car to a specialist in the city, just a short ferry ride away. But that might take several days.

My mechanic friend took me aside. 'Just go,' he said. The car would hold out.

Of course it would: Subarus were bullet-proof. That's what people said. I'd had a string of them. They could go anywhere, even places you never intended them to go. Once I found myself in the middle of an icy mountain stream, much deeper than it looked, with the only way out blocked by a lump of rock that had somehow missed its vocation as a war memorial. The car clambered over it with scarcely a groan.

Not one of them ever died on the job, nor had I been forced to put one down. Of course this one would hold out.

So the car ferry arrives in Putiki Bay, Waiheke Island, its ramp shrieking on the concrete. A queue of cars is loaded aboard with a convoy of trucks, part of the supply chain carrying everything needed by an island with a permanent population of 10,000, a few thousand more in holiday homes, and tourists swamping the place any good day. I drive on too, with various parts of my body crossed for luck.

The ferry chugs out of Putiki Bay, passes Motuihe Island then Motukorea, Browns Island, still bald after being being swept by a fire lit by a woman stranded on the island in mysterious circumstances the previous year. The vessel slips into the Tamaki River and passes Bucklands Beach, a mountainscape of its own. We sail beneath tinted plate-glass escarpments and bluffs of ice-white plaster and berth in Half Moon Bay.

The ramp shrieks. The cars land. We file into Pigeon Mountain Road, through the wilds of Panmure, thread and jerk along the Mount Wellington Highway and turn onto the motorway, heading south.

Ah, you think, the motorway, the freedom of the road, the highway abandoning traffic jams and snarls and whisking you off to soft roads and easy pastures.

Here is the motorway phenomenon: traffic expands to fill the space available. All lanes are crowded except at peak times, when they're packed to a standstill. What do these people do? Where do they come from? What's their business? Do they have lives? What did they do before motorways? What's the point?

There's no gain in building new roads, for this is a zero-sum game, and all of this means that I am crawling south at thirty kilometres per hour with almost 1600 kilometres still to go and a Cook Strait ferry to catch.

Around the Bombay Hills the traffic begins to thin, and I pass over the top heading south into a land of which legend says Aucklanders know nothing.

The New Zealand Transport Agency has heard of it, though. Alongside a picture of a smooth, graceful motorway disappearing into infinity and carrying five — yes, *five* — cars, the Agency says:

The Waikato Expressway project will improve safety and reliability and reduce travel times and congestion on SH One by delivering a four-lane highway from the Bombay Hills to south of Cambridge. The expressway is being built in seven sections.

Any one of which you're bound to encounter, just around the next bend. What a joy this new expressway will be, when it's finished. On my experience to date, I doubt I'll live to see it. I cannot remember ever driving between the Bombay Hills and Cambridge without traversing thickets of signs urging me to slow to a crawl, detour this way or that, or mind my windscreen from shrapnel spat by passing cars, although I've never known how you'd avoid it. It has always been an obstacle course from one end to the other and the only difference I can see now is that the graveyards, groves of wooden crosses beside the road once so numerous that it seemed a toss-up whether you passed or passed away, have been either removed or paved over. Usually I can count on at least one absolutely stupid, potentially lethal piece of driving per trip, and this is where it happens. A queue of cars forms at a dogleg crossing on the Cambridge bypass road. Someone gets impatient, passes the entire queue, speeds out onto the crossing and finds himself in the way of a truck.

Miraculously, everyone escapes.

The NZTA should consider a driver's licence endorsement proclaiming, 'I drove from Auckland to Hamilton and survived.' A kind of merit point, which could be offset against demerits.

This kinky little road turns off SH One past Taupiri and zig-zags through the countryside to Cambridge, avoiding Hamilton. I do not want to insult Hamilton. Once, when I was a writer for the *NZ Listener,* I referred to the 'four main centres', which excluded Hamilton. The grandees of that city heaped coals upon my head. They didn't mind being demeaned, they said, but they hated being overlooked. I could say that one of my close friends lives there, except that he hasn't been so close for several decades because, yes, he lives in Hamilton and I always choose the zig-zag. Driving through Hamilton is just such a bitch.

We no longer have to drive through Cambridge either, because the new expressway bypasses it. From a news report: 'The tidy tree-lined streets of Cambridge will become a lot less congested from next week when thousands of rumbling trucks and cars get funnelled onto the Waikato Expressway.' In other words,

Cambridge loses a lot of business, including my own, for the bypass seems to have so dispirited the owners of my favourite café there that they departed, presumably on the new four-lane. The Expressway is everywhere, creeping across the country, perhaps looking for other territories to colonise.

By now it is late afternoon. I contemplate the immediate future. Ahead lies the first of two deserts, of which Putaruru and Tokoroa are the high points.

Can I survive without a long black? I pull out my Thermos, have a strong white, curse the bypass and plug on. Is that judder the clutch giving up, or just the car shuddering in sympathy?

If there is a motoring limbo, then surely this section of highway is it. You go in one end and lose consciousness until you awake near Taupo and wonder what has happened in the couple of hours since. Am I still the same age? Has war broken out?

By now it is dark. The Desert Road lies ahead. Rain has been forecast. It begins to spit. The forecast proves wrong. Instead of mere rain, this is the beginning of a full-scale storm. Drizzle becomes a downpour, which turns into a full-scale wind-blasted deluge.

The world becomes a sparkle of lights. Whole towns seem to be approaching. They turn out to be trucks that are better-lit than some of the small towns on this route.

The Desert Road has just two conditions: open or closed. Snow and volcanic eruptions close it. Rain and darkness do not.

Some people love the bare beauty of the place. Having suffered a time in the Army here, I do not. Oh, bare beauty is all right, if you're not marching through it, or freezing in it, or wrapped in a thin Army blanket pretending there's an enemy out there who is worse than the Army itself. Moreover, it has to be seen to be properly appreciated, and I can see nothing except silver rain slicing across my headlights.

Whatever is going on in the wet darkness tonight, I know one thing for certain: here you are beyond help. You need to be somewhere else, just as soon as possible. If something is not happening at that moment, something is going to happen.

Something disastrous, usually. Perhaps a truck driver forgetting his lines. Or Ruapehu hiccupping. Or simply getting lost in space. The Desert Road at night is either glaring or so black the world is empty. There's no hint of the fried landscape in the dark.

The highest point in the state-highway network lies along this road. Also the lowest. At least, that is my view this dark, wet night.

The road is sixty-three kilometres long.

No one lives here, voluntarily. That includes the occupants of the Rangipo prison at one end and the Waiouru military camp at the other, although I might be prejudiced about the latter. You feel alone here, and you are. The Black Gate of Mordor scenes for *Lord of the Rings* were shot here. They needed no special effects.

I drive up the long uphill stretch from Turangi. I think. The road turns into a knot, twisting through gullies. I think. A kaleidoscopic assembly of orange signs warns against everything from roadworks to whooping cough. I keep a careful eye on where I think Ruapehu might be.

The night is a wet splashy thing and some idiot is setting off fireworks. Which turn out to be trucks.

Then a convoy, a road train, a ragged blaze of light appears far away. It turns out to be not trucks, but Waiouru. It looks so welcoming I almost stop. I once did, one dark wet night like this one, and ate a steak the size of a doormat, although more chewy. Tonight, I have another cup of Thermos coffee.

Then it is downhill to Taihape, whose night life consists of a man and a woman leaning against a car in the rain with a single stubby on the roof. His or hers? Are they sharing?

Through that dismal country south of Taihape. Do I imagine the car picks this moment to shudder?

Through Foxton and Levin and on to the outriders of Wellington's new Northern Corridor, eventually running to somewhere north of Levin.

The NZTA is promising everything from this new road: more trucks, more business, riches, safe sex. If we're to believe them, the Kapiti Coast will revert to its former persona as the Golden Coast.

With the Waikato Expressway racing south and the Northern Corridor rampaging north I imagine them colliding somewhere on the Volcanic Plateau in a furious eruption of diggers. New Zealand will become even smaller and in my view, which right now is murky, less interesting. Small towns are taking yet another hammering as the Cyclops gallops by, or over, or beside.

Oh, those nice little escapes that form a breathing tube for claustrophobic Wellington — Manakau, Otaki, Waikanae, Paraparaumu, Paekakariki, Pukerua Bay — are they all to wither on the shrine?

By now the rain is so heavy I can scarcely see them. We slither down the Ngauranga Gorge, turn off the motorway and into the Bluebridge ferry terminal. It is after midnight. The ferry is not due to leave until 2.30 a.m. but the woman behind the desk says we'll be loading early. After all, she says, I booked a cabin, and it would be unfair to have me dozing in the car. 'Especially your car,' she says, eyeing the old Subie. Superstitiously, I hope it doesn't hear.

I like this sailing in the small hours. Usually, you go aboard, find a few vacant seats together, stretch out and go to sleep. It is an odd sailing, favoured by introverts, xenophobes and insomniacs.

On a previous trip I'd woken a couple of hours after we sailed, disoriented. The ship rose and fell gracefully. It was silent but for a faint thudding. But the alarming thing was, it was deserted. If there were other sleeping forms, I could see none. The cafeteria was abandoned. It felt like the *Marie Celeste*, a meal on the counter but no one on board. What had happened to the passengers? The crew? Was I the only one left alive? The thought so terrified me that it was, oh, a full five minutes before I went back to sleep.

This time I am prepared. For $30 I have a cabin of my own. I expect a bunk inside some narrow cell. Instead I have a bed, a real one, with an en-suite bathroom. For $30! And a full-length mirror, which tells me this trip is taking its toll.

I climb into bed. Oh yes, this is the way to go.

Two hours later, I feel the engines thud and the ship move. We're leaving.

I know this because I'm wide awake. The Thermos of coffee I brought to keep me company on the long journey down the island has worked very well.

For four hours, the ship moves gently across Cook Strait, calm as custard, emitting phantom bangings and bumps, noises of the night. I hear them all, because I'm sleepless in my comfortable little cabin.

Then comes that marvellous stillness of the ship leaving the Strait and entering the Marlborough Sounds. They give me an entirely unnecessary wake-up call. Out on deck the hills ghost by, black against the grey dawn.

The cafeteria is serving bacon and eggs on ciabatta. Ciabatta? My first crossings between the islands were on the overnight ferry from Christchurch. Then, you were jammed into cabins full of narrow bunks whose occupants were either drunk or sick or both, and you were woken at six by a stern steward who demanded that you drink his tea and eat his two wine biscuits, for the Union Steamship Company didn't trust you to get up on your own.

We are told to go to our cars. Is there anything more desolate than a ferry's vehicle deck at dawn? The steel echoes, the ship's ribs are open for inspection, and all around are drivers wearing looks of grim determination. Trucks look like behemoths, like an All Black in the kitchen. Drivers, start your engines! We file down the valley towards Blenheim. The valley seems full of water. This has been a wet winter.

We turn right at Spring Creek. State Highway One has been closed since the Kaikoura earthquakes, and this is the start of a huge detour that runs almost to the West Coast before turning south over the Lewis Pass.

The detour runs through Renwick and heads west, along a beautiful green valley. In all the decades I'd lived in the South Island I'd driven this lovely road only rarely. The grape vines are dark and spidery in the early spring. The rain, the *rain*, here in a region famous for sun. A sign warns of winter weather conditions. Another points to the world's most boring historic place, a concrete water trough. It turns out to have been the only watering place for a very long way in either direction.

The government built a monitoring station here which is claimed by its detractors to be a foreign spybase on New Zealand soil. In 2008 three protesters broke in, damaged equipment, were charged — and were acquitted by a jury that agreed with the defendants' 'claim of right' that they were protecting human life. The government sued for damages and won, but did not pursue its claim.

Waihopai remains the subject of an annual protest camp near the Wairau River mouth. The protesters have succeeded, at least, in making this valley one of the world's worst-kept secrets. It is known as Spy Valley. It even boasts its own wine label.

In fact, this peaceful place has seen its share of excitement, starting with the so-called Wairau Affray at Tuamarina downriver in 1843, when settlers tried to take the rich valley land. Maori won, four dead to twenty-two Pakeha, followed by a moral victory when Governor Fitzroy ruled the settlers at fault. But Maori lost the land anyway.

The long, braided Wairau River follows a fault line, appropriately enough. It remains a wild waterway — so far, for it is still being fought over. This time it's Pakeha on Pakeha, mainly. Electricity generators have laid covetous eyes on it. They want to divert the river into canals for electricity and irrigation. The plan is currently on hold, but its opponents are fearful that it would ruin the river. I spend a little time staring at it from the roadside. Who knows whether it'll be there next time I pass?

But permanence in this valley is a shaky thing. In the 1855 Wairarapa earthquake the valley's eastern end dropped by a metre.

Wairau Valley town is the centre of civilisation here. You come on it quite suddenly: school, memorial hall, a church without a steeple, fire station, garage, golf course, a space where a shop used to be and a pub that has served travellers for a century and a half and is for sale when I pass through.

Far to the west a snowy peak, the end of the St Arnaud Range, stands against a patch of turquoise sky. Suddenly I'm driving into sunshine. Prospects go from bright to sparkly. Mountains rise in proper majestic fashion all around. The Red Hills rise in sharp abutments from the valley floor, with the perfectly named Mount Patriarch glowering above.

Right ahead, in this uninhabited place made lonelier by its huge sky, there's a purple sign. 'Coffee', it says. Nothing around it. Just the sign.

A track leads off the road. I take it. There's a kind of tent in the wilderness, and a caravan. Inside the caravan, working busily although there isn't another soul to be seen, is a woman. From the Philippines, she tells me later. She doesn't just sell coffee. She makes bacon butties, and chicken curry, and banana smoothies. A balanced diet.

I ask for coffee and a buttie. The coffee is good and the buttie comes in a beautifully light ciabatta. As she passes it over she slaps my hand, leaving a smear of blood. 'Sandflies,' she says. I'd forgotten about those.

A man appears. He introduces himself as the woman's husband. He points out their house. It's a nice place on the other side of the road, alone in its landscape. They have two houses, he says. The other is on the Whangaparaoa Peninsula north of Auckland.

We have the kind of comforting talk South Islanders have, assuring each other how wonderful the south is, and the north is not. He talks of retiring. Where to, Whangaparaoa or Wairau Valley? He looks at me with pity in his eyes. 'Down here, of course.' Pointing at his house. 'Who'd want to live up there?'

The road begins looking ragged. Rerouted trucks are tearing it apart. Road gangs are patching it up, moving from one spot to the next, trying to keep up.

The road is a maze of '30' (kilometres per hour) signs and one-way stretches. They're promising to reopen the old SH One just as soon as they fight their way through the earthquake rubble blocking it near Kaikoura. Will the poor Wairau Valley highway last until then? It will take some serious work to restore.

I pass the turnoff to the Rainbow Road, once part of the old stock route between Nelson and Canterbury and still one of the wildest roads in the country. A short-cut? I'd been through there, and didn't think so. Another turnoff almost directly opposite leads to the Tophouse, one of the old accommodation houses built a day's cattle drive apart. Several survive.

New direction signs are appearing, pointing to Christchurch. Another sign warns of kiwi on the road. I didn't like their chances at night, with a road train coming through.

And here's St Arnaud, New Zealand's least-known lakeside resort. It's quiet and beautiful. It verges the Nelson Lakes National Park. It was called Rotoiti after the lake it stands beside until the Geographic Board decided that too many people were confusing it with the other Rotoiti near Rotorua, and changed the name. Some are protesting that decision still. The Geographic Board refuses to budge.

The lakeside subdivision looks as sparse as ever. No shopping malls or big hotels clutter the place.

Volunteers have reduced pests to a level where, if you stop on a track, you're surrounded by bush robins. The morning chorus still rings through the forest here. A short walk into the bush and you're gloriously alone.

Ahead lies the Kawatiri junction: Nelson one way, Murchison the other, Christchurch a latecoming third. The end of the line for the ambitious Nelson railway. A lonely platform marks its grave. The station was open for five years and twenty-one days before the line was abandoned. Now you can walk through its tunnels and along its embankments.

I expect Murchison to be bustling with new life as the traffic doubles, triples. It is, but it's the same little town. The butchers still sell their award-winning honey-cured, Manuka-smoked bacon and ham, and sausages to make the most fastidious forget their diets. Hodgsons, a good old country-town general store, still sells everything from bread and milk to kerosene to children's clothes, and it's a Post Office too. The big old pub's airy verandas gaze upon the main street. The junk and antiques store sells the same amazing clutter of crockery, glasses, paintings, old tools. Some of my favourite New Zealand books have come from here.

This was the site of another mighty earthquake, in 1929, but it wasn't the first time Murchison held the world stage. A plaque on the site of the old courthouse records another explosive event: a 'gentleman farmer', one Joseph Sewell, was taken to court in July 1905 after a dispute with another farmer, Walter Neame, over a white-headed heifer.

As the case proceeded, Sewell opted for rougher justice. He put gelignite in his waistcoat pocket and in the courtroom declared he was 'going to blow the devil to hell'. Fearing that the court injunction 'All rise!' was being taken far too literally, policemen ushered him outside, whereupon Sewell blew himself to bits, injuring two and knocking several others senseless. The courthouse was shifted off its foundations. He is now remembered as the world's first suicide bomber.

Now we head west, and once more I note a difference between driving in the North and South islands. Despite horrific accidents, North Island drivers behave better on open roads. They're so much more crowded. In the South Island's wide and empty highways, drivers just go for it.

The highway branches at the Maruia River. I head west and stop at Lyell, whose fortunes have waxed and waned. This was once the biggest gold-mining area in the entire Buller district, where miners poked into every crack and crevice. Lyell had a peak population of 2000. The pub was the last survivor, of course. The Post Office Hotel was nearly a century old when it was razed in 1963. Most of Lyell's history, its relics, treasures and keepsakes, were burned with it. Nothing was saved, and more than a half a century on from that blaze all that can be seen of Lyell is a few flat spots and a couple of cemeteries.

This is classic West Coast. Houses for the living were the first to fall, pubs lasted a little longer, and only the cemeteries of iron and stone have a life after death. The oldest is up a steep track. Forty or fifty people are believed buried there, and you had to be a miner to entomb them in the hard rock. The declining population settled for an easier route to the hereafter, and took to burying their dead on the flat.

But Lyell lives on. Now it's the start, or the finish, of the Old Ghost Road, a cycling and tramping track running along the old miners' road between Lyell and the Mokihinui River. I'd tramped up the Mohikinui a few years previously, when Meridian Energy was proposing to build a dam and power station on conservation land there. I wanted to see the river before it was ruined, and grieved for its beautiful heart.

The old coal mining town of Seddonville, near the Mohikinui River mouth, was torn by the controversy. Of the sixty or so good souls who lived there, some foresaw a return to prosperity, some wanted peace and quiet, and some didn't care much one way or the other. The project went to the Environment Court but Meridian abandoned it, citing high costs and environmental concerns.

Now the eighty-five-kilometre track is one of the country's best-known and loved, and Lyell is mining the new gold, adventure tourism. A camping ground, toilets, huts and shelters have sprung up as quickly as the old mining village once did.

By now I've been on the road for twenty-four hours. The caffeine has finished twanging my strings. I put the seat back and doze among the ghosts.

To be awakened by a bellbird. A little later I'm in Inangahua Junction, named for a phantom: the junction between the Stillwater to Westport railway line, which still runs, and the Nelson railway line, which was never finished.

The town gave its name to the 1968 earthquake which killed five people and forced the hundred or so souls who lived there to leave en masse. Some residents were said to be better off than they'd ever been with the relief supplies coming into the town. Many never returned.

Today the hall storing the earthquake's history is closed and the café is for sale, along with the church hall. A fine old blue Ford sits outside with a mysterious sign announcing that it was built by spanners not chopsticks. Further down the Coast it has just been announced that a cake decorator has won a contract to build a $7 million sewage plant. The Coast has a life of its own.

Now I sit among little houses half-hidden in the bush deciding whether to go west through the Buller Gorge or south to Greymouth. The easy drive to Greymouth wins, but the West Coast's capital has fallen on hard times. Only six hotels remain of the forty-seven once there.

As a child I stayed at Revington's Hotel in Greymouth when it was among the flashest in the land, a fine building in a city full of fine buildings. The Queen and Prince Phillip slept there, in 1954, in a suite since declared a holy place. They came from Hokitika by a road so rough even by the West Coast standards of the time that the authorities decided something had to be done. But oh dear, the expense of tarsealing! The local council couldn't afford it.

They came up with a truly Coast solution. The royal couple were travelling only one way. So they sealed just that side of the road, the seaward side. Perhaps the theory was that the royal couple would be so transfixed by the view they wouldn't notice anything amiss. In any event, they proceeded smoothly into Greymouth and for many years after Coasters called that part of the road 'Lizzie's side'.

Now both lanes of the road are in fine condition but Revington's is empty and derelict, for Greymouth has fallen on hard times. The grand old pub was so run-down the town's mayor, Tony Kokshoorn, personally paid for its frontage to be tarted up.

Mines have shut, native forests are no longer being milled, floods have soaked the place and the main alpine fault line passes not far away, demanding new earthquake standards for buildings which their owners simply cannot afford. They're walking away. Greymouth looks as if it could become one of the Coast's ghost towns. Tourists are the new boom industry on the Coast, and they're quitting the gloomy old town in favour of the brighter Hokitika down the road. It's very sad. Standing on the abandoned

Mawhera Quay, once so busy, I get an end-of-the-world feeling. Perhaps it's exhaustion. I have to stop. I join the tourists, head for Hokitika and check into a backpackers.

I've never stayed in a backpackers before. I get a double bed in a room just big enough for it but nothing else. There's me and the bed. And Ches 'n' Dale, the cheese characters painted on the wall. I have nothing else to do but stare at them. After an hour or two I see there's something more than selling cheese going on here. Dale — or is it Ches? — is a fine, upright figure of open, cheerful demeanour, a man in gumboots and singlet who works hard. Ches — or is it Dale? — wears city boots and a dressy shirt. He's a townie, and he looks up to the honest cocky with an admiring, even fawning grin. Farmers carry the cities on their backs. They're the salt of the earth, and should you think that too much salt does the earth no good, you're certainly a townie and probably a greenie to boot. Dale keeps his own boots fair square on the ground.

I go for a shower in the shared bathroom, which seems to unsettle the young women backpackers a bit. So I forgo the TV room for a beer in the Railway Hotel and lamb shanks down the road. They're of such girth I hope never to meet one of those lambs in the wild.

Next morning I pass the Lake Mahinapua pub, once famous as the set for a Mainland cheese commercial ('I've never seen them so excited'). I stayed there once, drinking in a bar full of hats. Next morning Les Lisle, the seventy-year-old owner, took me for the hardest run I ever had, along a steep beach of soft sand and shingle, and made up for it with a breakfast of whitebait fritters the size of trailer wheels. He had a very long beard, didn't drink, and he died in 2013 at the age of eighty-eight, only twenty years or so younger than his pub.

Anyone with anything to look at, or do, or ride in or on, has set up an adventure tourism business on the West Coast. A stream becomes the greatest kayaking adventure of your life. An old shed is transformed into a traditional café. A swamp becomes a floating gold challenge, old goldfields a chance to strike it rich. The rimu forests which Coasters once wanted so much to fell are now national treasures.

We tunnel into the tall, still forests of South Westland and through the old timber town of Hari Hari, where an effigy of Guy Menzies, a fag hanging out of his mouth, is being photographed busily by a busload of Asian tourists. Some of them wear pollution masks. They're breathing some of the world's purest air but best take no chances.

Menzies left Sydney in January 1931 intent on making the first solo flight across the Tasman, heading for Blenheim. He ended up circling flat green pasture near Hari Hari. He landed. The pasture turned out to be a swamp. The plane flipped but behold, here's a replica of the plane surrounded by people taking selfies.

Even the alpine fault has been pressed into service at Whataroa, which previously had to rely on the kotuku, the white heron, whose only New Zealand breeding place is right here.

Do I imagine a faint air of resignation in Franz Josef? A million tourists a year pass through this place. So does the alpine fault: you might be taking your life in your hands when you stop for petrol. I never imagined buying a soy latte could be so fraught.

Between Franz Josef and Fox the road has been hewn from the mountains, which then do their best to strike back. The famous pair of towns have had no need to do very much at all: they've always been tourist resorts because of their glaciers. But those glaciers are now calving faster than a Canterbury cow and the urgent question is, when will South Westland come out of the warm? Will there be no end to the golden weather?

I am stuck behind a tourist bus all the way to Fox Glacier. The car shakes contentedly, like a dog preparing for a nap. But the one-way bridges here are wonderful, especially the suspension bridges over the big rivers. Long may plans for tourist highways gather dust on some minister's desk.

At Fox it begins to rain again, that thick, heavy, unrelenting West Coast rain measured here not so much in millimetres as in metres. I fancy I hear the car glugging.

We drive southwards, through Jacobs River. A tiny school, a church with no steeple, a few houses. No reproachful cows.

The last time I was here I'd come over the Haast Pass in the early hours after waiting until after midnight for a slip to be cleared. It was very dark in South Westland, black as the insides of a black cow, two of which happened to be standing in the middle of the road, invisible in the black night. I tried to steer (that is not a pun) between them. There came a huge thump. The front of the diesel 4WD I was driving was stove in. God knows what happened to the cows. I went back, expecting corpses, but they were still standing. Their eyes glittered in the faint glow of my remaining headlight.

I tried to call the police, really I did. Left a message. Police headquarters in some urban centre far from the Coast answered, and a female voice told me that stock on a major highway were a menace. I said I knew that. I had the dents to prove it. She said, in the firm tones of someone trying to communicate with an idiot, that I should track down the owner. I said this was black country, with no houses, no lights, no driveways and no visible sign of life except two reproachful cows. She said something would have to be done. I wished her luck.

Now I keep a wary eye out for crippled cows with vengeance on what is left of their minds.

I've always felt an affinity for Bruce Bay, for obvious reasons. But I don't like its chances. Rising sea levels are making the Tasman ever more testy and the West Coast is feeling it. Already only a lot of rock stands between the road here and oblivion.

At Knight Point a clutch of tourists huddle under umbrellas and peer into the grey. Somewhere inside it, they've been told, is a view.

Just over the Waita River bridge I see a sign. 'Whitebait patties', it says. I remember Les Lisle's beauties. The car shakes into a tight turn.

A little road leads into a settlement I never knew existed. It is one of those West Coast whitebaiting places, a bach town whose hopes rise and fall on the numbers of tiny fish in the river. Right at the end of the road is a house, more substantial than most of the others, with an outside shed and barbecue. I stop. A woman comes out. I ask for a pattie. She ladles a scoop of whitebait mixture onto a hot plate. Several more people arrive. She says she's a school counsellor, down here helping her brother. She likes making whitebait patties, she says. Her customers are usually on holiday. They are happy people who don't need counselling but, she adds politely, if I had any worries she'd be pleased to listen.

The whitebait sizzles on the grill.

'What was the biggest catch here?' someone asks. Once, she says, the run was so big everyone jumped into the river with gumboots, singlets, anything that might hold the 'bait. But now there's hardly anything. The season has been bad, again.

She brightens. A few baches have changed hands and last night was initiation night. The newcomers were given a choice.

Either they could run through the local visitor lodge naked, or they could jump into the river and catch a trout. They were a modest bunch. All of them opted for the river. How many trout? Quite a few, she reckons. As for the patties: they are large and light, perfect.

Ahead lies the Haast Pass. Oh dear. Its history hangs over it like the clouds before me today, threatening. On the day the road was opened, little over half a century before on 6 November 1965, Prime Minister Keith Holyoake cut the ribbon and ran for cover. The rain poured down so heavily the road was closed by slips a few hours later. That's its history, really.

The previous time I went over it a large sign at Hawea announced that it was closed by slips. A barrier at Makarora stopped traffic. The woman behind the bar at Makarora predicted it would reopen around midnight. I drove around the barrier and went up to the top of the Pass, knowing the slips were on the Coast side. Half a dozen cars were already there. I parked and slept until I heard a car pass from the Coast direction. The Pass had to be open.

The road's grim history made that night even darker. The Canadian couple trapped in their motor caravan by slips on the road then swept into the wild Haast River by another slip: only one body was ever found. The many crashes. Most of all, the constant slips, especially around the Diana Falls area. Slips there had closed the road to night-time traffic for fourteen months. It had been reopened to twenty-four-hour, two-lane traffic not long before.

They'd just cleared one slip that night. Road cones marked the spot without any clear indication of a way through. On one side of the road I risked rock falls, on the other a sheer drop to the wild river below. I picked my way through the middle. Half my brain told me to go for it, to get the hell out of there. The other argued that if it was dangerous they wouldn't have reopened the road. Would they? And why weren't any other cars on the road? That fear of demons in the dark which overlaid everything pictured the billions of tonnes of rock in the blackness above, held back only by Kiwi ingenuity. No one believed it was a permanent fix. Would it hold for just a little longer?

In fact, a few days later the *Greymouth Star* told its readers that the Pass was closed, again. It reported that house-sized boulders were blocking the road, 'adding to the nervousness among South Westland business owners.'

Nothing could add to my own nervousness that night. For the first time I didn't shudder crossing the bridge marking New Zealand's most famous unsolved murder, of Jennifer Mary Beard, whose body had been found beneath it. In fact, I was joyous, because it meant I was out of danger, pretty much (who could have predicted the two black cows?).

But today the cloud clears suddenly. The rain has stopped. The sun is shining. Who can believe awful stories on a sunny day? I scoot upwards. Tourists are stopping for photographs. At the Diana Falls, that complicated lacework of steel and rocks looks like a vertical garden, green growth poking through and waving gently in the sun. I nip smartly over the top. I'm not going to tempt fate.

The deep green forest gives way to that distinctive Otago country, brown turning gold, snow on the peaks, the wind blowing whitecaps across the lake. I cross the low saddle to Lake Hawea into country that is sharper, steeper — although somehow gentler. Perhaps it's the Haast receding and the rounded ranges of Central Otago appearing to the south. Ahead lies Wanaka, fat and happy in the sun. The sign at its entrance announces, 'Puzzling World'. It advertises a business, not the town, but I'm not arguing.

I've been on the road forty-eight hours but I'm not counting either. The car gurgles. This was always going to be a wild journey, but it became a strange one too.

And is there a grander journey anywhere? No use asking me. I'm irretrievably biased. Of course there isn't.

11

Passing muster

The Valley is a commonplace name for a place of uncommon beauty. It is a route between the Rangitata River and Lake Tekapo, an ancient track probably known to Maori and certainly to generations of high-country musterers.

The Valley lies between the Two Thumb Range, named for mountainous digits which thrust at the sky, and the Sinclair Range, marking the boundary of the mighty Mesopotamia Station. It is a deep and mysterious place, almost unknown to the outside world until it became part of the national pathway, Te Araroa.

The Valley runs parallel to the Rangitata River in the Upper Rangitata Valley, the 'desolate pathway of destruction' described by its most famous early resident, Samuel Butler. In this country the tough company who followed later often clutched their crucifixes. Chas Dunstan, who drove an eight-horse wagon across the Rangitata and into the Ashburton Gorge, once the main route in and out, reached for Ecclesiastes: 'Pity anyone who falls and has no one to help them up.' He wrote:

> To gaze on the headwaters of the Rangitata and the vast
> panorama of hills up the great divide ... one was reminded
> of [from Elizabeth Barrett Browning] ... 'Truly earth is
> crammed with heaven and every common bush afire with
> God but only those who see take off their shoes.'

Butler was searching for land which he could claim for a pittance, develop for sheep and double his capital in as short a time as possible. He found it here in the Upper Rangitata, claimed it for himself, named it Mesopotamia (the Greek word for country between two rivers), built it up to some 24,000 hectares and four years later sold it for twice the sum he paid. He was not much respected as a sheep farmer, but as a writer he was superb. His best-known work is *Erewhon*, a utopian novel whose setting is based on Mesopotamia and the mountain passes he could see from the station.

He first saw this place when he turned into the river valley, now the Upper Rangitata, from the opposite side of the Rangitata River and found his way up a tributary, Forest Creek, which was to become the boundary of his new station. It was autumn. His blankets were icy, his tea leaves frozen. He climbed along Forest Creek, which is not so much a creek as a wild river hemmed by mountains, until he reached the top of the range, and he was overwhelmed by the country he was in:

> Suddenly, as my eyes got on a level with the top, so that I could
> see over, I was struck almost breathless by the wonderful
> mountain that burst on my sight. The effect was startling. It
> rose towering in a massy parallelogram, disclosed from top to
> bottom in the cloudless sky, far above all the others.

The mountain he saw that day was Mount Cook. He probably saw it from a saddle which later became known as the Bullock Bow. It's a pass which leads down into the Bush Stream Valley, known simply as 'The Valley'. Butler was probably the first European to see that, too.

The Valley became part of Mesopotamia Station. It stayed within its boundaries until the introduction of the government process known as 'tenure review', which led to high-country pastoral leaseholders getting freehold title for part of their stations in exchange for handing over the rest of the property to the conservation estate. On Mesopotamia the vast, wonderful tract of the Valley became public property.

It is still lonely enough. The grandeur of the place diminishes everyone who goes into it.

Even now it is part of Te Araroa not all that many *do* go into it. It is a long and difficult walk. The logistics are tricky. Tramping from the Rangitata to upper Lake Tekapo can take five or six days and the walk goes from one remote place to another. How is it to be organised? At one end the track runs from the Upper Rangitata Valley. From the other, the track begins, or ends, from a point well up Lake Tekapo from the township. There's no public transport either way.

Some walkers get around the problem by dividing their party in half, leaving cars at both ends, and exchanging keys when they meet in the middle of the track. Or they take a shorter route, drive up the Rangitata, walk up the Valley, cross back over the Sinclair Range by way of the Bullock Bow and follow Forest Creek back to the road.

It is complicated, but worth it. Generations since Butler have been inspired by this land. Geoff Chapple, architect of Te

Araroa, described the journey through the Valley — the Two Thumb Track — as one of the real highlights of Te Araroa. Peter Jackson filmed part of the *Lord of the Rings* trilogy here, using the Rangitata Valley as a location for Edoras, capital city of the Rohan people. Poets have wiped sweat from their pens as they laboured to match words and subject.

I walked the Valley one autumn, when the air was still and the mountains still bald, the last warmth of summer leaking from the rock. I was with three companions. We'd spent the night in the old Mesopotamia shearing quarters, a labyrinthine wooden building overlooking the station's stables and woolshed.

The cookhouse kitchen was huge, one of two in the building, with two electric stoves, fridge, industrial-sized freezer, toasters, microwave ovens and generations of appliances, pots, pans and assorted instruments. The vast table in the dining room could seat thirty. There were great padded armchairs and, mysteriously, a toy box. The antiseptic smell of split pine rose from the woodbox beside the open fire.

One side of the shearers' quarters was given over to the cooks and reflected their place in the station hierarchy: bathroom and two bedrooms each with a queen-size bed and two bunks, and a private sitting room with its own armchairs and sofa and fireplace. The décor was high-country station: fencing-wire toilet-paper holder; chunks of wood; staples the universal fixer.

The shearers lived in the rest of the building, in a crush of bedrooms. The washhouse boasted three sinks, two concrete and lead tubs, and two washing machines. This was not so much shearers' quarters as a warren, a whole, self-contained community.

The wood floors were bare. Wide hallways led through the labyrinth. A billiard room ran off one, a library another. It was filled with the books of another age, one in which Gideon of the Yard investigated a murder and robbery on the top floor of a London bus, approaching his main suspects, Teddy boys, in a mannered and decorous way. Whodunnits, romances and histories distracted legions of shearers from the yards full of greasy merinos waiting below.

Now, shearing gangs arrived in vans in the mornings and went home at nights, and we had the place to ourselves.

Very early in the morning we headed away from the station buildings, following the road leading up the valley. We crossed a bridge over Bush Creek, built by eye by Laurie Prouting, the second-generation Prouting of the three running Mesopotamia, a delicate-looking structure but immensely strong, like good furniture.

Nearby Dr Andrew Sinclair lay in his lonely grave. Secretary to the government under the administration of Sir George Grey, Sinclair accompanied Julius von Haast, German geologist and founder of Canterbury Museum, on his exploration of the then virtually unknown mountain ranges of Canterbury. They were searching for the Rangitata's source in 1861 when Sinclair drowned as he attempted to cross the river, the first European of many to die that way. According to a contemporary account: It was a sad spectacle, 'this fine old man we all loved and respected so much, only a few hours before full of life and health, now a ghastly corpse, his hair and long white beard lying dank over his cold white face and glaring eyes. The scene was rendered all the more weird and awful by the surroundings, the still dark night, the rushing water, and overhanging cliffs under the red glare of the torches.'

***

We found his grave at the end of a faint path through the matagouri. It had been lost for decades until a shearing gang combed the river flats and found it hidden in undergrowth. Now it lay in the tiny Upper Rangitata Cemetery, last resting place of some 17 people.

From here the track followed Bush Stream, cut deep between the Sinclair Range on one side and the Brabazon Range on the other. Oh, it was wonderful, for fifteen minutes or so. Then we started to get wet.

The track followed Bush Stream all right, but more correctly it was *in* Bush Stream. It dived in and out of the water as if it had gills. Tricky in the spring thaw or after heavy rain, but this was autumn.

The Brabazon Range, named for an early partner of Butler's, reared up in cliffs and abutments with the Two Thumbs sticking up behind. On the other side lay Mount Sinclair, quite a friendly looking mountain compared with the truly savage peaks rearing and roaring to the west, although I was to climb it later and revise that thought: mountaineers might not so much as sniff at it, but it was a pretty stiff hike all the same. Steep on the Bush Stream side too and a tough muster in the bad old days.

Poor old Charlie Gillman died not far from here. According to Peter Newman, the musterer, writer and high-country balladeer, Gillman's gang was mustering over the back of the Brabazon when Charlie was sent back to round up some sheep stuck in bluffs. As it turned out, the sheep were safer than Charlie was. When he failed to return the gang went out into the dark and by the pale light of the moon they found his body lying at the bottom of a cliff.

We sloshed our way back and forth across Bush Stream, sometimes a torrent, today gentle enough, if freezing. In the gorges and ravines the track abandoned the stream bed and ran over jerky little spurs and through stunted bush. The worst of them was Sawtooth Bluff, whose name said it all, really. The idea was to wade around it, which could be tricky if the stream was up, but preferable to climbing over it. Climbing scares me, and the fear is transmitted to my boots, which will always slip, stumble or trip if that is in the slightest way possible.

Today we kept to the stream bed, until the track finally left it and headed for the Crooked Spur Hut. This was the starting point for the great Mesopotamia musters. The sheep were mustered, the flock growing as men moved down the Valley, eventually flowing over the Bullock Bow into the Rangitata Valley in a vast creamy tide.

The Crooked Spur was a classic musterers' hut, there for generations, rebuilt by Malcolm Prouting, patriarch of the clan, and absolutely fit for purpose. In the mountains that meant, essentially, that it would not blow away or fall down, would protect and shelter its inhabitants from gales and snowstorms, and provide rudimentary kitchen and bunks. Musterers would arrive late and worn out, get some food inside them and crash. They'd leave the sheep in holding yards, their dogs in rough kennels. The remains of those lay alongside the old huts in the Valley, ruins from another age.

The last musterers left these huts only when the Valley became part of both the conservation estate and Te Araroa. The Department of Conservation's contribution to their ambience was, essentially, thin modern squabs for the bunks and outside dunnies. Both were much appreciated, especially the outhouses, all of them scenically located for the best views in the Valley.

Sitting on the long drop with the door open, contemplating the wonders of the universe, I felt just as Chas Dunstan had, if from a more comfortable perch: 'Truly earth is crammed with heaven and every common bush afire ...'

Two hunters arrived. They set down their rifles and produced from their packs some choice cuts of venison. Now, one of our party was a chef. I can report that the combination of tenderloin, cook and ambience was an advance even on the company of musterers and their tucker.

Next morning, the track crept away from the hut and climbed over a saddle behind Crooked Spur. The majesty of the Valley burst upon us.

High in the Valley the tussock was golden and skylarks celebrated and the peaks stood to attention for their ceremonial dressing of snow in a few weeks' time, and the orange throats of the spaniard flashed like fire.

Valleys conjure images of peace and tranquillity. Happy families live in them and sit down to Sunday dinners. When people had talked of the Valley to me, I'd imagined a long smooth groove between mountain ranges, possibly green as the song, certainly tranquil. How could it not be, set so deep in the mountains that not a squeak from the outside world could penetrate?

Oh, how wrong. The Valley was deep all right, but not smooth. Spurs, ridges, abutments, crenellations, breastworks, parapets barricaded our path. Matagouri threatened to spear us from thatch to pizzle.

Every gully contained its own mountain stream, coursing and cold. The Valley was made up of a hundred little valleys. Inside each one you were totally alone. You imagined that climbing the next ridge would lead you into open country. The next ridge, though, led you only to another part of the maze.

Perhaps there was a track through here. I saw little of it. I walked up and down and around. I looked up at the Two Thumb Range and was 'struck almost breathless by the wonderful mountains bursting on my sight', and so on, but I was glad I was not up there.

It was a five-hour walk to Stone Hut. We crossed over Bush Stream on an old stock bridge and there it was. It wasn't much, a classic musterers' hut all alone on its terrace, but out here it was paradise.

The old hut had been constructed from boulders rolled up from Bush Stream. They formed the hut's walls and chimney, without mortar, cement, or anything else to keep out the sharp winds and frosts. 'There were no bunks or table and all hands simply unrolled their swags on the floor and gazed out through the chinks in the rocks,' wrote Peter Newton. 'However, it had a good corrugated iron roof and that, I suppose, was considerably better than a tent.'

Newton told of a mustering gang holed up in the Stone Hut for two days as the snow piled up against its walls and the streams ran high. The dogs were starving. They'd had no food for five days. Finally two men volunteered to risk the ice and snow and cross the Sinclair Range for supplies. They returned to find their mates existing on kea soup.

Eventually the hut was rebuilt and now it stands alone on its terrace, picturesque, everyone's idea of the perfect musterers' hut. Architects would labour to copy the pitch of its roof, the symmetry of its walls.

The hut was warmed by a big open fire, dry brush sparking. DoC's new lavatory faced on to the river like a telescope. Its seat was weighted with a cast-iron oven lid, which slammed it shut. You had to be nippy to avoid serious injury.

In the late evening a chamois stag climbed a narrow rock spiking up from the river bank opposite and posed against the pale evening sky like the Monarch of the Glen. I was glad the hunters had stayed at Crooked Spur. Inside, the firelight flickered on the walls as we ate a meal our chef had conjured from dehydrated food and shared a single thought, common to all who wander the back country: *This is the life!*

The track forked just south of Stone Hut. We could keep to the Bush Stream, cross the Two Thumb Range by way of Stag Saddle, Te Araroa's highest point, then follow Camp Stream and pass under the Richmond Range to emerge at Lake Tekapo by Boundary Stream. That way we would pass the last of the old Mesopotamia musterers' huts in the Valley.

Formerly Tin Hut, built by the original Malcolm Prouting of Mesopotamia, it was later renamed the Royal Hut. For this was the hut visited by the young Prince Charles and Princess Anne during the 1970 royal tour, to give them the flavour of the high country. We took royal tours seriously in those days. The royal youngsters were accompanied by a retinue including the Diplomatic Protection Squad and, for good measure, the Cliff Rescue Squad.

Laurie Prouting once told me he'd been drafted in as an extra for the performance. He was posted high on a spur, the idea being that the young royals could look down from their helicopter upon a picturesque shepherd boy going about his lonely work. His role in the royal tour went unrecognised. He waited, and he waited, and eventually he waited no longer and left his post. As it happened the helicopter pilot had changed his mind and flown in by a different route.

Our other choice was to go over the Bullock Bow and back into the Rangitata Valley. That was the route we'd chosen.

The morning dawned calm. Three days in a row, unusual in this high country. Sure enough, the weather was reliably unreliable.

The day soon lost its poise. The nor'-wester sneaked from its mountain lair, puffed into the sky and flexed its bulk for the day. Its warm breath spread around us. We hoped for the best. Nor'-westers up here are fierce, dangerous, not the hot winds I grew up with on the beach at Christchurch, which whipped sand into your eyes, shortened tempers and raised the divorce rate.

We left Bush Stream for the last time and walked up towards the Bullock Bow. After the Valley it felt like a highway, a long broad track with no vices.

At its top the saddle was broad and easy, giving musterers either their first glimpse of civilisation or their last, depending on their philosophies. The iron bow, once used to yoke bullocks to their loads, rattled in its little pile of rocks. I stood there imagining the passage of centuries. Long before Butler first laid eyes on the saddle, Maori were crossing the range into the Rangitata Valley, and why not here?

The Felt Hut was still on Mesopotamia Station land and was private. It huddled in a patch of bush below the saddle on the Rangitata side of the range. A stream below it flowed down to Forest Creek. Beside it sat an old iron bath with a fire below. When they'd rousted their sheep out of the nooks and crevices and the gullies and bluffs and precipices and driven them down the Valley and over the Bullock Bow, musterers bucketed water from the stream, lit the fire and waited for a hot bath, their first for, sometimes, a very long time. They must have wondered who could wish for anything finer.

The hut itself seemed as old as the hills around it. It looked frail but it had stood against the weather, the snow and the gales, for a century or so. I thought of all those fine houses built in the 1980s and '90s, with reams of permits and whole armies of inspectors, that had leaked and rotted away. No consents here. The hut was built of corrugated iron inscribed with the names of musterers, dozens of them, hundreds perhaps, going back seventy years or so. The iron was nailed to a framework of mountain beech dried to the consistency of iron itself. Once it had been lined with felt, which gave the hut its name. The same beech was used for table legs and odd bits of furniture. Kapok mattresses lay on the bunks, stained with god knew what, but who cared when the hard day was over?

Laurie Prouting once told me, 'I've always appreciated an abode for what it is. One of the huts at Messie has a dirt floor and you can't stand up in it. But when you're there on a stormy night you think it's a palace. You think you're a lucky bastard for the shelter it gives.'

The route out to the road lay along Forest Creek, where Butler built his own version of a musterers' hut. He called it a V-hut. It was shaped like a tent, or an A-frame. It leaked, and it was cold, and he spent a miserable winter in it.

With the station's permission we took the road out, but on the way I detoured to the ravine cut by Forest Creek and looked down on Butler's old hut site. It was cold and forbidding. I imagined it a century and a half before. Even colder and more forbidding, and no help to be had. And the musterer's life now gone from this valley and the Valley behind.

12

Feeling the heat

Looking deep into the heart of New Zealand is easier than you might expect, but more alarming. In the South a fault line, only too active, threatens to split the island into two, or three, or more pieces. In the north a different kind of line, red-hot, angles from the centre of the island, every now and then erupting in pustules or hurling rocks and mud high in the air. In this country we live on the brink, and to me the most remarkable aspect of our edgy existence is how equably we get through it.

Earthquakes have riven Christchurch, and Kaikoura, with the mighty alpine fault still threatening to blow, but people in those places haven't ducked for cover. They live their lives and when the worst happens they pick up the pieces and put them back together.

In the North Island people live in a cauldron yet dangle their toes in it. They cope with eruptions and nasty accidents in hot pools. They not only live alongside the beast, but profit from it. They dance with the devil and mambo with the magma.

The Taupo volcanic zone is mainland New Zealand's crucible. A row of active volcanoes reaches from Mount Ruapehu across the Volcanic Plateau, past Rotorua to White Island in the Bay of Plenty, a seething track with swathes of bubbling mud and boiling water.

I'm an expatriate South Islander and know all about earthquakes, but the fiery north is foreign country. I wanted to run that red line, all the way from Taupo to White Island.

Whakamaru seemed innocent enough, a good place to start. It sits in a corner near Lake Taupo, largely overlooked by tourists, an old power-station village dating from a time when the government constructed power stations and looked after the people who built them. It was briefly famous when police combed its streets for the prison escapee George Wilder (see Chapter 1). It's a quiet place now, even cute.

Lake Whakamaru formed behind the dam they built then. Black swans waddle in the sun. The lakesides are trimmed and clean. Grassy slopes run up to pine forest. But once, this place seethed and boiled.

For this is a very old volcano. Whakamaru sits in a crater that once measured thirty by forty kilometres, a truly massive passage into the earth's soul. It erupted regularly, the lava cooling into rock sculptures, gargoyles and giants standing guard over their territory.

Well, it's peaceful now, not a bubble in sight, although the last eruption was a mere 1800 years ago, a geological blink. The village is full of neat houses where not a single soul seems troubled by more than a power bill.

That is the remarkable thing about the red line. People live happily in the caldera, around the vents, along the hissing, cracked surface of the earth. Many make a dollar or two from their fiery history.

The road runs down past the lake to Tokaanu. Its heyday was the 1960s, when the power station was built. Now it's a town settling beside the southern end of the lake, quite beautiful, a hot-water tourist town. All it lacks, it seems to me, is tourists.

It has a thermal pool resort and a thermal walking track ('hidden gems'). A sprawling hotel was built in headier days. People here have their homes and spa pools thermally heated. It should be booming, but is not. Turangi stole its mantle, hydro-wise, later in the 1960s.

Turangi offers fishing and walking and biking but you have to go to the less-popular Tokaanu for a dip in a hot thermal pool. Life just isn't fair. Or perhaps tourists are more wary of the red line than the natives, even if the people here have felt the hot breath of the devil below.

The Tangiwai disaster began when Mount Ruapehu erupted in 1945. The crater lake emptied and its outlet blocked with debris. A new crater lake slowly formed behind the de facto dam. The monster grew slowly until Christmas Eve 1953. Then it tore itself loose and roared down the mountain and into the Whangaehu River.

Disasters have a way of compounding. The Tangiwai railway bridge crossed the Whangaehu a little way east of Waiouru. A bridge pier had already been weakened by the river. The lahar, a lethal mixture of mud, rock and water, finished the job. An express train was approaching and as it was Christmas Eve the train was crowded.

Warned by a brave man with a torch, the driver braked. Too late. The locomotive and five of the nine passenger carriages, then a sixth, plunged into the river. One hundred and fifty-one people died.

In the days of National Service I was drafted into the Army and spent quite a long time — it seemed forever — on the Volcanic Plateau. It was the scariest time I'd had in my young life. We'd be marched over the Plateau in various mystifying exercises which gave me plenty of time to watch the steam over Ruapehu, the neat cloud over Ngauruhoe, and the blasted top of Tongariro.

Of course I wanted to be somewhere else. Every young man plonked into uniform and sent to the coldest, loneliest, most barren place not just in New Zealand but, in our minds, the entire world, wanted to be somewhere else.

Those volcanoes appeared to us to be biding their time. At some intergalactic signal they'd explode, and we'd be atomised.

We camped on ground that seemed to be not soil but a kind of pulverised paste of unearthly colour. The farmers among us discussed trace elements; they felt that a little topdressing was all that was needed to bring the whole Plateau into production. To the rest of us, it was just scrubby and cold. It felt bleak. Its history seeped from the rocks: eruptions, lahars, a million times more violent than the Army with its tanks and shells blasting away. Much later, when Peter Jackson used this area as a setting for the Black Gate of Mordor in *Lord of the Rings,* the common thought among those young recruits grown older was: *Good choice.*

New Zealand soldiers sent overseas to dubious battlefields, such as Yugoslavia, Iraq or Afghanistan, clambered over, shot at and dug into the red volcanic soil here. To anyone who has baked their bones under its brassy summer sun, or been frozen brittle in its icy dark, the Plateau seems an appropriate prelude to the military adventure *du jour.*

Except for tourists, who are always incomprehensible, few stop on the Desert Road running over the Plateau. Even on the tarmac you can feel the thin, rent fabric of the earth's surface. In places the road dives into the entrails below, and you become a science-fiction adventurer, twisting and turning inside the layers of lahars and volcanic ash and boiled mud and rock ruddy as old blood. As you come spluttering to the surface there's little relief, for the landscape is sombre, threatening. You do not want to linger. The road traverses the Rangipo Desert, a landscape crisped by thousands of years of volcanic eruptions. Nothing survives here but low bush and wild Kaimanawa horses.

The Desert Road is only sixty-three kilometres long, but you always give a sigh of relief on the sixty-third. It wasn't a road at all until quite late in New Zealand's motoring history. It began as a rough track for an intermittent coach service between Taihape and Taupo, but most people didn't want to go anywhere near the Plateau. They preferred a long detour through Napier and later through Ohakune.

The Desert Road remained little more than a track until the country was tidied up for the royal visit by the new Queen Elizabeth in 1953–54. The road might have been all right for her subjects, but it was far too rough for Her Majesty. Royalty achieved what world war could not: the road was widened and sealed.

I found myself cruising the Volcanic Plateau in 1995, writing about a massive eruption. Volcanologists had first sensed trouble when the Ruapehu crater lake warmed. Steam spouted from its vents. There'd been quite a few smaller eruptions; lahars had run down the mountainsides, some into the Whangaehu. Crater Lake was leaking down the flanks, again.

Then it blew. This was no prelude; it was the main body of the work. Ruapehu wasn't mucking around. It was really, truly blowing up. For days, lahars smoked into the Whangaehu, the Whakapapaiti, the Mangaturuturu, filling them with volcanic excrement. The snowfields were streaked black. The Army began evacuating families from Waiouru. Sheep and other livestock died after feeding on ash-dressed pasture.

I was working for the *New Zealand Listener* then, based in the South Island. The editor wanted me to write about the eruption. I flew to Auckland, the pilot staying well clear of Ruapehu's ash cloud shooting ten kilometres into the air, spreading over land even 300 kilometres away. Perhaps he was thinking of British Airways Flight 9 from London to Auckland, which flew into a cloud of volcanic ash near Jakarta and lost all four engines. If he wasn't thinking about that, I certainly was.

In Auckland I rented a car and headed for the Plateau. The closer I got the less I liked it. My idea of volcanic activity was to go to Rotorua's wonderful Blue Baths and lie in geothermally heated water surrounded by art deco architecture and 1930s jazz.

Taupo was excited. People sat in cafés and eagerly discussed the eruptions. Every truly awful thing fascinates people, as long as they're safely out of its reach.

For three days I swanned around with a photographer. I stayed at a motel in Ohakune. The proprietor was disconsolate. The ski resorts had been closed: skiers had fled the scene with the eruption nipping their backsides; the volcano blew up just as the skiing day was ending.

Boulders were scattered like marbles. Steam and ash were blasted twelve kilometres into the air. A lahar flashed by Whakapapa while departing skiers mopped their brows and fretted over their likely fate had the mountain erupted just a little earlier. Black ash was rotting roofs and ruining pastures and corroding the turbine blades in the Rangipo power station.

I stayed in Turangi. It wasn't as disconsolate, although I was; Turangi at the best of times can be a little glum, for visitors at least.

The Desert Road was closed, of course. Who would want to get closer? From the gates we could see dirty smoke pouring from the mountain. We could smell the rotten-egg stench of fire and brimstone.

On the world scale Mount Ruapehu is ranked as especially dangerous because of its lethal lahars and its crater lake, millions of cubic metres of acidic water ready to pour down the mountainsides through any crack in the crater wall.

We took the circular route around the mountain, through National Park on the western side. Maps showed that lahars generally laid waste to the eastern side of the mountain. The western side was less beaten-up. Barren on the east, bush on the west. Still, it wasn't so much that the roundabout road was safer as that it was open. The map showed it dangerously close to a mountain which was at that very moment consolidating its position among the world's most badly behaved volcanoes, but that didn't seem to worry the clutch of thrill-seekers who formed an impromptu convoy on the route. Amateur photographers yapped around the mountain like terriers.

There was a vintage car and a couple on a motorbike. The occupants of the old car proceeded sedately. The two bikers and ourselves stopped often, and we had earnest discussions about how to get closer to the action. My own interest was academic. I smelled the volcano's stink, saw the granite column of ash, imagined the fire and brimstone, and had no intention of getting nearer to it. I was a moth drawn to the flame only by reason of my craft, and I was certainly not going to be burned.

But I was cowed.

The huge energy of the eruption, its ferocity, its reach, its implacability had shaken me more than I knew. For weeks and months afterwards I imagined the reek, shrank from the force.

The following year Ruapehu erupted again. Ash blasted over the skifields, which opened anyway. Volcanologists were examining that crater lake through leery eyes. What would happen when the acid waters rose so high that they would burst through the dam of volcanic ash blocking its outlet? Why, it would be 1953 all over again.

By January 2005 the lake was up to its brim. The next year, 2006, it erupted; a small eruption, a mere burp by Ruapehu's standards. Still, a great plume of water shot into the air and mighty waves beat the crater wall.

On 18 March 2007 the mountain again spat its contents over the countryside. The crater lake smashed through its dam. A huge lahar crashed down into the Whangaehu River. But the authorities had been warned and had closed roads and railways. A family were trapped in their home when their access way was swept away. All scary, but not too serious by Ruapehu standards.

On the evening of 25 September 2007, the mountain repeated the performance. This one was seriously frightening. There was no warning: the eruption simply sneaked up and let loose, taking everyone — volcanologists, local experts, the mountain industry — by surprise.

William Pike, an Auckland schoolteacher and mountaineer, lost the lower part of a leg when a boulder crashed into the hut he and a companion were sleeping in, crushing his leg. The rock was too heavy for his friend to lift.

I could imagine them both struggling in the dark while the world crashed around them. The terror, and oh, the pain.

Pike didn't waste the experience. He became a motivational speaker and led a youth-development programme.

Ruapehu erupts constantly. In 2012 it spewed huge boulders up to two kilometres. A vast ash cloud twenty-five kilometres long and fifteen wide travelled at sixty kilometres per hour. The sulphur could be smelled in Nelson and Blenheim. State Highway One was closed along with the surrounding airspace, and people in nearby homes legged it for safety.

***

A little north of Ruapehu lies Mount Ngauruhoe, a child's drawing of a volcano, beautifully symmetrical with a puff of smoke at its top. The mountain is judged to be peaceful — at the moment. New Zealand volcanoes are rather like the tiger in the Cambridgeshire zoo, which was peaceful and beautiful right up to the time it killed a keeper.

The huge boulders which lie around the Plateau, the weird shapes and colours of the hammered earth, the reluctance of any living thing, animal or vegetable, to put down roots into the ruddy ground, all proclaimed this to be a place best left alone.

One of the best descriptions of Ngauruhoe was penned by an early explorer and climber, John Bidwill, who toiled up its flanks in March 1839: 'Had it not been for the idea of standing where no [Pakeha] man ever stood before, I should certainly have given up the undertaking.' Then he peered into the crater and was aghast: 'The crater was the most terrific abyss I ever looked into or imagined'.

Staring into the raw innards of the earth reduces the watcher to a wisp.

***

Then Tongariro. The top of the mountain tells of tremendous explosions, because most of it is missing. Instead, the volcano ends on a jagged line of cones at odds with its comely neighbour (and vent) Ngauruhoe.

A geologist who climbed the mountain on New Year's Day, 1893 (on a jaunt with women and children), after an eruption the previous November, reported that 'the mountain ... was rent in twain by an enormous fissure ... Vast quantities of poisonous gases were rising from the rift, and the whole area on the north side of the rift was a seething mass of sulphur.'

The short story is, you don't mess with volcanoes. You try to have nothing to do with them. You get as far from them as possible, and especially from the Volcanic Plateau, which is among the world's most active.

Unless you're part of what is called the visitor industry. For many, the stink of sulphur is the sweet smell of success.

Further down the red line, along the highway between Wairakei (itself a thermal resort) and Rotorua, lies a faded little town called Golden Springs. It has a thermal stream running through its holiday park, but it seems rather lonely. No one I could find knew why it was called 'Golden', for no hint of the precious metal or its colour hangs about the place.

***

Not far from Rotorua's hot water and bubbling mud, Mount Tarawera crouches.

On 10 June 1886 Tarawera erupted, destroyed the Pink and White Terraces on Lake Rotomahana and killed some 120 people. Today you can visit the so-called Buried Village and walk over their bones. This is proclaimed as New Zealand's most-visited archaeological site. Currently, it will cost you $30. Of the Pink and White Terraces, said to have been the eighth wonder of the world, nothing remains.

I went back to Rotorua for the night. It's the red-line capital, where anyone with so much as a bubble in their backyard advertises a thermal pool. This is the place where the fiery underbelly turns a buck, where a whole industry balances on the hell below, rather like balancing on the lid of a kettle.

I stopped at an inviting motel, defined as one advertising spas in their units plus special rates. I was cautious. Several people have died after falling into boiling mud pools, and more have expired from hydrogen sulphide poisoning in motel hot pools.

This had a spa pool right in the unit, half as big again as the combined living-bedroom. It was a worn, cracked affair, so noisy the manager asked me not to use it too late in the evening so others could get to sleep. I took one look and resolved not to use it at all, then discovered it doubled as the shower base — the shower head was sticking out of the wall above. Truly, I was looking deep into the heart of volcanic New Zealand.

***

I'd been curious about White Island since I sailed past it once in an old wooden boat, making my way from Auckland to Picton. At first, I was astonished by the smell: a scorched, eggy stench that rolled across the ocean and left its taste for hours.

I knew that White Island lay alongside the route, but was unprepared for the presence: a reeking, smoking heap, red-hot, glowing and fading like a coke fire in a breeze.

This is the far end of that red line from the Volcanic Plateau, a light in the dark, a boil on the surface of the sea, a supernatural presence in the night. Beyond White Island the line disappears into a string of undersea volcanoes.

The island stands forty-eight kilometres offshore in the Bay of Islands. Most of it lies unseen, for it is the top of a volcano rising from the sea floor. If you stood on its top, which is not recommended, you'd be as far above sea level as another of New Zealand's great tourist attractions, Queenstown.

White Island is New Zealand's most active cone volcano. Its danger levels ebb and flow like the tides around it. A pohutukawa forest once survived on its scratchy slopes until eruptions in the early 1980s disposed of it. Now the island looks like a molar in serious decay.

White Island was more active between 1975 and 2001 than it had been for centuries. It blew rock, gas and ash as high in the air as its big brother Ruapehu at the other end of the line. What might a truly massive eruption, one that White Island is certainly capable of, do to the populous Bay of Plenty? That's a question the people in this calm and beautiful region don't even want to contemplate.

Amazingly, people want to visit this island. They are, mainly, international tourists rather than New Zealanders. Perhaps the natives live too close to the fiery mountains to tempt fate by walking right *inside* one.

Volcanoes are part of the New Zealand vernacular. Not so for foreigners. The chance to look inside a volcano and come out uncrisped is too attractive.

That's how I felt too. That's why I was aboard a big White Island Tours launch skimming over the forty-eight kilometres of water between Whakatane and White Island. The volcanic alert level was currently one, the lowest, indicating minor volcanic unrest. While people are still taken to the island when activity reaches level two, indicating moderate to heightened volcanic unrest, I was happy with level one. Volcano-watching could be dangerous to life and limb, as many of those who observed the Mount St Helens eruption in Washington State could testify — the ones who survived, that is.

Levels three to five describe actual eruptions from minor upwards, during which the island is off-limits to even the most dedicated thrill-seekers. But the tour operators warned that volcanic alert levels were shifty and not to be entirely trusted, for volcanoes are impetuous beasts and can erupt at any time. If this one did, advice on what to do was remarkably similar to that dispensed in the event of the eruptions' near cousins, earthquakes: avoid as many dangers as you can, find cover and hold. It reminded me a little of the old line about what to do in a nuclear explosion: assume the brace position and kiss your arse goodbye.

But nothing prepared me for the reality. I stepped off the beach into another world. Toxic craters bubbled all around. Had Macbeth's witches appeared, everyone would have congratulated them on their choice:

Double, double, toil and trouble;
Fire burn and caldron bubble ...
For a charm of powerful trouble,
Like a hell-broth boil and bubble.

It was a Shakespearean world with Disney overtones. The setting was in Technicolour: primitive purples and reds and yellows. Craters were named Donald Duck, Noisy Nellie, Big John, Gulliver, Rudolf.

Gouts of steam rose from vents like ghosts, and one of them might have been Donald Pye, who was a fireman when the island was producing sulphur. He disappeared one night and all they found of him were his boots. Yet it was easy enough to imagine what might have happened. The track ran alongside solid-looking mounds whose crusts were in fact fragile. If you stepped on one, that might be the last step you ever took.

Eleven sulphur miners (the number is still uncertain) vanished, atomised along with their buildings, in 1914. Men and buildings disappeared forever under a lahar of boiling mud, ash and rock. A single tabby cat survived, dubbed Peter the Great. The rescuers took him back to Opotoki, where he became famous, fathered lots of kittens and lived happily on his rep for the rest of his life.

So no one took any chances. We were glued to the track. We wound through the sulphuric morass without putting a foot wrong.

Grains of silica in the rocks glittered in the sun: silica adds power to eruptions. The occasional stream crossed the path, the water so sharp and bitter it seemed to corrode your tongue.

We walked over an angry-yellow terrain. Water boiled, mud bubbled. The whole business looked like some giant pot of hellish brew, certainly not one you'd ever want to taste, but I did. The water from a tiny stream was acrid.

Pure sulphur is tasteless, but when I licked a film of sulphur powder, my tongue curled in shock.

All the while the cracked cliffs hovered like spectres.

It was a beautiful, evil place, the scariest I'd ever been to, and the most memorable. Vents hissed. We carried masks, for sometimes the thick air seemed to reach into your body. People coughed and wheezed. When we left we took great gulps of the clean sea air. Some of us might have been gasping with relief. It seemed to me to be the proper end to a journey along the red line.

13

Passing by

Whitcombe Pass is named after a man who thought it might be a fine route between Canterbury and the West Coast. He died trying to prove it.

Maori knew the Pass, for they needed routes between the Coast and Canterbury for the same reason Pakeha did: the passage of treasure. For Pakeha it was gold, for Maori the precious pounamu, or greenstone. But they preferred a pass to the north.

Time has not improved the Whitcombe Pass, nor its reputation. The Department of Conservation warns novices away: only the fit, well-equipped and experienced should try it.

It is a very tricky route over the Southern Alps and perhaps the best that can be said is that it's not the trickiest. As a wild journey however, its pedigree is impeccable. It burst onto a wider stage through Samuel Butler, the young English immigrant who was then searching the peaks for sheep country and would make his fortune founding Mesopotamia Station in the Upper Rangitata Valley (see Chapter 11).

Just as Butler was probably the first Englishman to see what later became Arthur's Pass, he was also the first to see the Whitcombe.

He set out from Mesopotamia with John Holland Baker, a young surveyor. The two travelled up the Clyde River, which flowed into the Rangitata, without seeing any clear country. They turned back down the Clyde to its fork with the Lawrence River, and headed up the Lawrence.

This was truly a grand landscape. The Arrowsmith Range rose on one side of them, the Jollie Range on the other, overtures to the full symphony of the Alps. Butler and Baker crossed the Jollies over what is now the Butler Saddle, Chowbok Col rising beside him. Ahead lay the Southern Alps. From where he stood he could see a pass. It looked accessible.

Butler could not reach it on that trip, but early in 1861 he approached by way of Lake Heron, slogged up a likely stream now called the Lauper, and there it lay: a pass leading through the Alps to the West Coast.

The journey carved itself into his soul. His later novel *Erewhon* described that route accurately. His fictional character had been searching for sheep country with his companion, Chowbok, when he saw the saddle far ahead. He thought it part of the main range, and his blood was 'on fire with hope and elation'. Chowbok was not as pleased; he sensibly abandoned the narrator.

The real-life Butler did not spend much time on the pass he'd found. He looked around him, declared the country unsuitable for sheep, and went back.

John Whitcombe, Canterbury's road surveyor, should have done the same. Had he looked over the edge into the horrid wilderness to the west and declared it unsuitable for roads, he might have lived to a contented old age, telling his story from winged armchairs in the gentlemen's clubs of Christchurch.

To get to his pass from the east you need to cross the Rakaia in its least unruly mood. On the way you pass Mount Algidus Station, where Mona Anderson wrote *A River Rules My Life*. The river ruling her life was the Wilberforce, which flows into the Rakaia, the two of them whittling the land to a point. The country impressed her with its primitive beauty, sheer mountains, rivers, gorges. It impresses everyone who goes there, and scares the hell out of more impressionable souls, like me.

In *Erewhon* Butler wrote of a sombre, sullen place, with gigantic forms and barbarous stone fiends, where the air was dark and heavy, making the loneliness even more oppressive. Bang on, although he might have added that the air often moves rather quickly.

Well, the pass itself isn't so bad, a rocky place but level, convincing those early explorers that there might be a safe passage here. But I looked into the void and my first thought was: Wow, is that the time? I have urgent business back down there on the Plains.

***

Years later I thought to have another crack at it.

It was spring. The Rakaia was high, and gushing, and as Mona Anderson described it with 'the spring thaw on its back, brown, ugly and raging, a killer river that no man in his senses would cross'. Every one of my senses agreed: it might be better to attack the pass from its other end.

Butler's hero crosses over the pass and speeds downhill into his utopian civilisation on the other side. I drove back down the valley, north along the edge of the Plains, through Arthur's Pass and over the top to the West Coast where Butler's mystical civilisation is these days known as Hokitika.

The town wears the utopian mantle modestly. I find it best considered from the public bar of the Railway Hotel. I can see the mountains from there. They look wet, wild and cold.

In 1863, two years after Butler, John Whitcombe made the crossing; or, the crossing unmade him, for he left his name on the pass but his body buried to its boots in West Coast shingle.

Gold had been discovered on the West Coast. The Coast was booming; Canterbury was growing quickly. But the two were separated by the dangerous bulk of the Alps. Something had to be done. The impassable had to be made passable, a route between the two had to be found. Surveyors and explorers were sent out to poke into every likely pass, and Whitcombe decided he was the man for this one.

He did not seem well-equipped for it. In the best traditions of English explorers he came from a prosperous family, possibly fell out with them over his marriage to a publican's daughter, and headed for the colonies. By 1863 he was the father of five and expecting a sixth. He might not have donned baggy shorts and a pith helmet, exactly, but he rushed in where novelists, sheep farmers and angels all feared to tread.

His instructions were to discover a mountain pass and return. He decided instead to go all the way through the Alps to the West Coast.

Most people have imagined him to be some sort of functionary; that is, if they thought of him at all, and scarcely anyone did until

John Pascoe, climber, explorer, writer, photographer and unusual public servant entered the picture in the late 1950s. Pascoe was no mean adventurer himself. One of his mountaineering achievements was his ascent of Mount Evans, not far from the Whitcombe Pass, on his third attempt in 1934. It was then the highest unclimbed peak in New Zealand, a vicious spike probably spied by both Butler and Whitcombe who, like right-minded citizens, kept well clear of it.

Pascoe uncovered a narrative in the *Canterbury Provincial Gazette* of 6 July 1863. It had been written by Jakob Lauper, Whitecombe's companion, a Swiss guide who wrote his original story in German.

The *Gazette* published the English version, which languished, forgotten, until Pascoe came along. It was republished as a little book in 1960 by that good old Christchurch firm Whitcombe and Tombs, founded by Bertie Whitcombe, apparently no relation to John.

Jakob Lauper felt to me like Phileas Fogg's Passepartout, or Don Quixote's Sancho Panza, an unfailing, faithful servant to a flawed master and the real hero of the story even if (like Phileas Fogg and Don Quixote) without Whitcombe there'd be no story. He was a Swiss guide treated by Whitcombe as a beast of burden, and Whitcombe ignored what proved to be Lauper's very good advice. He lived as long as he did only because of Lauper, who did his best to save his boss from himself but eventually failed.

Surveyors were heroes of the day, men who pushed into the unknown and left their names on the maps they made. People such as Thomas Brunner and Charles Heaphy were immortalised. Their work was dangerous; starvation, drowning and falls from high places were part of their job descriptions.

Perhaps John Whitcombe struck out in search of fame. After all, he was a roads surveyor. No likely roadway had yet been found through Canterbury's Alps for a very good reason: the mountains were high and dangerous. There were other possibilities, more attractive than Whitcombe's. The Dobson brothers, Arthur, Edward and George, were already working on easier routes.

The Harper Pass was the most likely. Edward Dobson was clearing a track through Hawarden in North Canterbury, past Lake Sumner and up the Hurunui River, across Harper Pass and down the Taramakau to join what is now the West Coast highway at Aickens. His brother Arthur meanwhile was investigating a path up the Waimakariri River. Maori showed him their pounamu route, cut deep into the rock of the Alps and descending to Otira. That pathway became known as Arthur's Pass and is still the main highway between the West Coast and Canterbury.

But Whitcombe fancied his own prospects. He climbed to the top of his pass and decided to push on, in the grand tradition of Scott of the Antarctic, or David Livingstone of Africa. Perhaps he thought being English was enough. He was poorly equipped and his food was awful, even for an Englishman. His idea of mountain clothing was a possum fur rug.

His only good decision was to take Jakob Lauper with him. Whitcombe took his rug and a dozen biscuits. Lauper carried the rest: hatchet, billy, rope, pannikins, tea, sugar, rat traps, tobacco, matches, salt, mutton, instruments, blankets. A third man accompanied them to the pass, laden; then he turned back and Lauper took the lot.

The Swiss could already see the flaw in the plan. The descent was 'very much broken everywhere. The valley gets narrower and narrower; water rushes forth from under all the rocks, and in a short time a large stream is formed ... From both sides of the valley small streams fall down nearly perpendicular.'

They reached an impasse. Huge rocks blocked their way, and whirlpools, and they were boxed in by cliffs. Whitcombe declared it impossible to go on, and not possible to go back. What was Lauper going to do about it?

The Swiss lowered himself into the water on a rope: 'The water boiled, and hissed, and foamed like a witch's cauldron.' Up to his neck, he managed to cross. He cut some poles and improvised a bridge for the boss.

The sugar dissolved. The biscuits collapsed into a soggy mass. Whitcombe declared himself weak and tired: 'He had no idea the road would be so fearfully rough.'

Whitcombe said he'd pay Lauper to carry his sopping, fly-blown possum rug and he would sleep under the guide's blanket. Lauper kept his head, although by then he must have had serious misgivings about the man. He even panned for gold, and found some.

It could take them a whole day to go less than 200 metres. 'We could not make a fire, we ate a little of the [biscuit] dough, which was getting worse and worse, and the last morsel of meat we had with us.'

Lauper's descriptions grew more desperate: ceaseless rain, long perpendicular walls, whirlpools. They were starving, and freezing.

After ten days they got to the bottom. They fought their way through a tangle of rainforest and swamps and reached the sea. They walked in warm sunshine, found an old pa. Whitcombe went to sleep. Lauper searched for food, found a handful of small potatoes and some Maori cabbage. It was their last meal together.

Whitcombe told Lauper the guide had lost weight, and asked how he looked himself? Lauper said he did not look so very bad, 'but, in reality, he could not be recognised — his eyes were sunk deep in his head, his lips were white, and his face was as yellow as a wax figure; you could almost see his teeth through his cheeks.'

They came to the Taramakau River. Lauper judged it impossible to cross, and if you see that mighty river after heavy rain, you'd know he was right. Besides, he could not swim. He wanted to follow the river into the bush, find a place to cross, catch some birds to eat.

Whitcombe had had enough of bush. He refused. He set about making a raft but then found instead the remains of two Maori waka. 'Hurrah,' he said. He bound them together. The canoe raft floated just forty centimetres above the water.

'You can see now you've got nothing to worry about,' said Whitcombe. 'Together they'll take us across perfectly safely.'

Lauper's heart sank even faster than the raft would.

It was later in the afternoon when they launched this flimsy craft into the river. 'It's going really well,' cried Whitcombe. 'Couldn't be better.'

They went under, of course. The raft went deeper, and deeper, and in a moment they were shooting towards the surf at the river entrance.

Whitcombe changed his mind. 'We are lost, Jakob, and it is all my fault,' he cried. He struck out for shore.

'I had no doubt he would save himself, but I thought I was lost — lost, beyond all hope,' Lauper wrote.

He clung to the wreckage. He was swept over the river bar. The first wave hit him: 'It was as high as a house and certain to swallow me up.'

Waves broke all around him. It was dark. Out to sea he went. He clung so tightly his hands seemed to be nailed to the remains of the canoe, which threatened to batter him senseless. 'I have stared death in the face before ... but I had never seen it so horrible and so close.'

Then he felt ground beneath his feet. The next wave swept him out to sea. Back and forth he surfed until, nearly senseless, he was shot headfirst into a pile of driftwood and clamped himself to it. He burrowed into wet sand, numbed, and not even daylight could stir him. At last, he realised he was alive.

He was stiff as a log. His hands were black with West Coast sandflies. He vomited sand and seawater, staggered to his feet. He was wearing only a pair of trousers and a flannel shirt. He felt like Robinson Crusoe.

He shuffled back along the beach. There was Whitcombe's possum rug. A parcel of tobacco. His hairbrush lay in the sand and a little further down, why, a pair of boots stuck up. He hurried along the sand. Tore away at it. Below the boots lay Whitcombe's body, drilled deep into the shore. He was, Lauper reported, quite dead.

The Swiss fought his way back to the shanty towns that comprised West Coast civilisation then. Later in Christchurch, in the best tradition of English explorers, Whitcombe was proclaimed a hero. He got the naming rights to the pass while, until John Pascoe's discovery, Lauper faded away.

The Swiss became known as 'old Jakob', and some accounts decided that Whitcombe had died saving the guide's life. The points that, first, Lauper alone had kept Whitcombe alive as long as he did, and second, that Whitcombe had endangered the guide's life by ignoring his advice, were put aside as inconvenient truths. Whitcombe was among the glorious dead and Lauper was still alive.

***

Well, Whitcombe's pass is as awful as ever and it is warm here in the Railway Hotel, and safe, and I don't really want to go into the mountains on my own. That is a stupid idea, usually, but I work it through like this: I'll walk up the Whitcombe Pass track to the Rapid Creek hut, two hours, say. If all is going well and the weather is holding I'll go on to the Frew Hut, another three hours, spend the night there and come down again. It's only part of the journey and Jakob Lauper would have had no trouble with it, but it'll give me an idea of the country he had to deal with, or the easier parts of it. And I have no alternative, no one to go with me anyway. Writing is a lonely business. I'm well-equipped. I've left a note of my route and a list of who to call if my wife Sally hasn't heard from me by a certain time.

She is not at all happy about this, reading it more as a suicide note. She shows it to a friend. 'He's mad!' shrieks the friend, so piercingly I can almost hear it here in Hokitika. I think of it more as a masterly composition, short and succinct. No wasted words. To the point.

She points out that the Department of Conservation still rates the Whitcombe Pass track among the most dangerous in the country. I rate it less risky than missing a deadline.

She is right, of course. People of my advancing, nay, galloping years should not tramp alone, and especially not in these mountains.

Yet I get up early and drive through farmland and dairy country. Civilised. Spring mists brush the land, a little drizzle hiding the mountains ahead. It parts every now and then, revealing that lowering green of the West Coast mountains. Mine is the only car in the parking area but I leave it anyway, telling myself that, oh well, I can always turn back.

The route follows an old farm track at first, with a bit of gorse here, some pasture there, the occasional piece of abandoned machinery, a Coast trademark. Coasters are very good at abandoned machinery. A bulldozer may sit fair square in the middle of a paddock, scrub growing through it, as if its driver had knocked off for smoko one day and never gone back. The occasional paradise duck complains loudly about my passing.

The track drops down into the Hokitika River bed, and the ducks form squadrons launching into a cacophony of complaint.

An old cableway crosses the river. It is no longer used, to my relief, for it looks feeble above the rushing grey-green river below hissing between boulders lying like spat pebbles. Close up they're more like giant pieces of rock strewn so higgledy-piggledy along the bank that you understand the immense power of this river and resolve to stay as far away from it as possible, unlike poor Jakob who, starving and worn down to his elements, had to cross the thing on his way north to the Taramakau.

This is a huge river, a torrent which would shade many more celebrated — the Manawatu, the Whanganui, the Waiau. I've been on the track for only half an hour and I'm already in awe of the man.

Those rocks are slippery, hard on knees. The track lurches out of the riverbed and becomes ... well, bless me, more of a road.

That is what it was intended to be, in fact. Some early officials in Canterbury and on the West Coast saw it as another likely route for a road between the two provinces, possibly even the best. It would run up the Hokitika and cross the Main Divide at the Mathias, a precarious pass through the tops to the north of the Whitcombe Pass. ('The whole difficulty in the Mathias Pass route is the pass itself,' the chief surveyor of the time reported in a rather odd statement of preference for the Mathias over Arthur's Pass.) They were so certain of their ground that men with picks and shovels were already cutting and benching a track through the valleys.

Oh, what a road-building jamboree this was! Those Victorians were always up for a slash and gash. Washouts? Trifling, said the official report. Big boulders? Roll them out of the way, 'a little cutting here and there'. Bush? Poof! The whole thing should cost no more than £2000. What an admirable thing was the pioneering spirit!

So now I'm strolling along the surprisingly good remains of all this enterprise, which have the atmosphere of the quiet before the storm. In a couple of hours I reach a cableway across the river. It is supported by pylons on concrete blocks at either end. A kind of carriage runs along the cable. It dangles above the middle of the river. It has a winch whose handle you turn to bring it over to your side. It would be grandiose to call it a cable car. Up close it is more like a tea tray.

The idea is to pile your gear into it, then climb in yourself, cast off and zoom over the river, rejoicing at the ingenuity, the spirit of the thing, the huge adventure of crossing this mighty river in a flash! The Rapid Creek hut is only fifteen minutes from the end of the cable.

I try it, empty, a couple of times. It works wonderfully. Of course it does. Things always work when nothing depends on it.

I put my pack into this contraption, climb in myself, cast off.

Oh the excitement, the speed! In a trice I'm over on the other side of the river.

The cable car/tea tray slows, stops. We're almost there. But we're not.

It starts going backwards. It zooms across the river, again. It goes much faster than I can think. Why, here I am, almost back where I started. Oh no I'm not. The damn thing is off across the river once more. Back and forth I go in ever smaller stretches.

It stops, swaying. One thing I hate more than heights is dangling high above a river. And swaying. Oh all right, that's two things, but I'm hating it twice as much, at least.

The river is rushing and roaring below, and snarling and sometimes sending up a spout to scout the intruder. I wonder how long it will be before someone comes along and finds me. I wonder whether I want to be found because then I'd have to explain myself as an idiot. I wonder why oh why did I ever leave home?

On reflection I think, a couple of days later when my brain cells have clasped hands and started to work again, that I should have grabbed the steel fork lying in the bottom of the tray, used it first as a brake to stop the tray rolling back, then as a lever to get it all of the way over. If there are two of you, none of this is necessary. One cranks the winch, the other hops in, crosses the river, and the two then swap jobs.

Now, alone in the middle of the river, I have three choices. I can stay where I am until someone comes along. But weeks later, when sensible people started using the track again, trampers would find my mouldering body stiff as a tombstone. I can go on, or go back. Going on means coming back, sooner or later. Bugger that.

I valiantly retreat, first pulling the tray along the cable by hand, then using that bloody awful fork. The going gets steeper as you near the end, of course, but desperation works wonderfully. A final heave and a curse and I'm back. Out I go in a flash, out comes the pack, out goes any notion of reaching the Rapid Creek hut, much less the Frew, that night. This trip has no mercy on sensitive souls. Look at what happened to Whitcombe.

I plod back, outwardly defeated, inwardly rejoicing and taking too little notice of the rocks I'm climbing over, for I slip on one and land squarely on my bottom. Swarms of sandflies hone in.

Lauper and Whitcombe must have done this a dozen times a day. Once is enough. I'm sitting there lamenting, wondering if I'll ever walk again, when I hear voices. Two possum trappers, a man and a woman, are working their way along the riverbed. They stop for a chat. I pretend I'm enjoying the view.

They're walking in to the Rapid Creek hut. It will be their base for a couple of weeks while they catch possums. They stopped counting when they reached 600 in the square kilometre around the hut last time they went in, and there's a good market for skins. He is spare and sparse, everyone's idea of a possum-trapping mountain man. She is every mountain man's idea of what he might come home to, none of it being spare and sparse.

He says the cableway is a bit hard to crank at this end. I agree. He says it rains a bit up here. We look at the clouds, not far above our heads. I agree.

He says that sometimes, at night, lying in a bunk in the Rapid Creek hut, he hears the growl of huge boulders being swept down the river and feels the hut shake.

You need to know what you're doing to tackle the Whitcombe, he says. I agree with that too. From somewhere in the mist smoking off the dark forest I hear a sigh. It has a Swiss accent.

14

Keeping count

Motuihe lies in the Hauraki Gulf not far from Auckland, looking from above rather like a ham bone. A long thin island spreading into lumps at each end, it is 179 hectares of subtropical paradise. It was once covered in bush and will be again, one day, when the trees being planted by an army of volunteers grow into a mature ecosystem. In the meantime it is one of the most popular islands in the Gulf.

Sandy beaches grace its flanks. When the southerly wind blows the eastern side is sheltered, and in a northerly the western side remains calm, so that on any fine weekend one side of the island or the other is crammed with boats.

You can float in clear, pale-green water tinted with gold and think, How wonderful, what a place to live, just above the beach there, or on that cliff, or among the trees on that gentle sunny slope.

Yet this island's history is all about people seeking to get *off* the island rather than onto it, and one of the strangest episodes in New Zealand's modern history occurred here.

Count Felix von Luckner, German raider and scourge of the South Seas in World War I, was imprisoned on Motuihe after his capture in 1917. The island became the setting for his escape, among the most daring ever seen.

A few years later, von Luckner was transformed into a romantic hero, an international star. He'd won the attention of a man called Lowell Thomas, who would now be termed a creative. Thomas was an American journalist and adventurer in the early twentieth century, a period Hunter S. Thompson. He started with print, starred on radio, and became a hit on television. One of his two best-known creations was Lawrence of Arabia, a little-known soldier until war correspondent Thomas recreated him as a war hero and made him an international celebrity.

The other was Count Felix von Luckner, the Sea Devil. Thomas may not have coined the name, but he made it world-famous. He was smitten with von Luckner from the moment he first saw him at Stuttgart airport in the 1920s. The Count had stepped off an arriving aeroplane. Thomas, who never used one adjective when half a dozen would do, described him as tall, massively built, saluting in all directions in the perfunctory manner of the Prince of Wales. He was with a small blonde woman, his countess, 'like a fairy who had arrived on a sunbeam'.

Thomas found himself flying through Germany on von Luckner's tail and watching the couple being greeted and idolised by cheering crowds at every aerodrome. And when they eventually met, Thomas joined the adoring throng. Von Luckner, he said, was one of the most powerful-looking men he'd ever seen, a rollicking buccaneer of the good old 'Yo-ho-ho and a bottle of rum type'.

Well, possibly. Photographs taken of the Count in New Zealand usually show him as languid, elegant and always good-humoured even when captured.

By von Luckner's own account he rose from the ranks, joined the Salvation Army in Australia, hunted kangaroos, boxed, wrestled, became a Mexican soldier, blistered through the Pacific in his windjammer sinking millions of dollars of shipping without killing a soul (history records one death) and roaming the oceans under sail.

Now, his was a truly great story but any modern journalist would suspect that the Count was a romancer or, in today's terms, a champion bullshitter.

Not Thomas, which might explain why he still occupies a place in history after his fellow hacks have turned to dust: people love a good story, and a good story-teller, and the devil take the sceptic.

Von Luckner was as much pirate as 'raider'. His ship was the *Seeadler*, 'Sea Eagle', even then a remarkable vessel: she was a square-rigged ship, the last ever to be commissioned as a warship. She set sail in December 1916, sneaked through the British blockade in Norwegian disguise, and set about dispatching as many merchant vessels as von Luckner could find. Eleven were sent to the bottom with the loss of just one life, a seaman killed when a steam pipe was ruptured by a shell.

The German raider captured so many sailors, almost 300, that von Luckner was running out of food to feed them. He cornered a French barque, slowed it down by removing some of its spars, loaded the prisoners aboard, appointed a captured British captain her commander, and wished the vessel bon voyage.

The *Seeadler* then rounded Cape Horn and entered the Pacific, escaping a British ambush when a storm pushed her well south of the waiting ships. Von Luckner had added another three ships to his tally when he came to Maupihaa, also known as Maupelia or Mopelia, a tiny, lonely atoll in the Society Islands. On 31 July 1917 he anchored outside the coral reef and went ashore, apparently for a picnic. But the wind and sea rose and, as many ships before her had been, the *Seeadler* was swept onto the reef and wrecked. Von Luckner later insisted it wasn't poor seamanship that cost him his ship, substituting the unlikely story that he'd been the victim of a tidal wave. The captain, crew and some forty-six prisoners were marooned.

The resourceful Count took an eight-metre ship's longboat and six of his men, intending to hijack another ship and return for his fellows. The heavily loaded boat sailed more than 3000 kilometres, its crew constantly bailing. They first reached Atiu in the Cook Islands, where they tricked the New Zealand Resident into giving them enough supplies to reach Aitutaki. The New Zealand Resident there was suspicious but powerless to detain them, and von Luckner sailed on to Fiji.

There they were captured by what von Luckner later insisted was a heavily armed vessel but was in fact a cattle steamer. Either way, the game was up. He was taken prisoner along with his crew.

Meanwhile, back at Maupelia the remaining crew, led by Lieutenant Alfred Kling, had done rather well. They had captured the French schooner *Lutece*, loaded with goods for sale around the islands: it was a floating supermarket whose cargo included Canterbury cake, plum pudding and loads of New Zealand butter. Off they went on a gourmet tour, leaving the unfortunate French crew on Maupelia. But the *Lutece* proved to be carrying some extra stock: scorpions, cockroaches and a nice range of vermin.

Pumping constantly, they reached Easter Island where Chilean authorities allowed them to put in for repairs. But the ship hit a rock and sank and the crew discovered her secret: she was so rotten she couldn't be fixed. They were interned for the rest of the war.

The remaining Maupelia castaways were rescued at about the same time von Luckner arrived in Auckland.

The New Zealand public was outraged by the German at first. Von Luckner was suspected of having sunk the passenger steamer *Wairuna*, along with her passengers and crew. It was untrue, and it would have been ironic if the German had been undone by a falsehood not of his own making. But he was tucked away in the Devonport naval base for safekeeping and later moved to Motuihe, together with government officials from Samoa, which, until 1914, had been a German protectorate. They included the pompous German governor of Samoa, Dr Erich Schultz.

The Germans by then must have become accustomed to paradise: South Pacific atolls, Fiji, and now an idyllic island in the Hauraki Gulf. Von Luckner described it as 'a beautiful strip of land'. They were trusted, especially by the good-natured camp commandant, Lieutenant-Colonel Charles Harcourt Turner. Turner had been beguiled by von Luckner, although according to the German's account the New Zealander had reservations: 'He apparently expected us to go breaking out of his camp breathing fire from my nostrils'.

If this was true rather than self-serving, then Turner clearly put his suspicions aside. Photographs and records of the Germans' lives on Motuihe show a gentle utopia: bushwalks, warm sea, a tolerant and kindly regime which even allowed shopping trips on Queen Street. The best of the South Seas for them. After all, who'd want to return to the carnage that was World War I?

In fact, some of the German population of Motuihe did. They included Walter von Zatorski, a German merchant navy cadet, who was intent on escape even before von Luckner's arrival. He and three other internees began building a boat in a cave on Motuihe, finishing its hull in mid-1916. He even devised a sextant to navigate with, painstakingly constructed from bits and pieces he found around the island — a brass hinge here, a mirror there, the frame fabricated from the brass of an old Primus stove, an adjusting screw from a safety razor — all of it so finely made it still lies in Te Papa in Wellington. Then a rainstorm struck. The cave collapsed, the boat was wrecked and that was that.

The Germans helped the canteen manager build a second boat but in true Kiwi fashion it was no sooner finished than it was sold.

Von Zatorski turned to a new plan. Lieutenant-Colonel Turner had acquired a launch. The Logan-built *Pearl* was his pride and joy. The prisoners and internees helped him with it. All the while they were collecting material for an escape: sails, munitions, food, navigation gear.

Von Luckner arrived. He found that the stage had been set, literally, for a Christmas show. Props were made. They became a useful cover for their escape equipment. Von Luckner claimed he built a radio set out of items he said were for the show, which he called the *Grosses Shauspielhaus* (after a theatre in Berlin). He said bombs were made in tin cans, pistols stolen from the camp arsenal, a fake machine-gun fabricated, a sail disguised as a stage curtain, a German naval ensign painted on a bed sheet.

Some of this was certainly true. The flag later flew on the scow they hijacked, the *Moa*. It is still on display at the Auckland Museum. The Count claimed to have stolen Turner's best dress uniform and even his sword and scabbard. If this were so, one imagines Turner must have noticed.

Von Luckner appointed himself star of von Zatorski's show. A photograph in the Auckland Museum shows him happily at the launch's helm. His account of the escape included setting a fire in a barracks, which he helped fight, as a diversion. That was untrue, but trying to untangle truth from fiction in his tales is a waste of time. Who wants to let facts get in the way of a story so good that a century later it is still being told?

On the night of the escape, Turner sailed the *Pearl* back from Devonport, leaving two of the Germans to moor his boat near the jetty while he walked up the hill. As soon as he was out of sight, von Luckner, von Zatorski and nine others cut telephone wires, boarded the launch and off they went, eleven of them. It was 6.15 on a December night. Broad daylight.

At a brisk seven knots they rounded Cape Colville on the tip of the Coromandel Peninsula at dawn, anchored off either Great Mercury Island or Red Mercury (accounts differ) and hid out until they saw two vessels approaching. They captured one of them, the scow *Moa*, threatening the crew with home-made grenades. The captain protested: the vessel was designed for New Zealand's shallow waterways, not the high seas. 'We are sailing for our lives, by Joe,' von Luckner responded, and raised all the canvas the vessel could carry.

They pointed her towards the Kermadecs with the *Pearl* in tow. The fine old launch was lost on the first night. It was a second disaster for Turner: although von Luckner's story had him vacillating between stupid and blind, he was merely kindly. But the theft of his launch was another matter. He was sacked, court-martialled and dismissed from the defence force altogether.

The Germans were intent on raiding the Government stores hut on the Kermadecs for enough supplies to reach South America and thence Germany, or possibly to rendezvous with the German raider *Wolf*, which at the time was busy sinking two ships near the Kermadecs and laying mines off the North Island coast which claimed two more, one of them the trans-Tasman liner *Wimmera*. It sank with the loss of twenty-six lives.

The *Moa* reached the Kermadecs all right, and successfully burgled the government store on Curtis Island. Von Luckner proclaimed the islands German territory and became the only German sailor to capture British territory in that war, however short-lived. Then they saw smoke from a steamer and made off as fast as the old scow could go, which was not very fast at all.

The ship was the government cable steamer *Iris*, for the authorities had guessed the Germans' intentions. It caught up with them, fired a shot across their bow and the Germans surrendered.

Back to New Zealand they went, this time amid a great deal of favourable publicity. New Zealanders loved von Luckner's daring escape, and he came with a character reference from the *Iris*'s captain: 'He was a good sport'.

They were locked up Mount Eden prison. Von Luckner claimed the inmates gave them a hero's welcome on the promise that if the Germans were victorious he'd be made Governor and pardon the lot of them. He and his second-in-command Karl Kircheiss, a smaller and rather portly man, were then carted off to the tiny Victorian fortress of Ripapa Island in Lyttelton Harbour. Most of the others went to Somes Island in Wellington Harbour.

***

One summer's day I begin following their trail, searching for traces of this amazing tale. I drop my anchor in the greeny-gold water of Horahia, the western beach on Motuihe where the ham bone is at its thinnest, so that you can go from one side of the island to the other in a minute.

On the edge of this bay is the old stone quay and the jetty, which in one form or another was there in von Luckner's time. It was perhaps twice as long then as it is now. From where I sit in my boat, which he'd have been far too smart a seaman to hijack for his getaway, he'd have been able to see Rangitoto still recovering from its last eruption, for its scoria surface was a good deal more bare a century ago than it is now. The young Auckland lay behind him. Now Auckland's skyline juts upward, the Skytower beyond even the Sea Raider's imagination. Motuihe, though, is intent on going back to what it once was, untouched by human hand.

I haul my dinghy up the beach and walk the easy slope onto the island. The day is blue, the sea warm, the island alluring.

The odd thing is that many people, Europeans at least, who lived on Motuihe for any length of time had to be dragged here, sometimes literally. Maori lived here once, but the evidence indicates there weren't many of them. They left remarkably few traces, a couple of pa, one large, one smaller. They preferred Motutapu just across the water, or the much bigger Waiheke nearby, where historians have counted dozens of pa.

Motuihe was covered in forest when Rangitoto erupted in the fourteenth century. It blew red-hot scoria and ash over its near neighbours, Motutapu and Motuihe, destroying the bush on those islands and probably on the western end of Waiheke Island too.

It's hard to see where Maori lived and cultivated their soil on Motuihe because in the early days of European settlement it was farmed. The farmers felled the remaining forest and cleared the land. Sheep and cattle efficiently disposed of the rest.

When economics and common sense put an end to it all, a wider public took over, cleared out the rats and ferrets, got rid of the weeds and began the long job of regenerating the native cover. On some nearby islands such as Motutapu and Rotoroa the shift back to past glories is working remarkably well.

Only eighteen hectares of coastal forest remain here, but the Motuihe Trust is planting much more, and kiwi now run in the undergrowth.

A Pakeha farmer bought Motuihe in 1839, paying its Maori owners one cow, twenty blankets, ten axes, ten hoes, ten spades, six gowns, two red blankets, twelve Dutch pipes, six pots and one shawl. It was a bargain, all right: Pakatoa, a small island nearby, just out of sight beyond Waiheke, was for sale recently for $40 million.

When the government bought Motuihe in 1872 they had a quarantine station in mind. One end was for animals. The other, the northern end, was intended for a possible smallpox epidemic. They built two big barracks buildings, a hospital, a brick fumigation structure with a high chimney and stables. One young girl died there of scarlet fever, and may lie in one of the unmarked graves in the cemetery.

But smallpox was overtaken in 1918 by a much greater tragedy. The SS *Niagara* had sailed from Vancouver via Hawaii and Suva to Auckland and picked up a highly contagious influenza on the way. Nothing, not even World War I, killed as many New Zealanders in such a short time as the 1918 influenza epidemic. Influenza was an even greater and certainly more immediate menace than Germans, who by then had signed the Armistice.

Some 9000 people died between October and December that year.

Auckland's death toll eventually reached 1100 and the city was in no mood for risks: thirty-nine men, twenty-four women and twelve children, all passengers and crew aboard the passenger liner RMS *Makura*, were landed on Motuihe in December 1918 and quarantined. One was dangerously ill, eight were seriously sick and the rest showed symptoms.

The ship proceeded to Auckland, to the dismay of Aucklanders. They suspected, probably rightly, that politics had overtaken caution. Two of the passengers were the Prime Minister, William Massey, and the pompous Joseph Ward, who fancied himself as co-prime minister. Aucklanders saw them as a toxic mixture, literally: they did not believe doctors' assurances that the remaining passengers were disease-free. They preferred conspiracy theory: politicians had prevailed.

The *Makura* berthed in the city under cover of darkness, over the protests of some passengers who objected to any suggestion of surreptitious entry, and sent everyone off to homes and hotels. She then left for Sydney, with Auckland's mayor, James Gunson, wailing in her wake: 'The whole business is reprehensible in the extreme.'

Some of those quarantined on Motuihe never left, and are buried on the island. The small cemetery there has seven marked graves. One is the final resting place of poor, brave Ethel Browning, wife of the *Makura*'s captain, who rushed to the island to help the sick and died nursing them. Another of the graves might contain the remains of a smallpox victim from the previous century. They all lie here, in a sheltered spot on Motuihe, where the wind sings a sad song in the pines. Little flax sculptures sit on the graves.

Oh, the view from this clifftop eyrie: Motutapu to the left, then Rakino, and the Noises, and the eastern end of Waiheke, and other islands peeking from behind, and the blue sea all the way to Great Barrier.

Maybe von Luckner and his fellow Germans sat here and dreamed of home and saw the Gulf as their pathway. But what an unimaginative view of this paradise.

Old fortifications lie nearby, a gun emplacement which once commanded the approaches to Auckland harbour. A great deal more effort went into its concrete than ever went Ethel's way. But the military are quite used to graves, and their constructions last longer.

The internment camp on Motuihe for Germans and Austrians classed as enemy aliens was designed, in keeping with the stratified society of the day, for a better class of person: German and Austrian businessmen and government officials, the governor of Samoa and a bevy of bureaucrats. They might have counted themselves lucky.

Less fortunate 'aliens' went to Somes Island, that weather-beaten pile in Wellington Harbour, and shivered their way through the war. On Motuihe they swam, fished, lived in quality accommodation.

The former governor did his time in a new house of six to eight rooms, flasher than the camp commandant's house behind it, and much, much better than the barracks for soldiers and guards. Motuihe boasted quite a little village then, buildings spreading down the hillside, a fine view from every one of them.

A century on, the question, to me, is why anyone would want to leave. New Zealand prisoners of war who had endured the horrors of Gallipoli and the Western Front and were imprisoned in a cold, dark land would have found this a paradise. It is, of course.

Passing by on the Waiheke ferry you can see only two buildings remaining on Motuihe. One is an angular structure on the north-west headland which I always believed must have been a barracks building but turns out to be nothing more than an old Ministry of Works shed, which, built of concrete, may simply have been too hard to remove with the rest. The other is the ancient water tower, too expensive to demolish but shaky: some worry that it is a risk to the public. A nearby concrete pad was the base for the navy's flagpole.

I walk up to the remains of the old pa on Te Raeokahu Point, and follow the angled trenches and ramparts. They run across the base of a small peninsula whose sides and bottom drop sheer to the sea. They're now guarded by Department of Conservation warning signs: 'Steep Drop-offs', 'Danger of Falling' and so on.

The earthworks are testimony to the pa architects' skill, for this is a perfect site: beaches for waka on either side, sheltered terraces.

Did von Luckner pause here to wonder? I doubt it. He was too immersed in notions of European aristocracy to consider traditional peoples. In 1918 he regarded himself as among barbarians born of a 'convict colony'. Yet the remains of Maori civilisation still lie on this island long after most traces of the Pakeha one have been obliterated.

In 1929, the quarantine station became a children's health camp. Hunger and disease, notably tuberculosis, were rampaging through the children of the poor and, on the threshold of the Great Depression, there were plenty of those. Health camps set out to give them good food, sunshine, exercise and structure.

Even when I was growing up they still had a fearsome reputation among children; you were 'sent' to health camp, which sat darkly in our minds as some kind of prison.

Whatever their regimes, they protected and healed vulnerable children, and still do. Children evacuated from the Napier earthquake in 1931 swelled Motuihe's numbers.

In World War II gun emplacements were built on the island to protect Auckland against a possible Japanese invasion. Meanwhile Motuihe became home to a naval training base, HMNZS *Tamaki*. Jolly jack tars, no doubt celebrating their good fortune, were accommodated in the old quarantine buildings, twenty-two of them then. Another fifteen were built, including food and clothing stores, canteen, gymnasium, chapel, school, hospital, dental clinic, dormitories — enough for 517 people.

The village had become a town. Photographs from the era show streets, lamp-posts, two-storey buildings, a town square which the Navy called a parade ground. The rest of the island was farmed. When the Navy left in the 1960s the island went back to farming and eventually became part of the Hauraki Gulf Marine Park.

So a slice, a cross-section of New Zealand history, is contained in an island of 179 hectares: drama, disease, war, adventure, pestilence, plague and disaster. If Motuihe itself has not been through the fire, the fire has certainly been through *it*.

What is left of all this? The enterprise, the history, the drama of von Luckner and his famous escape? Nothing, really. A few graves in the cemetery, some remnants of the wartime gun emplacements.

I tramp around the northern end of the island, past the old Ministry of Works shed and the water tower, stop at the cemetery, admire the view from the gun emplacements, stroll back down to the isthmus. For all of its history, a walk around this part of the island doesn't take very long.

Everything has disappeared: the governor's house, the camp commandant's, barracks, village buildings, the twenty-two quarantine buildings, guns, the naval training establishment. It's hard even to see where they've been, for the Navy's parade ground, roads, and building sites flattened the land. Some roads remain.

Only the derelict navy surgeon's cottage still stands, an old yellow-ish weatherboard house with a chimney and boarded-up windows. I rest beside it, in the quiet, beside the fallen remains of a giant tree.

* * *

Somewhere on this island artefacts from von Luckner's time are said to be hidden. Some of them are in the boat-builder's cave used by von Zatorski and his companions to build the craft for their intended escape before von Luckner arrived. The cave collapsed in a storm, burying the boat and, presumably, all the heavier gear that went with it mast, oars and so on.

Some are in another cave. The Count's tale of his time on Motuihe says that after their capture in the Kermadecs the Germans planned another escape from the island, and hid supplies, pistols, even a folding boat, in a cave. The Count said the cave was dug into the side of a dry riverbed and disguised. The plan was to hide in it while giving searchers the impression that they'd escaped over a cliff and been picked up by a boat. They would wait until the hue and cry had died down then hijack a passing sailing ship. The plan, von Luckner claimed, was an excellent one but was interrupted by the Armistice, when the Germans were released and repatriated to Germany in May 1919: 'If it had been delayed a week, there would have been another escape at Motuihe.'

Can this be true, so close to the end of the war? None of his fellow Germans ever mentioned the cave. Still, the Motuihe Trust believes that it exists, that it has collapsed and buried the Germans' gear inside it.

When von Luckner returned to New Zealand and cheering crowds in 1938, the *New Zealand Herald* accompanied him back to Motuihe to search for his cave. Von Luckner wanted to recover his supplies, including, he said, a kerosene stove, bottles of rice and beans and other items, all stolen from the camp storehouse.

A 1927 report in the *Herald* claimed that a rifle and two flame werfers, shields and a collapsible boat all manufactured on the island, along with a stolen automatic pistol and ammunition, were also hidden in the cave.

The 1938 article had von Luckner and his party climbing into a bush-clad gully then up a small hill. For some time, the newspaper reported, the Count was at a loss, but then he saw two trees which had been growing at the cave's entrance lying on the ground, beside a deep, overgrown hole. Eureka! The Count asserted that this was what was left of his cave, and a Mr Hill, the city council caretaker on the island, said he knew of the hole as sheep often fell into it and he'd had to pull them out. He'd never suspected a German cave lay below. Neither had anyone else, and the stage was set for a fascinating treasure hunt. But no one excavated it or found the other, the boat-builders' cave.

Many years later David Veart, a former Department of Conservation archaeologist and historian, and a fellow archaeologist spent a lot of time scrambling around the island searching for any trace of either cave, unsuccessfully. Were there two caves? Or was von Luckner simply cashing in on a good story, von Zatorski's?

I go looking for the boat-builders' cave, 'Bootshohle' on a map drawn by von Zatorski. It seems to me the more reliable of the two stories. Von Zatorski certainly planned an escape, and the evidence survives in Te Papa. According to the map the cave should be on the south-eastern side of the island, in a gully, but I can find no trace of it by land.

From the sea there are two places in the area shown by von Zatorski where you might build an illicit boat. They're both in gullies beside the coast, well out of sight of the settled area, within easy reach of the water. I row ashore and rummage around. Not a sign.

Well, the plan is now a century old. There've been plenty of floods and slips and erosion since — and gullies, after all, are carved by water.

I take the 1938 *Herald* report and search for the alleged second cave. I reason that it would be on the eastern side, within carrying distance of the coast and well away from the built-up area. No fallen trees, of course; they'd have rotted away or been chopped up. No overgrown hole either.

The island has no sign of von Luckner and his fellows. Except for a few artefacts in museums, they've left no trace.

***

Ripapa was once a tiny island of rock in Lyttelton Harbour, joined to the mainland by a reef exposed at low tide. Its pedigree is similar to Motuihe's, although the Maori pa here was much stronger, a bastion covering the entire island. It became a quarantine station for immigrants (renamed Humanity Island) and an internment camp for some of Te Whiti's people after their passive resistance at Parihaka. Conscientious objectors were jailed there in 1913.

During the Russian scare of 1885 the young New Zealand nation grew paranoid after a fake newspaper report of Russians invading Auckland and taking the mayor hostage. In 1886 Ripapa was turned into a fortress called Fort Jervois, a medieval construction right down to a drawbridge to the mainland. Stone walls were thrown up where the pa palisades once stood, tunnels and emplacements were built, and huge guns pointed towards the harbour entrance. They were never fired in anger, which was just as well, for the authorities feared that firing them all at once would shake the fort to pieces.

The most warlike figures to emerge from the grey Southern Ocean here were the recaptured von Luckner and Kircheiss, who seemed to fit perfectly into this melodrama. Von Luckner was placed in an old hut, the former battery hut, and for the 109 days he was there moaned about his bitter quarters.

He didn't need to exaggerate. Ripapa is beaten up by the easterly wind from one direction and bullied by the southerly from the other. Even on a good day it is cheerless.

The island was open to the public by sea until the Christchurch earthquakes. I clambered over it as a boy, scrambling over the reef at low tide and scaling the stone walls, breaking in rather than out as von Luckner longed to do, and so easily!

The island was worth the trouble. Its greatest prizes, for boys, were the two surviving guns, one of which is very rare, one of only a dozen left in the world. The remnants of two further guns lay around too. Mysterious barred tunnels vanished into the rock below. Altogether it was a perfect playground, although the two Germans didn't see it that way.

When he returned to tour New Zealand in 1938 von Luckner wanted to revisit Ripapa. The authorities wouldn't let him: it was a military installation, no Germans allowed.

'By Joe [his favourite exclamation], what a pleasure it was to see that old weary Ripa island again,' he wrote in the visitor's book of the launch *Awatea*, which had taken him to the island. 'But there certain fools wouldn't let me land for fear I didn't know it well enough!'

A pleasure? He lied. All the time they were there he and Kircheiss complained of the cage-like barbed-wire net over their heads. Kircheiss inscribed his sentiments on the wall of his room: '109 weary days held in this dreary place ... We are fed up with this monotony and off we go to Motuihi [*sic*]. Thank God.'

My memory says I saw this inscription. But the hut is no longer there. The inscribed wood was later kept in the sea cadet base in Redcliffs, Christchurch, not far from where I lived. But when I went to check, that had disappeared too. I kept a grip on myself lest I vanished with them.

Now that chunk of wall, grey tongue-and-groove wood, lies behind glass in the Torpedo Bay Navy Museum in Devonport, alongside a room key with a wooden tag carved with the name 'von Luckner'. The Navy says his 'cell' had a concrete floor to prevent him tunnelling out. Tunnelling was unlikely, for Ripapa Island is a rock fortress built on rock.

The Count's fellow Germans on Somes Island in Wellington Harbour were no better off. The island is the final resting place of dozens of immigrants quarantined here who died of typhoid and other diseases. Kim Lee, a Chinese man was suspected of having leprosy (probably wrongly), thrown onto a nearby rock and left to die in a cave.

Not a proud history, although the Germans fared better: I visited the single remaining barracks building on the island, which must have held some sixty men. It was lined with wood and had wooden floors and must have been an icebox in a Wellington southerly.

Von Luckner's men may have left a ghostly residue. Three German prisoners twice attempted to escape from Somes in World War II, first by stealing the lighthouse keeper's dinghy, then later by sailing on a raft of empty oil drums using — shades of von Zatorski! — a beautifully made sextant of scrap wood. This fine instrument is now under glass in the island's visitors' centre.

While on Ripapa von Luckner grizzled to Sir James Allen, Minister of Defence, whom he saw as his social equal among lowly Kiwis. He complained that he and Kircheiss shivered in the easterly and cowered in the southerly and slept under newspapers padding their bedclothes. 'This is scarcely imaginable for educated men,' he wrote to Allen, who agreed. The Germans got the woolly underwear they asked for and in May 1918 were sent back to balmy Motuihe as a bonus, although they lived in considerably more straitened conditions than before. On their way back they spent a night locked up in the Chippy's Shop, the carpenter's room in the Torpedo Bay base. It is there still, now kitted out as a wardroom and much more to the Germans' taste.

***

Von Luckner returned to New Zealand in 1938 to mixed reviews. Some thought him a spy for a government intent on conquering much of the world. Many others cheered him. The Australian military later claimed they knew all along the Count was a Nazi agent, although he'd been feted by that nation's social elites.

New Zealanders were sometimes suspicious, more often cordial and frequently rapturous. Historians, notably James Bade, have produced evidence proving that his Pacific voyage was a propaganda journey not only encouraged but also financed by the Third Reich, in particular by Hitler's propaganda head, Joseph Goebbels.

In return von Luckner praised Hitler's policies while denying he was doing so. He had had nothing to do with politics, he claimed, and had not spread any Nazi propaganda. In the same breath he said he had not favoured the Nazis at first, but had changed his mind. In New Zealand he publicly applauded the invasion of a 'corrupt' Austria as 'a powerful factor toward the peace of Europe'.

Von Luckner was greeted with rather more scepticism when he returned to Germany. Hitler's government accused him of damning them with faint praise. He was told to shut up for the rest of the war, to go inside and close the door.

On balance, New Zealanders liked him. We were at the outer edge of our age of innocence. He was a gentleman raider. He hadn't hurt anyone except for that lone sailor, and we were inclined to accept the view that the death was accidental. He was gallant and handsome. He'd made the authorities look like fools then starred in a 'daring escape' from Motuihe and that made him a hero to many.

They loved the aristocrat with the common touch.

A retrospective article by 'A Local Lad' in the *Auckland Star* in 1941 gave an account of one of the Count's pub crawls: 'I believe that New Zealanders ... would not be so prone to regard him as a romantic character, a glamorous German, if they could have seen him setting forth ... Poor Felix! When he went on the scoot (which was pretty often) he was worse off than the average husband making the most of a meagre allowance for beer. The Countess, who controlled the exchequer, usually handed him a florin.' ('"He drinks like a horse water [*sic*]," she would scream in moments of anger.')

Often he would auction his cap in bars for funds. The Local Lad accompanied the Count on a tour of the country, reporting that Auckland businessmen fawned over him but also that, after being in close contact with him, 'I cannot now believe he was the clever adventurer that he would have us believe.'

Newspapers also reported that the Count, who was sailing to New Zealand in his own yacht, the *Seeteufal*, 'Sea Devil', had called at Maupelia on the way. He claimed to have dug up money, gold, uncut diamonds and pearls he'd hidden there twenty-one years before, and sent perhaps £10,000 worth of buried treasure (he had no knowledge of the value of such things, he said) back to Germany. He would give no details to the avid reporters, whose bullshit detectors must have been stowed away that day. Desert island? Buried treasure? The essentials of any good South Seas romance. The evidence is that von Luckner did not land on Maupelia, much less dig up his loot.

The chief postal censor, who had read and translated many of von Luckner's letters, responded to the Count's claim that he'd been made a Maori chief by a Maori princess. The censor dubbed him 'Baron Munchausen the Second', the Baron being a fictional character who claimed to have ridden on a cannonball, fought a twelve-metre crocodile and flown to the moon. Officials seem to have been more direct and colourful then.

Apart from newspaper accounts and a lingering scepticism not very much else remains of that great adventure: a few relics in museums. Practical New Zealanders have eliminated the rest, pulled it down, grown it over, thrown it out and cleaned up.

Von Luckner died in Sweden, his wife's home country, on 13 April 1966, aged eighty-four. His body was returned to Germany.

Oh, and what happened to the staunch old *Moa*, the captured scow that took the escaping Germans to the Kermadecs? She's long gone too. A Greymouth newspaper in 1935 carried a small advertisement for the sale of a wreck: the *Moa*, carrying a cargo of timber-mill machinery, had become stranded while trying to cross the bar of the Wanganui River near Hari Hari south of Greymouth. It is a wild river on a dangerous coast. The bar was seldom used. It had silted up and the *Moa*'s crew realised, too late, that it was too shallow to cross. The ship stuck fast and was pounded by heavy seas. People came from Hari Hari and saved what they could but the *Moa* was lost. Her remains were sold at auction.

From this distance, what are we to make of von Luckner? Oh yes, he was a character, an entertainer, a great storyteller and a romancer. He was a Nazi sympathiser, at least. Perhaps he was a fool who rushed in. But there's no doubting his courage, his abilities, his skill. His was a huge adventure.

A century on Aucklanders still recall him. I asked a dozen or so people at random what they remembered about him. 'Romantic,' they said. 'Cavalier.' The gentleman pirate.

There may be few physical reminders, but he left his mark.

15

Travelling first class

For a long time the notebook lay on my desk unopened, a small, oddly sized journal, somewhere between a diary and an exercise book. It had a mottled brown paper cover and the remnants of what looked like leaves stuck to the front.

Someone had given it to me at my father Hec's hundredth birthday party. He didn't make his century, for he died at seventy-six, but it seemed a good time for friends and family to celebrate his life. Old photographs, drawings, books, logbooks, school reports, fragile newspaper clippings and club minutes appeared — the things that people save because they say something about a person they loved.

I took the notebook home and put it on my desk. It disappeared in the clutter for months. And, in the course of one of those grim assaults on disorder which satisfy for a week or so before chaos triumphs again, it resurfaced.

I looked at it more closely. What was that mottling effect? Why, it seemed like grease. Like a brown paper bag after the pie has been taken out of it. And those leaves, now khaki, crumbling away from the paper. Surely they were, yes, lacebark, houhere. We had a big lacebark tree in the back yard of our parents' home. Small boys could climb its smooth trunk and hide in its branches. It was a refuge, and the tree was obliging. We tore off pieces of bark and looked at the creamy lace beneath. The tree was forgiving, too.

The book measured 205 by 165 millimetres. Too big for a notebook. Every second page was blank. The pages in between were standard exercise-book format, with a red margin. Where would such a book have come from?

The answer to that, of course, is from long ago — from the days when everything was written down, and written by hand, the only alternative being a typewriter the size, complexity and price of a pocket battleship. (As for photographs, my big Kodak camera had a front door like a safe, from which unfolded a bellows outfitted with levers and distance rulers, which sometimes — rarely — got the subject in focus but was not often used because the price of film and developing at the chemist's was far beyond my sixpence-a-week pocket money.)

The opening page of the book revealed it was not a journal, but a log book. It was addressed, in yellow letters, outlined in red ink, to:

Mr N. Reeder
D.C. Kowhai District
Christchurch

It had a drawing of yellow kowhai flowers and their tiny leaves in the top right-hand corner, and below the address a picture of a resolute young fellow in broad-brimmed hat, long brown shorts, green, beautifully squared backpack and stave, marching beneath rounded brown hills. The D.C. stood for District Commissioner, of the Boy Scouts.

At the time the District Commissioner was more impressive than the Governor-General, closer to God even than cleanliness. We promised, on our honour, to do our duty to God and the Queen, and we thought omitting Mr Reeder from the list was a serious mistake on somebody's part.

The inscription below the drawing announced that this was the Log of the First Class Journey made by Bruce Ansley, P.L. (patrol leader) of Karoro Patrol, Bishop Troop, following NZ Topographical Map S84, in the company of a boy called John.

The dates surprised me, for they covered only two days. I remembered that journey very well. It seemed to go on forever. It was wild, all right. At certain times on the route I was lost in space. It went on for weeks. Oh, all right, a week at the very least.

Two days? There must be some mistake.

I remembered the Karoro Patrol too. At the time I hoped *that* would go on forever. We were eight boys who did everything together: camps, hikes, bottle drives. We'd graduated from the Cubs. My mother Jess was the pack leader, the Akela. She gave us structure and purpose. She battled the chaos of her six children and had enough energy left over to help generations of others, for she gave much of her life to struggling kids.

The Cubs gave a two-fingered salute. This was before the two-fingered salute took on new meaning and became universal. Scouts used three fingers for their salute. This meant you had to join your thumb to your little finger. Some boys could do this easily. Others, like me, had to put their hands behind their back and surreptitiously join the two. What's a boy without the three-fingered salute? Not a good Scout, that's what. My hand still looks like a crow's foot whenever I try.

Nor could I remember what hand to shake with. Scouts have a secret handshake: they shake with their left hands. Normal people shake with their right. Giving a good firm handshake is part of a man's measure. Forgetting which is which is not a good start.

We lived by the Scout Law. We promised to be trustworthy and dependable, to tell the truth and, of course, to keep our promises.

We were to be true to family, Scout leaders, friends, school and nation.

We were to be helpful at all times, without pay or reward, friendly to all, respectful of difference, courteous and well-mannered, kindly and gentle, cheerful, thrifty, conservation-minded, brave in the face of danger, courageous in the teeth of injustice, clean in body and mind, reverent towards God yet respectful of others' beliefs.

From the outside we were pimply, wavering thirteen-year-olds. Inside, we were paragons.

We in the Karoro Patrol promised to do our best, to do our duty to God and the Queen. We promised to obey orders without question, and even if we didn't like them, to obey immediately, because that was our duty as Scouts.

We listened in awe to Bill Liddy, schoolteacher by day and Scoutmaster nights and weekends. Bill was the most popular schoolteacher in New Brighton and hence the whole world. He was defined by school and Scouts. When he fixed you with his level grey stare you knew you'd been outed, that he'd spotted the worm inside.

As a returned soldier he recognised the enemy. He called them the Skirt Brigade. They were a rival group to be feared and, eventually, they won. The Skirt Brigade made off with us, one by one, until we were lost to the Scouts forever.

In the meantime we undertook to be clean in thought, word and deed. The Founder, Baden-Powell, had declared, on the subject, that decent Scouts looked down upon silly youths who talked dirt, and did not let themselves give way to temptation. A Scout was pure, and clean-minded, and manly.

But that was a step too far. It was the first promise to go. We spent Sundays in a macrocarpa tree whose branches had matted into a kind of platform where we were invisible from the ground. We'd sit in a circle and wank and I can guarantee that not a single clean thought passed through our minds.

Our world at the time was constructed of staves. They were long manuka poles, stripped of bark and polished by use. Bishop Troop had dozens of them, perhaps hundreds. Naturally, we fought with them on every possible occasion, until Bill's stare caught up with us. Then we built bridges, stretchers for evacuating the injured, complicated derricks for lifting things, ladders, walls, emergency shelters.

There was nothing you couldn't do with manuka staves. We grew up believing the world a much better place for them. It was a manuka stave I'd pictured myself holding as I marched along the front page of my log, the happy wanderer with his knapsack on his back.

When we went on a Scout camp we built washing-up benches, plate racks, drying frames, clothes hangers, shoe shelves, platforms, dining tables and seats, all from manuka staves. We made kybos of them too. 'Kybo' was the Scout name for a dunny:

Keep Your Bowels Open. You'd go behind a scrim screen held up by manuka poles, and sit gingerly upon a seat constructed of, yes, manuka poles, and there you'd be suspended above a malodorous hole in the ground. Naturally, this taught us everything we needed to know about knots, for a failed clove hitch, or a granny knot instead of a reef, or a dodgy sheep shank, could end in unspeakable disaster.

Reef knots don't slip. Also, they lie flat, so that when someone broke their arm — scaling a mountainside, say — and you had to put their arm in a sling using your Scout scarf, you always used a reef knot. I still do the chant: 'Left over right and under, right over left and under.'

A bowline doesn't slip either, so it was the knot to use when, say, someone fell over a cliff when out hiking and you had to take the rope you always carried, construct a derrick from your staves, tie a loop using a bowline and lower yourself down after them. I still use the bowline-tying chant too: 'The bunny comes out of the burrow, goes round the tree and dives back into the burrow.'

We had the bodies of stick insects but our hearts were of steel.

All of this was encased within our Scout uniform. Our uniforms were to us as the telephone box was to Clark Kent. We'd put them on and fly out transformed. Superman had a cape and a cozzie (tight, but Scout-like in that no untoward bulges showed).

We wore the Scout scarf in the colours of Bishop Troop, yellow and black. It was folded in such a way that each end presented a twist of colours, which should have come together in perfect Vs but seldom did. The two sides were held around the neck by the magnificently named woggle, usually made of plaited leather, although a rubber band was sometimes pressed into service. My own was made by my father from stag's horn. A white lanyard, usually rather off-white, wound around the scarf.

By that time the military-looking lemon-squeezer, differing from the old diggers' hats only in the creases in the crown (the Army had one crease to the front so the four were in a diamond pattern, Scouts in a square — or was it vice versa?), had vanished. A beret had taken its place.

We wore Scout belts with fleur-de-lis on the buckles. Our socks had ribbons attached to the gaiters. We had khaki-ish shorts and shirts with big pockets for carrying a compass, pocketknives, odd bits of lashing rope, bandages, maps, pencils, even the occasional handkerchief. Our shirts were adorned with ribbons and badges. The ribbons denoted Karoro Patrol. Somewhere on the shirt, the breast I think, was the famed fleur-de-lis, the Scout emblem. The badges told other Scouts everything they needed to know about the wearer.

There were badges for housekeeping, bushcraft, first aid, knot-tying. There were, in fact, badges for everything, and so many of them that a truly diligent Scout could end up looking like a pine tree at Christmas, hung with so many baubles, bits and pieces that he glittered, which, of course, was the whole point. A Scout's badges were the measure of the boy who wore them. The more badges, the more worthy.

Among the most coveted was the First Class badge. It was a rite of passage, a marker on the way to Scout heaven which was, then, Queen Scout. Scout literature to this day has Queen Scout as the 'pinnacle of effort and achievement' and promises a presentation at Government House.

Well, I was a Queen Scout, but certainly I never made it to Government House.

Wellington was a world away. A privileged few went by air, on a DC3. The rest of us had to climb aboard the *Hinemoa* in Lyttelton, endure a night in a tiny cabin with three other passengers who invariably snored, and be woken at 6 a.m. by a warder with a cup of tea and two wine biscuits. I would have remembered that.

No, it's more likely that I would have been given mine by God's representative in New Brighton, Mr N. Reeder, D.C.

Before reaching such ethereal realms, however, Scouts had to get their First Class badges. They were an essential rite of passage. Every good Scout needed one to progress. Without a First Class badge you remained, I imagine, second class. I can't remember whether there was a Scout Second Class. It seems rather a shabby label to hang on someone. But there was certainly a First Class, and we all wanted it desperately.

As part of your First Class badge you needed to complete a First Class Journey. When I was a Scout the essential mechanics of the First Class Journey were these: you, two small boys, were assigned an area you'd never been to before, and had no idea about; you were given a rough route, with several outstanding features you were required to note; you were provided with sparse instructions for each stage of the route; you were carted to the starting point, ejected from the car, and left to yourselves. There was no Child, Youth and Family then, and health and safety rules had yet to wriggle onto the national stage.

We were taken to the start line by John's father, leaving home, according to my journal, at 8.40 a.m. He bought us an ice cream on the way. I hadn't been sent into the wild on my own before, and certainly not when I had to provide all essentials — food, water, shelter — for myself. For some reason the ice cream made me feel even more desolate, like, perhaps, the condemned man's hearty breakfast.

It was a very long way to the edge of the known universe. At 9.20 a.m., my log records, we arrived at the Tai Tapu Memorial Gates. The journey into the wilderness had taken forty minutes. It only seemed like hours.

We unloaded our gear. There appeared to be an awful lot of it. Possibly because there *was* an awful lot of it. Spare clothes. Raincoats (parkas came later). Food, including a big cake my mother had made. A large, heavy canvas item known jocularly as a pup tent. Poles. Pegs. Cooking gear, kerosene primus, something you tried to start with methylated spirits and never, ever, worked. Toilet gear (we did not so much as clean our teeth, of course, but you had to keep up appearances.) Toilet paper and spade for emergencies, for by now the old Horlicks highway was so puckered with fear I could not imagine passing anything ever again. Our Scout motto was 'Be Prepared.' We packed all of this stuff into borrowed packs only slightly smaller than we were.

Recently I read an article in *National Geographic*, which noted that when Ed Hillary and Tenzing Norgay climbed Mount Everest, they carried loads of about twenty kilograms apiece. A mere twenty kilograms? Perhaps we carried the same weight, but *we* were less than half the weight of Ed and Sherpa Tenzing.

We could see something very like Everest as we stood at that lonely roadside.

That illustration on my frontispiece showing a resolute Scout striding along with a perfect pack square on his back was rubbish, of course. No matter how we packed and repacked them the result was the same: two very large packs with stuff — pots, poles, pegs, bags — hung all over them, so that when we eventually staggered to our feet we looked like a garage sale with legs. We clanked off up the road, the start of a very wild journey indeed.

I remembered all of that when I opened that old logbook. The next time I was in Christchurch I resolved to retrace my steps.

***

That's why, this fine spring morning, I'm standing at the Tai Tapu Memorial Gates. The day is much the same: blue sky, slightly chill in a way that precedes a baking-hot afternoon. These handsome portals are made of the red volcanic Banks Peninsula rock. They commemorate the servicemen and women of both world wars. The dead have an X beside their names: thirteen of them in World War I, four in World War II. The gates are impressive and they make a full-page drawing in my log. Years later they're exactly the same. They lead on to the Domain and playing fields, but then, John and I were looking in the opposite direction, towards the hills, and the long haul upwards to the rim of the old volcano that is now Lyttelton Harbour.

Banks Peninsula is close to the city but it's pretty much as wild as ever. In Christchurch's early years, and even later ones, people died up there, either caught out in the dark as they stumbled along the paths linking settlements, or snap-frozen by the southerlies which can fall upon the place in an instant.

We all knew the story of the two young boys who'd left their Christchurch homes to climb over the Bridle Path and go fishing in Lyttelton Harbour. They set out to walk back over the Port Hills as night was falling. A sudden storm swept over the hills. Three days later one small body was found clutching his fishing rod and 'staring peacefully at the sky'. Almost two months after that the second was discovered, not far from the first.

So we were prepared for the worst. What's more, we were expecting it, for those hills seemed a very long way away as we set off on the endless shingle road leading towards the bottom of them. Twenty minutes along, my log records, we 'arrived at first bridge. This was wooden and the wood was fairly rotten.'

Five minutes later (the times were recorded meticulously), 'arrived at second bridge. This was also made of wood but in a lot better condition.'

Obviously, I was describing a foreign landscape, one where men and women had seldom trod before: 'The surrounding countryside did not appear to be affected by the drought. Everything was green and I could not see hardly any [sic] dry places. The road is lined with willow trees on one side and silver birches on the other. Sheep and cattle are grazing and lying about on the fields.'

Lying about this morning are languid locals, for a well-known café sits on one side of the road now, although on the other cows still graze and do their bit for local water quality. This is affluent country suburbia now. Rhodes Road, our long-ago path, is nicely lined with poplars on one side and trimmed macrocarpa hedges on the other, a long straight thoroughfare. A concrete truck passes, then four women on foot. That would have made this road a bustling thoroughfare then, although we probably would have wondered about the women: they're doing this for *fun*?

'The hills formed a semicircle around us,' I wrote. 'I could see two or three farmhouses.'

From this distance I can see the beads of sweat on that composition, the despair of a young writer with little to write about. The raw material is rather skinny, until: 'Arrived at Otahuna. Otahuna turned out to be a very pretty place. We saw a large grey house which looked to us like a mansion. It was half hidden by trees with a large lily pond in front of it. John and I took a photo of this and moved on.'

Oh, such masterly understatement. In fact, both of us were stunned. Such beauty! Such perfection! We had never seen anything like it, not even in the flicks. Who could own such a place? Even Mr Reeder was not grand enough.

We didn't move on for quite some time. We lay in the green grass outside the fence, overcome by splendour. We didn't know such a place could exist in Christchurch. Porticos, arches, verandas, turrets, vast windows, a thicket of windows, a panoply of grand architecture spread across the green lawns. Pools, ponds, fountains, sculptures and hedges were set amid the finest gardens we'd ever seen, far back from the road, a metaphor for the distance between the mansion and the two awe-struck boys lying in the long grass outside. This wasn't just a journey, it was a transcendental experience. We had found paradise, and it wasn't very far from Tai Tapu.

That image stayed with me for many years. I couldn't bring myself to explore it, for fear of puncturing the dream. But one day, a very long time afterwards, I was researching an article about the Rhodes family and I discovered the truth. This wasn't just a house. It was Canterbury to the core, its heart and soul.

Heaton Rhodes had built it, and Heaton Rhodes was as much ingrained in the Christchurch consciousness as the First Four Ships and the Four Avenues. We always believed that Rhodesia was named after him, and probably rhododendrons too. He possessed not just one but two knighthoods. He and the future

King George VI collaborated over their stamp collections. He gave land for a Christchurch school, named Heaton Intermediate. It stands in Heaton Street. He could speak fluent Maori. He was, in short, a big noise, although we heard it only faintly in far-off New Brighton.

Rhodes was educated in France and England and Oxford, in that order, became a lawyer, inherited his father's fortune, built a fancy house in Christchurch and a fancier one at Otahuna with forty rooms, three storeys of wood and slate, and became a country squire, or rather, *the* country squire. Horses galloped over the polo ground and the good burghers of Christchurch clippety-clopped over hectares of manicured lawns, and flower beds, and woods. A yellow storm of daffodils heralded spring.

The great man was not long dead when we peered through his fence and marvelled.

I find the spot where the two awe-stricken boys paused that day. The place is as grand as ever. It's a very expensive lodge. The gardens and the lily pond are immaculate. The lawns run up to the white house in perfect stripes. The trees and shrubs clothe the house just so. The wood is half a century older, more a forest now.

The neighbourhood has changed, however. Much subdivision has gone on, of the lifestyle-block kind. Lots of rustic architecture. Signs warning of horses on the roads.

The two Scouts had to get permission to cross the farmer's land before tackling the hills. We knocked on the door of a neat little storybook house, which I sketched for my log: cream walls and a red roof. The log says, 'The farmer was a nice sort of man and told us the way to the track. When he answered the door, he said, "Oh, more Boy Scouts." He finished by saying, "I'd rather you than me."'

I follow a gently curving road and find the farmhouse all right, but it no longer seems to command access to very much. My map shows two public tracks running down from the crater rim, both of them ending, well, right here.

Perhaps I was better at reading maps then. I walk hither and thither. I search. Darned if I can find even one track from the road. Fences and gates bar access. Signs forbid it. There's a broad driveway leading in from the road in the place a track should be. Several other driveways branch off it.

A man stands by a gate marked 'Private'. Tanned legs below tailored walk shorts. Short-sleeved shirt. Very clean, well-trimmed, kempt, like Rhodes's gardens. The kind of fellow who'd refer to the shop down the road as 'the village'.

I ask him whether there's a public track through here. He gives me a hard look, shakes his head. *Public?* Will I have to go up to the top and climb down? 'Yes.' Abrupt. It is loathe at first sight.

So back I go, down Rhodes Road to the domain, around the foot of Banks Peninsula, up Dyers Road through Cashmere, past those grand old Christchurch emblems of the Summit Road, the Sign of the Takahe and the Sign of the Kiwi, the rest houses built by the dream of Harry Ell, who saw this wonderful scenic highway reaching towards heaven, past the remains of the Sign of the Bellbird, past charred hillsides, bare rock, scorched pines, ruined bush, blackened and barren, awful reminders of the Port Hills fire a few months before. I drive along the summit road until I reach the Omahu Bush, a protected bush remnant at the crater rim.

Now I'm at the top. My Scout log starts at the bottom. So, a walk down a good track. It doesn't take very long, really. The climb uphill in the opposite direction, however, seemed to take two Scouts forever.

'We started up towards the given map reference,' I wrote then, 'but soon forgot the farmer's directions. We picked up what we thought was the right track. We walked up the hillside but the track soon petered out. We looked around for a place out of the wind to have lunch. We ate in the shelter of some rocks. When we had finished we left our packs and went looking for the track. Failing to find the right one we decided to carry on towards the summit road. It was very hard going as the hill was very steep.'

Oh, what living hell is disguised by that sentence. It was also very hot. We were very tired. Our packs were very heavy. We were very sick of the whole thing and we'd hardly started. Mutiny was threatened, although I cannot remember by whom. Perhaps both of us. But as Scouts we swore cheerful comradeship. So we had our own version of the old ditty: 'When in trouble, when in doubt, *don't* run in circles, *don't* scream and shout — lie instead.' My log sanitised the disagreements.

'We found Rhodes Springs. It is a stone building about two metres square. Inside is a pipe pouring water into a trough that never seems to fill. I sketched this and set off towards the summit road.'

Sure enough, here's the sketch. A red rock building with what looks like a palm tree at the side. (Perhaps we were starting to have delusions, like marooned sailors.)

The Springs building is still there, but here's the thing: it's closer to the bottom of the hill than the top. It might take a fit walker twenty minutes to walk up to it. For the two of us then it seemed to take hours, days, and my word, that had to be a mountain dead ahead.

For Gibraltar Rock reared its pointy head far above. 'We didn't have to look at a map,' I wrote. 'We guessed it was Gibraltar Rock as soon as we came within sight.'

Within sight? That's like the Tibetan Buddhists in Rongbuk Monastery saying Mount Everest is 'within sight' instead of just being rather big.

Gibraltar Rock glowers over the landscape. Its virtue is that once you're up and onto it, you're quite close to the top of the hill. We didn't see much virtue in it then. The log reports matter-of-factly, 'We could hear the crash of guns.'

Guns? Could that have been the final stages of exhaustion, the thudding of two tormented hearts?

But I remember those guns. They were up in the Godley Head battery overlooking the Heads into Lyttelton Harbour. The last gun was fired in 1959, so we could in fact have heard the artillerymen popping off. Let's give the two Scouts the benefit of the doubt.

I follow their path up to the summit. It is quite couth now, and hard to lose your way, and it doesn't take long. Wild pigs have been rooting on the track. Wild pigs, this close to civilisation? Later I talked to one of the invaluable band of volunteers who foster the Omahu bush reserve and tracks here, Paul Tebbutt. He said pigs had often been released here, possibly by hunters. They also battled possums, rats, stoats, wild goats and the occasional deer. If we'd known about all this wildlife then, we'd have retreated, rapidly. Maybe there was a badge for that too.

Omahu lies at the top, sixty hectares of bush regenerating so successfully in this harsh climate that the understorey has returned and bird life is flourishing. This reserve, and Gibraltar, and surrounding land, 148 hectares in all, was sold to the Summit Road Society by a family of property investors — for a dollar.

A lovely, rare white clematis laces the bush. A riroriro trills, a bellbird answers. A stream tinkles at the top, rushes into waterfalls below. But I remembered crashing through scrub and falling into holes (the packs made us top-heavy) and staggering from one side of the valley to the other. Did we stray into that frieze of golden gorse on the other side of the valley? I don't know, but according to my log the climb took four or five hours. A photograph, taken on my huge bellows camera, shows a pile of gear apparently struggling up the hill on its own. Looking closer, I can just see a tiny John below, on all fours.

Now, I can see far across the Plains to the mountains on the other side. Canterbury is not short of splendour.

'We had a lot of trouble finding a track on the other side,' I wrote.

I'm not surprised when I look over the edge. The way down is a lot steeper than the climb up. I'm gazing into the crater of an ancient volcano. In parts here the drop is all but sheer. I skirt the cliffs now, as I did then, and look for an easier route.

My log says, 'We could see a track down the bottom of a valley leading to a non-metal road which led to a metal road going along the coast. We set off down the hill which was very steep and slippery. We had to go through a lot of bush and found that a bush with milky white spikes can sting very badly.' Welcome to ongaonga. Not much of that in New Brighton.

I make my way down. It is still very steep and slippery. What's more, there seems to be a lot more bush getting in the way. I'm not sure whether this is public land or private property. I worry about trespassing. But if it was good enough for a couple of small Scouts ...

'We were just getting a bit fed up when we sighted a tent which turned out to be the Cashmere Scout Camp.' We found those other Scouts a rather prickly lot, actually. Perhaps they hadn't heard of the world-wide fellowship.

But now, oh joy. I'm on more or less open ground. I slink along, trying to stay out of anyone's sight. I reach the bottom.

'Found coastal track (an old road),' my log says. It's still there, the old coach road from the early 1880s, which carried passengers and mail twice daily around the edge of the harbour.

Rounding a bend the two boys came across some Rapaki Scouts, Rapaki being an old Maori settlement near Lyttelton. The Peninsula seemed full of Scouts this weekend. They asked who we were. 'Upon being told they called out to us and said we might as well camp with them as they'd had a hard time finding a camp site ... We made a fire and pitched the tent.' The world-wide fellowship was back in business.

After tea (lamb chops, peas, tinned peaches, bread and jam) we walked up to the Governors Bay shop and sat down on a seat. A sinister note crept into the narrative: 'A man was watching from the bar window of the hotel opposite. He remained watching until we went away.'

The Scouts went back to their camp and found the others had tea and biscuits ready. I fished out my mother's cake. Oh the joy, not only of eating it but knowing that something the size and weight of a brick would be missing from my pack next day. I offered everyone another piece. 'While we drank they told us they had seen movements in the bush that definitely (so they said) were not opossums. We hunted for a while and went to bed.'

Late that night, the Rapaki Scouts woke us up. 'They had seen a torch flashing. We searched around in pyjamas for a while but all we could hear was a few opossums. We went back to bed.' I should have added that we were terrified. The night was black. Monsters were afoot. One of us cried. The great brotherhood of Scouts still prevents me from saying who it was.

In the bright light of morning the night's alarums seem to have vanished. 'We packed our kits and gear and burned or buried all the rubbish we could find. Somebody had left tons of rubbish lying about.' And, having done our good deed for the day, we set off for Lyttelton.

The road between Governors Bay and Lyttelton hasn't changed much. It still bends and bumps its way around the harbour edge. It is still ten kilometres. Then, it seemed much, much longer. 'The day was boiling hot without a breath of wind,' I wrote. 'In the cool, green sea below we could see people swimming. It was sheer torture.'

Then came a gap of three hours in my timeline. I still remember that day. It was, indeed, boiling hot. The road was hard. It shimmied. Each bend brought nothing but another bend. We were convinced it would never end. We were lost in an alternative universe, and it sizzled. Now, I drive it in perhaps fifteen minutes. But then, we struggled on, hour after hour. One whole day passed, then another. It must have, mustn't it?

A car pulled up beside us and a young man leaned out of the window 'Want a lift?' he asked.

The two Scouts looked at each other. This was dishonourable. This was a breach of trust. This broke not just the Scout Promise, but the Scout Law too. This could never be mentioned in the log. We'd have to lie. This would have to remain secret forever.

But we'd discovered the truth about wild journeys. They're uncomfortable, and exhausting, and are much better viewed from a safe place a long way away, such as a sofa. For once we were in accord. 'Yes,' we said.

ACKNOWLEDGEMENTS

A lot of people helped me with this book. In particular I thank Sally Ansley, Rhys Buckingham, Antonios Papaspiropoulos, June Peka, Craig Ansley, Bob Reid, Anne Main, Alex Hedley, Dave Veart and Robert Dwane.